MW01630228

RESISTING THE PLACE OF BELONGING

This richly evocative text investigates the strangeness at the heart of home through explorations in poetry, film, contemporary art and popular culture. The spiritual challenges of dwelling in familiar, intimate and yet dangerous spaces are addressed with creative candour and academic rigour demonstrating our intense preoccupation with issues of security and identity. It is a compelling but unsettling read.

Heather Walton, University of Glasgow, UK

This is an impressively interdisciplinary volume that repositions our understanding of home. In a world where displacement seems to be the ruling sense for so many, even when "at home", the essays here set out important bearings – literary, philosophical, religious and cultural – in helping us negotiate any return home or, as may be more the case, reconstruct the place we once thought was home. To engage with these various discussions is to displace, significantly and uncannily, displacement itself.

Andrew Hass, University of Stirling, UK

People often overlook the uncanny nature of homecomings, writing off the experience of finding oneself at home in a strange place or realizing that places from our past have grown strange. This book challenges our assumptions about the value of home, arguing for the ethical value of our feeling displaced and homeless in the 21st century. This book explores occurrences of home in places ranging from digital keyboards to literary texts, and investigates how we mediate our homecomings aesthetically through cultural artifacts (art, movies, television shows) and conceptual structures (philosophy, theology, ethics, narratives). In questioning the place of home in human lives and the struggles involved with defining, defending, naming and returning to homes, the volume collects and extends ideas about home and homecomings that will inform traditional problems in novel ways.

For David Klemm,
whose character, grace and integrity continue to inspire the
pursuit of truth.

Resisting the Place of Belonging
Uncanny Homecomings in Religion, Narrative and the Arts

Edited by
DANIEL BOSCALJON
University of Iowa, USA

ASHGATE

Published by
Ashgate Publishing Limited
Wey Court East
Union Road
Farnham
Surrey, GU9 7PT
England

Ashgate Publishing Company
110 Cherry Street
Suite 3-1
Burlington, VT 05401-3818
USA

www.ashgate.com

British Library Cataloguing in Publication Data
Boscaljon, Daniel.
  Resisting the place of belonging : uncanny homecomings in religion, narrative, and the arts.
  1. Homecoming. 2. Homecoming – Religious aspects.
  3. Homecoming in literature.
  I. Title
  128.4-dc23

Library of Congress Cataloging-in-Publication Data
Resisting the place of belonging : uncanny homecomings in religion, narrative, and the arts / edited by Daniel Boscaljon.
     p. cm.
  Includes index.
  ISBN 978-1-4094-5394-9 (hardback) – ISBN 978-1-4094-5395-6 (ebook)
  1. Home–Religious aspects. 2. Homecoming–Religious aspects. 3. Home. 4. Homecoming. I. Boscaljon, Daniel.
  BL588.U53 2013
  204--dc23

                                                                    2012018680

ISBN 9781409453949 (hbk)
ISBN 9781409453956 (ebk – PDF)
ISBN 9781409473534 (ebk – ePUB)

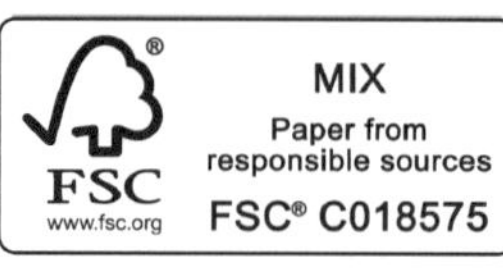

Printed and bound in Great Britain by the MPG Books Group, UK.

Contents

Notes on Contributors

Thomas J.J. Altizer, currently Professor Emeritus from SUNY Stony Brook, is renowned for his pioneering work in "Death of God Theology." The author of several works of groundbreaking theology, he is best known for *Godhead and the Nothing*, *The Gospel of Christian Atheism*, and his recent *Living the Death of God*.

Michael Baltutis is Assistant Professor of South Asian Religions at the University of Wisconsin, Oshkosh. His recent publications analyze the refashioning of dialogue and religion in Kathmandu, the capital of contemporary democratic Nepal, through a number of local strategies: the performance of classical Hindu festivals, the state-sponsored installation of political billboards, and the renovation of a temple to the dangerous divinity Bhairav.

Daniel Boscaljon received his doctoral degree in Religious Studies from the University of Iowa in 2009 and is working on a second doctoral degree, also from Iowa, in English. His work in Religious Studies focuses on questions of faith in post-modernity, and his work in literature examines narrative theory with an emphasis on gothic spaces in nineteenth-century American literature. His first book, describing vigilant faith, will be published in 2013.

Kimberly Carfore is a graduate student in the Philosophy and Religion program at the California Institute of Integral Studies in San Francisco. With a background in psychology and a former career as a wilderness therapy instructor, her current research includes feminist theory, deconstruction, critical theory, object-oriented ontology, and environmental ethics. She is currently working with the Women's Earth Alliance.

Forrest Clingerman is an associate professor in the Department of Philosophy and Religion at Ohio Northern University. His scholarly interests include the issue of place in environmental thought and the interconnection of theology, hermeneutics, and culture. His publications include *Placing Nature on the Borders of Religion, Philosophy, and Ethics* (with Mark H. Dixon).

Nathan Eric Dickman is Assistant Professor of Religious Studies at Young Harris College, GA. He researches and teaches in the comparative study of religions, religious philosophies, critical methods in religious studies, and philosophical theology.

Janet Donohoe is Professor of Philosophy at the University of West Georgia. She has published many articles covering a broad range of issues from Heidegger and Benjamin on technology to feminist phenomenological ethics, to the phenomenological shift of parenthood. She published a book on Husserl's ethics with Humanity Books, and most recently has been working on issues involving the role of place in collective memory, focusing her research on monuments and memorials.

Verna Marina Ehret is Assistant Professor of Religious Studies at Mercyhurst College in Erie, Pennsylvania. She holds a Ph.D. in Modern Religious Thought from the University of Iowa, an M.A.R. in Philosophy of Religion from Yale Divinity School, and a B.A. in Philosophy from Hamline University. Her primary fields of study are philosophical and constructive theology. She has given a number of presentations on redemption and globalization, and her current research focuses on religion, humanism, narrative, and globalization.

Hanna Janiszewska will receive her Ph.D. in English from Stanford University in June 2013. Her dissertation, *Romantic Lives of the Mind*, examines the emergence of a new form of intellectual life in the Romantic period in Britain. In particular, she looks at how literary activity became both a vital component of any program in life and the hermeneutic model best suited to interpreting it. She is also interested in the history of ideas, philosophical approaches to literature, and theories of poetry.

David Jasper is Professor in Literature and Theology at University of Glasgow and is the Changyang Chair Professor at Renmin University of China from 2009 – 2012. Professor Jasper's most current work centers on interdisciplinary projects in literature and theology in contemporary culture. Publications include: *The Sacred Body, The Sacred Desert, A Short Introduction to Hermeneutics*.

Joni L. Kinsey received her Ph.D. from Washington University in St. Louis in 1989. Her research focuses on nineteenth-century landscape painting and Western art, but she has also written on other subjects, such as nineteenth-century popular prints, Grant Wood, and women artists. She is the author of four books and is also the curator of the Eve Drewelowe Collection.

Ayesha Malik is a Ph.D. candidate at the English Department, SUNY, Buffalo. She is a Fulbright Scholar from Pakistan and is currently working on her dissertation on the political aesthetics of Virginia Woolf and James Joyce.

Christopher Merrill directs the International Writing Program at the University of Iowa. His most recent book is *The Tree of the Doves: Ceremony, Expedition, War*.

David Seamon is Professor of Architecture at Kansas State University in Manhattan, Kansas. Trained in geography and environment-behavior research, he is interested in a phenomenological approach to place, architecture, and environmental design as place making. His books include: *A Geography of the Lifeworld; Dwelling, Place and Environment* (edited with Robert Mugerauer); *Dwelling, Seeing, and Designing*; and *Goethe's Way of Science: A Phenomenology of Nature* (edited with Arthur Zajonc). He edits the Environmental and Architectural Phenomenology Newsletter.

Rachel Wagner is Associate Professor of Religion at Ithaca College in upstate New York. She has numerous articles and chapters in books, most dealing with religion and popular culture and especially religion in digital contexts. She recently published her first book, *Godwired: Religion, Ritual and Virtual Reality*, in 2011.

Acknowledgments

This volume represents a small portion of the 2011 Religion, Literature and the Arts Conference at the University of Iowa, a conference that began with the vision and direction of David Klemm. Many of the contributors in this book are indebted to David's pioneering scholarship in the field of Religion, Literature and the Arts. The Department of Religious Studies at the University of Iowa not only has continued to support conferences in Religion, Literature and the Arts but was also helpful in allowing this book to come together. I would like to thank the following people involved in helping to plan and organize the Uncanny Homecomings conference: Nellene Benhardus, Justin Cosner, Kerry Doyle, James Lambert, Jennifer Loman, Michelle Petersen, Andrew Williams and Lacey Worth.

Ezra Plank's artistic vision provided a rich background to organize and hold together the ideas at the conference and within this book, and his dedication to envisioning an Uncanny Homecoming is breathtaking. Sarah Lloyd was extremely helpful in answering questions along the way, and I am very grateful to Forrest Clingerman for his time and patience in helping me understand what all is involved in editing, and for supporting my initial decision to edit a book. Finally, I would like to thank my family for providing me with both time to work and with breaks from working.

Introduction:
Uncanny Homecomings: Becoming
Unsettled in Religion, Narrative, and Art

Daniel Boscaljon

Poets and philosophers long ago identified the human yearning to find a geographic and emotional environment that allows for a feeling of integration, a place where we understand our situation in the greater whole. Informed by our memories and anticipated in our futures, our homes provide us with spaces that nourish us in a prolonged present that seemingly defies change. Our familiarity with our home allows us to be comforted by its physical persistence, to receive consolation from its steadfastness. Even as commercial spaces attempt to become more homelike in their furnishing and amenities, such attempts to replicate what symbolizes home merely result in reinforcing everything that makes our home unique. Homes are the places we recognize and the spaces that mediate the ways we recognize ourselves, revealing the seemingly timeless truths at the foundation of our own self-conceptions.

Perhaps the invariability of our homes causes us to resist them: suffocated, we leave our homes and strike out toward what is unknown and undefined. Leaving home has been a staple of human narratives from Abraham to Odysseus, a trend encouraged by mass transportation available today. Whether voluntary or enforced, permanent or temporary, most people depart from their natal inhabitations before their deaths. When prolonged, we experience a break from home as an illness, a disease, a sickness. It is difficult for us to flourish apart from a place that provides a center for our lives. Once we have left our home, even if our leave-taking was voluntary, our desires often become focused on the possibility of return. The importance of home, the role that it plays in centering our lives, becomes impossible to ignore at those times of crisis that result in our feeling most lost.

Although few attend to or discuss the peculiar tensions associated with homecomings, many people discover an odd tone of dissonance that disrupts the triumphant solace that had been desired upon return. Something *unheimlich* haunts our efforts to return home: this lesson manifests in the agony of Gilgamesh, the plight of Odysseus, the struggles of the Prodigal Son and still echoes today for those facing crises of homecoming in twenty-first-century Palestine or Algeria. Two explanations for this curiosity present themselves. On the one hand, homes that remain unchanged and undisturbed reflect the extent to which our journeys have changed us, revealed by the fact that we no longer fit a space that we remember having enjoyed as perfect. The sudden revelation of our own metamorphosis can come as a shock, revealing that we have become strangers in a familiar land. On the other hand, places can change as much as people do—when we return to a space that we remember, we may find that the place we left has been altered beyond recognition. What we remember has been lost beyond our ability to reclaim, relegated to a memory that we know as a poor substitute. Unlike other new places whose novelty we enjoy, finding an unfamiliar place existing in a space we once knew well causes us to suffer in a unique way.

In addition to these personal and subjective experiences of uncanny homecomings, history has shown that home often has a darker side within it. For example, the postcolonial turn has forced us to grapple with the fact that myths of homecoming lack the allure of innocence that we have long desired to find there. Homes are places that pre-exist us, whose histories are marred by violence and loss that cannot be redeemed. Additionally, the quality of home that we most enjoy—the sense of timeless permanence that it offers—is defended at the cost of difference and openness. The space of home can quickly become tyrannical and can urge us to violently war against change that inevitably comes. Those who return victorious from wars often find that the home they fought to protect no longer recognizes what they have become. Even though we desire to make our homes where we feel we belong, it is nonetheless better to *resist* this impulse.

Just as odd as finding that what had been familiar has become uncomfortable, is finding ourselves at home in a place that we have never been feeling a familiarity in a place that holds the memories of other lives. These moments of homecoming are attended with a shock similar to what occurs as one confronts the loss of home, and forces us to re-evaluate ourselves in a parallel fashion. Such encounters of something familiar within an alien context refer us back to the mystery of both our homes and our selves: to *feel* at home in a new place means, perhaps, that we are more vast than we had credited ourselves as being. We can make ourselves at home in the world in delightfully unexpected ways, participating in a localized gathering whose familiarity overwhelms the strangeness.

This volume attends to the ambiguous role that home plays for humans and to the consequent ambivalence that defines our homecomings. In German, an etymological bridge connects home with the uncanny—*heim* with what is *unheimlich*. Undergirding these chapters is the assumption that we cannot see what is uncanny in our home as we dwell within it: the precondition for the possibility of experiencing the uncanny is leaving the home and becoming different from the place where we first learned to know ourselves. In lingering with the revelation of the uncanny that occurs in our returning home, the volume reflects on the roles that religion, narrative, and art perform in providing foundations for our homes as well as mediating journeys of leave-taking and homecoming that result in our appreciating our homes in new ways.

Additionally, the chapters collected in this book probe and unsettle our myths of home by inquiring into the process of what it means to make a home, and by questioning whether finding oneself at home should persist as an ideal. The specific topics that localize how homecomings are—or should be—accompanied by the uncanny differ widely, and show the many ways in which our understandings of home are being altered and manipulated. Building on the tension that Freud identified at the heart of the term *unheimlich,* each chapter provokes questions of what it is that makes homecomings uncanny; while some emphasize the importance of incorporating what is strange into what is familiar to us, others emphasize how what should be familiar is also rendered strange. The emphasis on *home* and *homecoming* in each of the chapters is an attempt to move the discussion from merely academic musings to uncover something that dwells at the heart of each of us, implicating our habits as well as our habitations. Each chapter, then, points to a different manifestation of uncanny homecomings that echo in how we live today. The first task of the book is to assemble a variety of sites that throw the uncanny dimension of homecoming into relief. Rather than an exhaustive account, this collection indicates only a few of the many ways through which art reveals the tension at the heart of home. Assuming that the tension of the uncanny within the home is valuable to us, the chapters that follow specify different possibilities for resisting the place of belonging.

Additionally, this collection discloses how our sense of home remains indebted to narrative, religion, and art. Homes allow us to merge our memories with our hopes in a process dialectically intertwined with our culture, and we rediscover possibilities of home through the imaginative structures provided by narratives. The continual creative effort required in making homes and making ourselves at home also occurs in creative work as the traditions, images, and narratives that inform us of the meaning of home are produced and received through these cultural artifacts. Several of the chapters expose the anxieties provoked by the narrative foundation of home and thereby indicate how the uncanny is necessarily gathered into the myths and stories about our homes—even when we attempt to ignore its presence. The chapters reflect on both the narrative logic and structure that enables homecoming as a human possibility, and on how the individual stories of homes and homecomings gripped by the uncanny gestures toward ways to consider our own personal narratives—as well as the stories we consume—to find the uncanny within them.

Moreover, the collection points to the importance of revisiting the role of religion in revealing what our homes have been, in tradition, and might be, in the imagination. Although few chapters deal directly with "religion," several of them examine the theological possibilities awakened by having our habitat unsettled. Instead of privileging one or another religious tradition, valuing the uncanny within homecoming allows us to grasp the necessity of a faith that transcends any given revelation or symbol of God that undergirds our homes. Displaced from what is familiar, these chapters hint at a possibility of religion that emerges only when we have turned toward what is foreign, after we have forsaken the traditions that constitute our homes.

It would be somewhat contradictory to approach a volume that resists the place of belonging from a perspective that respected traditional disciplinary boundaries—resting in one home instead of becoming unsettled. Therefore, this volume brings together several disciplinary perspectives in order to disclose a complex vision of "home" that exists between and among them. It is within these rifts, or fissures, that a kind of truth may emerge that manifests the courage to exchange the comfort of certainty for the ineffable pleasure of insight. Beyond the juxtaposition of disciplines, several of the chapters are interdisciplinary in nature, entangling religion, literature, art, theology, philosophy, and cultural studies in a way that reveals how these sometimes strangers can be at home together. The interdisciplinary nature of this collection underscores the complex process through which homes can be questioned at all, as a strict adherence to a "field" tends to revert to the myth that homes are possible or desirable.

A haunting interdisciplinarity emerges in the two introductory chapters that open the volume in Part I, "Uncanny Homecomings." David Jasper's "Knowing for the First Time" and Christopher Merrill's "Staying Found" are simultaneously autobiographical chapters that look back at moments when the divisive nature of home was revealed, works of literary criticism and interpretation that disclose the power of poetry to perform the opening of new worlds, and theological musings about the mysteries that comfortable lives conceal. David Jasper looks to his past homes in India and England as a way to show how betrayal is the blessing that lurks in the heart of home—and homecomings—in literature and in our lives. Christopher Merrill looks at the poets and the poetry that have offered a foundation for his life in order to explore how becoming lost is required for being found, and how staying found serves as the necessary precondition for having something like a "home" at all.

Part II, "Unsettling Foundations of Homes," examines the logics and structures that we use when assuming the function of home, providing a foundation for how we can resist the places that invite us to belong. In other words, these chapters expose the internal flaws hidden in the concept of home that makes every homecoming an uncanny one. The task is to reveal how all homes rest on foundations that— when we contemplate them—*are* unsettling. In drawing our attention to the fragile grounds that we all too frequently dwell upon unthinkingly, these chapters also question the possibilities of having a home.

This part begins with a chapter by Forrest Clingerman that interprets how two pieces of modern art reveal our forgetfulness relative to problems of home, underscoring the unique role that uncanny homecomings play in opening up the healing possibilities offered by the imagination. Daniel Boscaljon extends Heidegger's understanding of poetic dwelling into the sphere of narrative, exploring how the houses featured in nineteenth-century American Gothic literature make readers uncomfortable by gathering them into their closed spaces as a way of warning against a desire for too much familiarity within the home. Kimberly Carfore discusses Derrida's *hauntology*, examining the ethical importance of creating a space within our homes for the others that homes are tempted to exclude, including the non-human. Verna Ehret advocates the wisdom of grounding the sacred depth of theological homes in the uncertainty of a transcontextual narrative, which requires the courage of the uncanny to balance the plurality of voices found in contextual narratives with our participation in a monolithic meta-narrative. Rachel Wagner explores the effects of virtual worlds on our idea of home and homecoming, investigating ways in which computer technology provides a new model for "home," seeing it as a hub instead of as a dwelling point. She then demonstrates how the model usefully interprets diasporas in virtual and "real" worlds, and the implications of this model for the study of religion. Nathan Eric Dickman argues that the polyrhythmic home within the human self requires us to pit faith against friendship, holding our desire for Kierkegaardian individualization in tension with participation in an Aristotelian fellowship. The part concludes with Thomas J.J. Altizer's proposal that Christian theology uniquely posits that the human home is damnation and thereby engineers a *coincidentia oppositorum* that allows humans to encounter a universe of joy that can be accessed only after having dwelt in a universe of absolute damnation.

Part III, "Uncanny Mediations of Homecomings," explores how homecomings are mediated activities, emerging dialectically between things we find and things we make. The chapters in this part examine how aesthetic artifacts and cultural products reveal the complex way in which culture supports our work of homecoming and homemaking. We cultivate and construct homes from the beauty and ugliness that we find in memories and in the material world. Each of these chapters looks at particular works of art as a site that reveals the tension that inheres within the home, and looks to what solace remains once we accept the ethical responsibility for living in a fractured home. These chapters concretize and problematize the slightly more theoretical approaches offered in Part I, revealing the complexity that underlies the habits and habitats that we all too often, and too forgetfully, tend to take for granted.

Joni Kinsey interprets the way that conceptions of home are central to tensions within art history and the visual arts, using conflicts about the opportunities and dangers of art's emphasis on home in the 1930s to inform current Localist trends. Michael Baltutis analyzes the urban uncanny as a way of describing cinematic works that depict characters who build model cities that allow the architects to merge what is terrifying in their world with what is familiar in it. David Seamon investigates how Alan Ball uses the uncanny to frame the house in *Six Feet Under* as a symbol capable of mediating modes of postmodern resistance and reaction to enable characters and viewers to move toward better futures. Janet Donohoe offers a phenomenological account of the work that cemeteries do in mediating homecomings, exploring how such homecomings function to mediate a Heideggerean awareness of our being-toward-death. Hanna Janiszewska examines how attempts by the British Romantics to use lyric poetry as a mode of mediating homecomings led to an uncanny paradox that split the idea of home between its physical and linguistic components. Finally, Ayesha Malik exposes the uncanny consequences of colonialism as mediated through fiction, examining James Joyce's *Dubliners* as an example of how political power disrupts and subverts our ideas of home.

The boundaries that separate these chapters are fictions of convenience: most chapters simultaneously identify what is foundational in our attitude toward home as well as what is problematic, and most include cultural examples that allow for reflexive thoughts. The cohesive thread that unites these chapters arises due to their central point of origin, a conference on "Uncanny Homecomings" held at the University of Iowa in August 2011, sponsored primarily by the Department of Religious Studies. These represent some of the key strands of the discussion that emerged among the scholars gathered there. Most importantly, we hope that these chapters are able to convey the importance of becoming unsettled, convincing you to linger in the uncanny moments that interrupt the everyday as gifts that gesture toward a more rich, full, open and ethical future.

PART I:
Uncanny Homecomings

Chapter 1

Knowing for the First Time

David Jasper

I begin with some words of the twelfth-century monk Hugo of St. Victor:

> It is, therefore, a source of great virtue for the practised mind to learn, bit by bit,
> first to change about invisible and transitory things. So that afterwards it may
> be able to leave them behind altogether. The man who finds his homeland sweet
> is still a tender beginner; he to whom every soil is as his native one is already
> strong; but he is perfect to whom the entire world is as a foreign land. The tender
> soul has fixed his love on one spot in the world; the strong man has extended his
> love to all places; the perfect man has extinguished his.[1]

When I was 22, I had been living and working as a school teacher for two years
in rural North West India and I was looking forward with an aching heart to my
return home to London and to my family, whom I had not seen in all that time: a
long time for a young man of 22. Arriving in London's Heathrow Airport—that
most transitory and solitary of places—I was embraced by my mother and father
and drawn back into the home and the familiar streets of which I had dreamt so
often. There was the sound of Big Ben and the sight of my beloved cat. But my
first night in my own bed, in the familiar room in which I had grown up, was a
sleepless one, for already I was yearning for India, for the little room which I had
shared for so long with my Keralan friend Babu Koshi, for the loneliness even, the
being on my own. I missed the absurd hospitality of the Bankipore Club in Patna,
its smoky lounge peopled by former officers of the Indian Army with magnificent
handlebar moustaches and their vision of an England that never existed or had its
origins in the lonely imaginations of English expatriates in the Colonial Service
before 1947, some of them the sad men and women of Paul Scott's novel *Staying
On*—people without a home or even a country to call their own. But part of me
longed to join them. The London to which I now returned had changed—or, more
precisely, I had changed—and home was no longer entirely home. My own family,
in their very love for me, could have no access to that part of me which had grown
used to being in exile, to being different and which had lived in a subjectivity
that was suspended between extremes of selfishness and selflessness. When I
much later came to read Adorno's *Minima Moralia*, subtitled "Reflections from

---

[1]   Quoted in Edward W. Said, *Reflections on Exile and Other Literary and Cultural
Essays* (London, 2001), p. 185.

Damaged Life,"[2] I understood exactly, though in my own way, what he meant by that fragile term "home" and the irony of his conclusion that "it is part of morality not to be at home in one's home."

Like Adorno, though for quite different reasons, I found refuge in texts and writing. Across enormous, almost limitless, spaces of human experience, my little period of voluntary exile in Bihar gave me a glimpse into the literature of displacement and a sense of something which might have remained incomprehensible to me if it had not been for that first sleepless night at home in Westminster, London. Years later, the last page of Imre Kertész's novel *Fateless* came to haunt me. It tells the story of Gyuri, a 14-year-old Hungarian Jewish boy who survives Auschwitz, finally returning to his family in Budapest and to his "uncontinuable life." In my own pale way I knew exactly what he meant, though without his ghastly experience. He says:

> My mother was waiting, and would no doubt greatly rejoice over me. I recollect that she had once conceived a plan that I should be an engineer, a doctor, or something like that. No doubt that is how it will be, just as she wished; there is nothing impossible that we do not live through naturally, and keeping a watch on me on my journey, like some inescapable trap, I already know there will be happiness. For even there, next to the chimneys, in the intervals between the torments, there was something that resembled happiness. Everyone asks only about the hardships and the "atrocities," whereas for me perhaps it is that experience which will remain the most memorable. Yes, the next time I am asked, I ought to speak about that, the happiness of the concentration camps. If indeed I am asked. And provided I myself don't forget.[3]

What is that we save of our experiences when we return "home?" Sometimes they are all that we have and the homecoming is tragically impossible, the barrier to it unforgiveable. Yet there is the presence, impossible as it might seem, of a "happiness" that seems ineradicable, even in the inevitable betrayals of homecoming or the miseries of the death camp. Is it, perhaps, the sense of life itself that endures, in spite of everything, even beyond the possibilities of forgiveness?

In another novel of the sufferings of the Second World War in Europe, Julia Franck's *The Blind Side of the Heart*, Peter, a seven-year-old German boy, is unaccountably abandoned by his loving mother on a railway station in 1945, just as hostilities have come to an end. Years later she returns to him in the home of his aunt and uncle where he has been living. But he knows that there is no going back and he refuses to see her and hides in a shed:

---

2   Theodor W. Adorno, *Minima Moralia: Reflections from Damaged Life*, trans. E.F.N. Jephcott (London, 1974).

3   Imre Kertész, *Fateless*, trans. Tim Wilkinson (London, 2006), p. 262.

> Peter would have liked to climb down and take a look, but it was too risky ...
> What had his mother imagined? She wanted to see him—so then what? Did she
> by any chance want to ask him to forgive her? Was he supposed to forgive her?
> He couldn't forgive her, he'd never be able to do that. It wasn't in his power;
> even if he had wanted to.[4]

In all homecomings there is a background of separation and walking out on
something that has come to an end—childhood, war, marriage. And there is
therefore inevitably always the element of betrayal and a rejection of what we
have become, so that sometimes the damage is irreparable. It is the risk we take
every time we leave home.

Exile can be voluntary (as in my case), enforced (as in the plight of refugees or
the victims of war), or the mysterious severance that happens when we desert one
another under the pressure of overwhelming circumstances. This last severance
cannot be healed (as in Julia Franck's novel), and so we can find ourselves in
circumstances which plunge us into a lethal mixture of betrayal, resentment, and
cynicism that even love itself cannot heal. We bear responsibility, but to what
extent can we be said to be at fault?

In Simone Weil we see the complexity of the exilic predicament, described
by Edward Said as "the sheer fact of isolation and displacement, which produces
the kind of narcissistic masochism that resists all efforts at amelioration,
acculturation, and community." And yet it is not all loss—in the complexity and
the displacement there is another voice that is less tragic and perhaps ultimately
religious in its tenor. More recently we have grown used to the post-colonial, exilic
voices of Said and Homi Babha, the latter with his oft-repeated call to the city of
Bombay (as he insists on calling it still), "I want to go home." It is a call which
demands dialogue, both within the self and between selves. Babha recalls us to the
"unsatisfied voice" of Adrienne Rich, hesitantly affirming—*I am ... I am*—and
the "insistent questioning" of the Mumbai Dalit poet Prakash Jadhav—*Who am
I? What am I?*—and from them he asserts the right to be heard (even by oneself),
the right to speak either at home (wherever that is) or abroad (or reverse the two):

> You are part of a dialogue that may not, at first, be heard of heralded—you may
> be ignored—but your personhood cannot be denied. *In another's country that
> is also your own, your person divides*, and in following the forked path you
> encounter yourself in a double movement ... Once as a stranger, and then as a
> friend.[5]

The word "home" has such heavy meaning. Coming back from India, "home" was
too much for me—something almost bovine in its security, its lack of risk. The

---

4   Julia Franck, *The Blind Side of the Heart*, trans. Anthea Bell (London, 2010), p. 422.

5   Homi K. Bhabha, *The Location of Culture* (London and New York, 1994), p. xxv,
emphasis added.

danger then is that one begins to long always for that which is lost, the stranger within one picking quarrels with home (like Joyce did with Ireland) to sustain the vision of the other. And Paradise itself can then seem oppressive: as Said has suggested of *The Divine Comedy*, "even the beatific peace achieved in the *Paradiso* bears traces of the vindictiveness and severity of judgement embodied in the *Inferno*."[6] I think I had always suspected this, though I never dared to admit it. Perhaps Dante also knew the sharp edge of the contrary vision that we find later in Blake—and for me, its consequences? That is, that it is only by contraries that we can ever progress—not contradictions, but sometimes painful paradoxes and the being caught between unreconciled alternatives. There is the sense then, perhaps, of the necessary transitoriness of what we call home and that dialogue between the stranger and the friend in each of us, our pilgrim selves, the ever new realization that the place known as home is always barely known as if for the first time, a place ever realized anew in each visit on our journey through time and space—like a sacrament. I think back to another time of brief exile in my life, a short period of solitary retreat in the Texas desert, and I look back to my notes made then: "I am where I am, touching base. This is my home for the time being, and it does very nicely." Well—perhaps that, at least, is a start.

"For the Time Being"—this takes me back to that most matter-of-fact of poets, W.H. Auden, who is not, perhaps, much in fashion these days. *For the Time Being*, Auden's "Christmas Oratorio," begins with the calling of Advent and whose narrative of birth is haunted by the cross. The eternal presses itself upon the creatures of time, making us restless even at Christmas, the most homely of all Western Christian festivals—Auden, it must be said, loved Mr Pickwick and the innocence of Dingley Dell. Yet our sense of well-being is oppressed, and even around the Christmas hearth we are not quite at home, strangers to ourselves:

> We who must die demand a miracle.
> How could the eternal do a temporal act,
> The Infinite become a finite fact?[7]

And at the end of his poem, Auden captures precisely the sense at the end of Christmas, even its failure perhaps, in our fallen world:

> Stayed up so late, attempted—quite unsuccessfully—
> To love all of our relatives, and in general
> Grossly overestimated. Once again
> As in previous years we have seen the actual Vision and failed
> To do more than entertain it as an agreeable
> Possibility, once again we have sent Him away...[8]

---

[6]   Said, *Reflections on Exile*, p. 182.

[7]   W.H. Auden, "For the Time Being," in *Collected Longer Poems* (London, 1974), p. 138.

[8]   Ibid., p. 195.

But the coherence in pilgrimage which eludes these familiar homely admissions is found mysteriously in the liturgical rhythms of another work—Auden's poetic sequence, which is based on the canonical hours of monastic discipline—*Horae Canonicae*. A meditation in seven parts on the mystery of the cross, upon fallenness, forgiveness, and restoration in coinherence (the word is deliberately taken from one of Auden's mentors, Charles Williams),[9] the poem explores the necessary complexity of our being at home in the world—at once the stranger and the friend, the one who returns like the prodigal son, finding forgiveness and yet feeling drawn back to exile in a far country, the soul rescued from hell yet still longing for the "home" of this provisional and fallen world which, as at the end of *Paradise Lost*, in spite of all is the world we want and love—even in the unthinkable happiness of the concentration camps. And so we can find ourselves saying with David Daiches that "God is justified, in a way that might perhaps have surprised him."[10] Or, as Auden tentatively puts it in "Nones," "It would be best to go home, if we have a home."

Horae Canonicae begins and ends at dawn in "Prime" and "Lauds" with the half world between sleeping and waking in the early morning:

> Recalled from the shades to be a seeing being,
> From absence to be on display,
> Without a name or history I wake
> Between my body and the day. ("Prime")

> Among the leaves the small birds sing;
> The crow of the cock commands awaking:
> *In solitude, for company.*
> Bright shines the sun on creatures mortal;
> Men of their neighbours become sensible:
> *In solitude for company.* ("Lauds")[11]

And so we begin our worship at the break of day, in solitude for company. At home in exile and in exile at home, we are divided creatures, the joining of two parts seeking an impossible solidarity in our "unhomely" (*unheimlich*) selves, caught, in Hannah Arendt's words, in the rent between "things that should be hidden and things that should be shown," discovering with what pain "how rich and manifold the hidden can be under conditions of intimacy." With our dearest ones we ache

---

[9]   See Charles Williams, *The Descent of the Dove: A Short History of the Holy Spirit in the Church* (London, 1939). The book is dedicated to "the Companions of the Co-inherence."

[10]   David Daiches, *God and the Poets* (Oxford, 1984), p. 49.

[11]   W.H. Auden, *Collected Shorter Poems, 1927–1957* (London, 1969), pp. 323, 337.

to share that which we dare not or cannot articulate to them, in solitude, for company.[12]

In Auden's meditation—he was never demonstrative in his religion—this finds its focus in his most deeply Christocentric and private/public acts of worship, in the Christ of the Passion and in the sacrament of the Eucharist caught between absence and presence in what he calls "an operation beyond our comprehension but not beyond our attention." In the rhythms of the daily offices, we finally turn away from our participation in what Auden describes as the "crowd," which is, in his friend Bishop Peter Walker's terms, "almost no more than a perverted way of seeing things: 'it looks on or it looks away,'" to a being in communion, oneself with the other and the other as oneself.[13] Here one is never more deeply alone and yet at the same time never more deeply at one with all—at home in one's very unhomeliness, taught us first and most excruciatingly and profoundly in the cry of Christ on the cross: "My God, my God, why have you forsaken me":

> Can poets (can men in television)
> Be saved? It is not easy
> To believe in unknowable justice
> Or pray in the name of a love
> Whose name one's forgotten: *libera*
> *Me, libera* C (dear C)
> And all poor s-o-b's who never
> Do anything properly… ("Compline")[14]

The words lodged in the poem are from the *Requiem Mass*, the *Responsorium*: "*Libera me, Domine, de morte aeterna in die ille tremenda…*" Edward Mendelson ends his book *Early Auden* with the words: "The only answer to the isolating will is the absolute gift of pardon."[15] That is what we find so hard, especially to pardon those whom we love most dearly, whose misunderstanding (a forsaking of us) wounds us most deeply. Here, in the mystery of the sacrament, which lies at the very heart of the *Horae Canonicae*, we glimpse the communion in the fragment of the bread, apart from the anonymity of the crowd. And here, paradoxically, is the most absolute losing of self to find the self—to know it for the first time, if but for an instant.

The same Peter Walker (who was, as it happens, the bishop who ordained me in 1976) once wrote that "it must be remembered that [Auden] died a communicant

---

[12]   Hannah Arendt, *The Human Condition*, 2nd edn (Chicago, 1998).

[13]   Peter Walker, "W.H. Auden's Horae Canonicae: Auden's Vision of a Rood – A Study in Coherence," in David Jasper (ed.), *Images of Belief in Literature* (London, 1984), p. 65.

[14]   Auden, *Collected Shorter Poems*, p. 337.

[15]   Edward Mendelson, *Early Auden* (London, 1981), p. 364.

member of his church, as I am humbled to remember recalling a Palm Sunday morning Holy Communion (his last) in Christchurch Cathedral, Oxford at which I was celebrant."[16] Auden appreciated Peter who, as a celebrant, had the extraordinary capacity to disappear from Mass, never to intrude himself into the words and actions, allowing self to be self utterly without ego, in communion.

Such self-effacement is all so much more gentle and even forgiving than the far better-known and oft-repeated words from the end of T.S. Eliot's *Little Gidding*:

> We shall not cease from exploration
> And the end of all our exploring
> Will be to arrive where we started
> And know the place for the first time.[17]

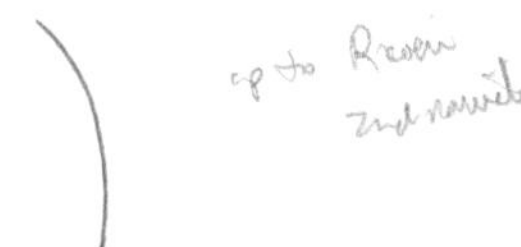

I know what Eliot means here, in a way, but it is finally too pious for me, too absolute for my divided self. It lives in the realms of what theology may call the spiritual, but I am not there yet—and I don't know if I ever want to be there, to be at home there. Somehow I feel more comfortable with the uncertain festivities of homecoming described at the end of Hölderlin's elegy *Heimkunft an die Verwandten* (*Homecoming to his Relatives*), as rendered in Michael Hamburger's English translation:

> Silence often behoves us: deficient in names that are holy,
> Hearts may beat high, while the lips hesitate, wary of speech?
> Yet a lyre to each hour lends the right mode, the right music,
> And, it may be, delights heavenly ones who draw near.
> This make ready, and almost nothing remains of the care that
> Darkened our festive day, troubled the promise of joy.
> Whether he like it or, and often, a singer must harbour
> Cares like these in his soul; not, though, the wrong sort of cares.[18]

How such cares afflict me—the distractions, the perplexities, which accompany the homecoming that is the realization of the absolute present even in our divided selves that exist ever in the inbetween of our lives. In literature they are found with most crystal clarity in the traditions of mystical writing. Here, for example, are words of the Spanish Sufi mystic Ibn 'Arabī, a wanderer all of his life:

> The Real made me contemplate [the light of] perplexity and He said to me, "Return!" But I did not find where to. He said to me "Approach!" But I did not

---

16   Walker, "W.H. Auden's Horae Canonicae," p. 59.

17   T.S. Eliot, *The Complete Poems and Plays* (London, 1969), p. 197.

18   Friedrich Hölderlin, *Poems and Fragments*, trans. Michael Hamburger (London, 1994), p. 281.

find where. He said to me, "Stop!" But I did not find where. He said, "Do not withdraw!" And I was perplexed…

Make them stay in perplexity and do not point Me out to anyone. Bring them to Me and let them know about Me but do not let them know My place, and let them know about My place without letting them know Me. If they hold fast to My place they will find Me. If they find Me, they will not see anything. If they see something they will not see My place. If they do not see My place, then perhaps they will see Me.[19]

If I try to understand this religiously or, even more presumptuously, theologically, it means little to me except in some vague theoretical sense. But as a reader of literature and poetry, and as a traveller, I know precisely what Ibn 'Arabī means— but I know as if for the first time. It is not even or just in the great literature, but at the end of something as humble as, say, Charles Kingsley's 'socialist' novel *Alton Locke* (1850), when Locke dies at peace seeing in his mind's eye the promised land which he will never see, and lying on the ship carrying him to America "as peacefully as if he had slumbered.". And I have known it, I think, from time to time, in the stuff of my life, even and perhaps especially in those moments of painful separation where true peace resides.

That is why, I suppose, the Christian poet can speak of the heart in pilgrimage, that we are a pilgrim people and only in being can we find ourselves uncannily at home. Thinking of my own Celtic homeland (though an adopted one), I can see a bit more clearly why the great Celtic saints did not build great stone cathedrals or centres of permanent residence, preferring to dwell (as in the Greek verb σκηνόω— to 'tent,' to 'have one's tabernacle'—as in John 1:14: "the Word became flesh and dwelt [ἐσκήνωσεν] among us") as wanderers. In the words of David Adam:

The Celtic church did not seek so much to bring Christ as to discover Him: not to possess Him, but to see Him in "friend and stranger"; to liberate the Christ who is already there in all his riches.[20]

The Celtic Christians were restless (finding their rest only in Him), wandering on pilgrimage as a kind of exile and a constant reminder that on earth they were far from perfect but, in the words of Adamnan, the biographer of St Columba, *"pro Christo peregrinari volens"*—"wishing to be a pilgrim for Christ." Journeying from place to place on the earth, they found the true pilgrimage to Christ which is of the heart and soul, in which they found their being and their home. Perhaps it is the true traveller who follows in the way of Christ who had no home in which to lay his head, like the patriarch in the Epistle to the Hebrews, desiring "a better

---

[19]   Ibn 'Arabī, *Contemplation of the Holy Mysteries*, trans, Cecilia Twinch and Pablo Beneito (Oxford, 2009), pp. 85–6.

[20]   David Adam, *The Cry of the Deer* (London, 1987), p. 28.

country, that is a heavenly one" (Hebrews 11:16). Yet, it is also here with us. The great seventh-century Irish missionary St Columbanus spent his life in perpetual pilgrimage, affirming that "it is the end of the road that travellers look for and desire, and because we are travellers and pilgrims through this world, it is the road's end, that is of our lives, that we should always be thinking about. For that road's end is our true homeland."[21] And yet somehow I am not quite one with the great missionary saint here, tinged as his words are, for all their piety and solemnity, with just a touch of morbidity. Pilgrims we may be, but in journeying we learn the paradox, at the same time, of purifying our restlessness, cultivating on the way the disinterestedness of the Desert Fathers, the Indian Yogis and the Zen Buddhist monks.

Thus, to be "at home with oneself" is to realize a purity of heart (with a beauty that is past change) always as if for the first time. Thomas Merton calls such purity:

> a clear unobstructed vision of the true state of affairs, an intuitive grasp of one's own inner reality as anchored, or rather lost, in God through Christ … Simply the sanity and poise of a being that no longer has to look at itself because it is carried away by the perfection of freedom that is in it. And carried where? Wherever Love itself, or the Divine Spirit, sees fit to go.[22]

To be thus is to be the perfect man—as opposed to the tender man or the strong man—of Hugo of St Victor, with whom we began. Oddly, one comes close, though painfully so, knowing it so remote, to this perfect freedom in the divisions experienced when one returns to the familiar hearth and find oneself longing for the far-strange country that has also become an image of home, and, in the words of Homi Babha, "this borderline existence inhabits a stillness of time and a strangeness of framing that creates the discursive 'image' at the crossroads of history and literature, bridging the home and world."[23] Only in our journeying can we learn such stillness—or at least the edge of it.

As I ponder upon this, I am reminded of an evening which has haunted me for years. My daughter and I went to an evening of jazz in a small theatre in Glasgow. We went to see the great jazz pianist Keith Tippett and he had playing with him a band from the Island of Mull in the Scottish Inner Hebrides. They came from the small town of Tobermory, which was familiar to me from childhood holidays, and they played music which had been inspired by letters written to one another by two sisters in the nineteenth century, both unmarried, who came from Mull. All their lives they continued to write to each other, though they rarely saw one another. For one was an example of those great Victorian adventurer travellers who spent

---

[21]   Quoted in Ian Bradley, *The Celtic Way*, new edn (London, 2003), p. 81.

[22]   Thomas Merton, *The Wisdom of the Desert: Sayings from the Desert Fathers of the Fourth Century* (New York, 1961), p. 8.

[23]   See Bhabha, *The Location of Culture*, Chapter 12, "Conclusion: 'Race,' Time and the Revision of Modernity," pp. 338–67.

her life journeying in remote corners of the globe from Africa, to India, China, and Russia: the other, as far as I remember, never left Mull, not even crossing the short stretch of sea between the island and the mainland—perhaps a mile at most. For she was a traveller in spirit, journeying in the stillness of her being "at home"— and the two sisters understood each other perfectly. One could feel this unity and disunity in the music—peaceful and yet also unearthly and slightly disturbing. But it had an immediacy that one responded to—and knew it, as if for the first time.

In conclusion, I want to draw the strands of these reflections on homecoming —personal, literary, theological—together in a moment that has been the focus of my thinking for the past few years as I have been writing a book which is entitled *The Sacred Community*.[24] It is the moment in the Christian liturgy, based on the vision of Isaiah in the Temple in Isaiah 6:1–3, when the community on earth joins for one eternal moment, ever new and endlessly repeated, in the hymn that has become known as the Sanctus: "Holy, holy, holy, Lord God of hosts, heaven and earth are full of thy glory." From the earliest days of the church, a word was added to the biblical text: "and earth"—"heaven *and earth* are full of thy glory." And so for one unearthly moment, we divided creatures are at home in the joining of heaven and earth. Thus, what is "done" in the celebration of the Eucharist is the focus for the totality of the Christian life, not only spatially but also in the totality of time, in an act of remembrance that unites the past, present and future of human history in eternity. Then we sing, with angels and archangels and the whole company of heaven, the restless oppositions of our beings brought, for one instant, together. Here, in a sense, there is no passage of time, of pilgrim time, but only a dwelling in eternity. One of the great and often-quoted passages in modern liturgical study, from the end of Dom Gregory Dix's work *The Shape of the Liturgy*, bears another repetition to make the point:

> For century after century, spreading slowly to every continent and country and among every race on earth, this action has been done, in every conceivable human circumstance, for every conceivable need from infancy and before it to extreme old age and after it, from the pinnacles of earthly greatness to the refuge of fugitives in the caves and dens of the earth. Men have found no better thing than this to do for kings at their crowning and criminals going to the scaffold; for armies in triumph or for a bride and bridegroom in a little country church…[25]

I will not go on. You will be calling me sentimental, and there are also the moments of betrayal, inevitably and always, as well as those of recognition and knowing: the liturgy knows this too, and in my book I dwell much upon the inevitability— even the painful necessity—of betrayal, for, as we have touched upon, without this, there could be no happiness of the concentration camps or the deep joy of

---

[24]   David Jasper, *The Sacred Community: Art, Sacrament, and the People of God* (Waco, 2012).

[25]   Dom Gregory Dix, *The Shape of the Liturgy* (Westminster, 1945), p. 744.

the cross, moments that comfortable familiarity can never understand. Indeed, to *understand* can never truly be part of our homecoming for it involves a knowing, or perhaps a moment of true being, that is known only in betrayal. In a faint way, my return to London from India was also a moment of betrayal—of my family and close friends—that I could barely admit to myself. But then I knew something that I had not known before and could not have known without the journey out and back. I suppose it was my passage to India.

To return, in this ending, to Auden's *Horae Canonicae*. The final poem in the sequence, "Lauds," bursts, with a transport of rejoicing, into a new day: "Among the leaves the small birds sing." Their song—like the Sanctus, but also like the crowing of the cock that Peter knew in bitterness of spirit—commands our awakening in solitude (Auden calls this man's real condition), but for company so that "Men of their neighbours become sensible.".[26]

And now I draw to my conclusion, which, of course, concludes nothing, with the words of Bishop Walker:

> Awake, that is the call, to a belonging that is real. There is a realm, there is a people, to whom you belong; the green world temporal is your world, no urban desert now, and there is God's blessing on it all.
>
> To say that this is a waking to a world renewed, redeemed, would be no more than a natural use of words. It is, in fact, precisely what the poet is conveying. At the heart of "Lauds" the mass bell—at the heart of the mass, it goes without saying, an act of redemption…[27]

But I end, finally, in curious irresolution. I have become, with the good bishop, too theological, too close to a sense of understanding and resolving the mystery, or at least imagining so. At home, back again, for the first time, I know that division in myself, with that hint of cruelty that is in all of us (betrayal again), far from the perfect man of Hugo of St Victor. I am home but I am not at home. Perhaps I have just begun, at last, to grow up and now that I have reached my three score years, I can begin to say this kind of thing, which would have been impossible before. It is like a small death, good to get over and done with, and in the impossible interstices of the present there is something new. For the first time, I can say, I know it.

References

Adam, David, *The Cry of the Deer* (London: SPCK, 1987).
Adorno, Theodor W., *Minima Moralia: Reflections from Damaged Life*, trans. E.F.N. Jephcott (London: New Left Books, 1974).

---

[26] Auden, *Collected Shorter Poems*, p. 337.
[27] Walker, "W.H. Auden's Horae Canonicae," p. 59.

'Arabī, Ibn, *Contemplation of the Holy Mysteries*, trans. Cecilia Twinch and Pablo Beneito (Oxford: Anqa Publishing, 2009).

Arendt, Hannah, *The Human Condition*, 2nd edn (Chicago: Chicago University Press, 1998).

Auden, W.H., *Collected Longer Poems* (London: Faber & Faber, 1974).

Auden, W.H., *Collected Shorter Poems, 1927–1957* (London: Faber & Faber, 1969).

Bhabha, Homi K., *The Location of Culture* (London and New York: Routledge, 1994).

Bradley, Ian, *The Celtic Way*. New Edition (London: DLT, 2003).

Daiches, David, *God and the Poets* (Oxford: Clarendon Press, 1984).

Dix, Dom Gregory, *The Shape of the Liturgy* (London: Dacre Press, 1945).

Eliot, T.S., *The Complete Poems and Plays* (London: Faber & Faber, 1969).

Franck, Julia, *The Blind Side of the Heart*, trans. Anthea Bell (London: Vintage Books, 2010).

Hölderlin, Friedrich, *Poems and Fragments*, trans. Michael Hamburger (London, 1994).

Jasper, David, *The Sacred Community: Art, Sacrament, and the People of God* (Waco: Baylor University Press, 2012).

Kertész, Imre, *Fateless*, trans. Tim Wilkinson (London: Vintage Books, 2006).

Mendelson, Edward, *Early Auden* (London: Faber & Faber, 1981).

Merton, Thomas, *The Wisdom of the Desert: Sayings from the Desert Fathers of the Fourth Century* (New York: New Directions, 1961).

Said, Edward W., *Reflections on Exile and Other Literary and Cultural Essays* (London: Granta Books, 2001).

Walker, Peter, "W.H. Auden's Horae Canonicae: Auden's Vision of a Rood – A Study in Coherence," in David Jasper (ed.), *Images of Belief in Literature* (London: Macmillan, 1984).

Williams, Charles, *The Descent of the Dove: A Short History of the Holy Spirit in the Church* (London: Longmans, Green & Co., 1939).

Chapter 2
Staying Found

Christopher Merrill

The first part of the trail I remembered from college. And nearly every summer since graduation I had hiked in the woods behind Middlebury's mountain campus, during the Bread Loaf Writers' Conference, usually in the company of the novelist Tom Gavin. He was on the faculty, I was an administrative scholar, and once the daily round of readings and lectures, workshops and cocktail parties began to taper off, it was our custom to steal away for an afternoon. There was an element of truancy involved—he had manuscripts to read, I had crises to address, we told no one where we were going—which added a certain thrill to our time together in the woods.

Tom cut a trim figure in a brown leather vest and white shirt, with his sleeves rolled and a satchel slung over his shoulder; he had a beard and a mustache, sleepy eyes, the richly modulated voice of an actor. On stage as a student, his fear of falling into the arms of his fellow actors had led him to give up any thought of a career in theater—a failing which would shape his teaching. Thus, when his daughter was quite small, he devised a game to cultivate her trust, standing her on his desk and coaxing her to fall, laughing, into his arms. This same trust he instilled in me in an introductory poetry workshop, and in the decade since he had transformed himself so gracefully from my mentor to my friend that it would take me many years to begin to grasp the selflessness of his gesture. In 1987, though, when the events described here occurred, I knew only that the subjects addressed in our correspondence over the previous year, which ranged from the books we were reading to the nature of inspiration to questions of belief, would animate our walk. Conversation with Tom plumbed depths which I found in no other literary circumstances.

From my first class with him I had relished his willingness to share his experiences as a writer, introducing not only the mysteries of the creative process but also methods of tapping the sources of literature—images and phrases, memories and observations, narrative and poetic strategies gleaned from other writers, the music of chance. The circuitous ways of the language, he explained, can lead to marvelous encounters with our deepest selves; from his vast reading he described some of the ways in which poets and fiction writers, trusting their instincts, discover new ways of apprehending the world around and within them. To illustrate the importance of developing sound working habits, he recalled the night that his young daughter, gazing out of her bedroom window, told him that the moon looked like a fingernail.

"I raced for my notebook," said Tom—a subtle admonition for those, like me, who were too lazy to take notes. To this day I carry a notebook everywhere I go.

On another occasion, he said that when he realized, well into his first novel *Kingkill,* that his main female character lay lifeless on the page, he stopped writing for three months in order to record in his journal every thought and memory, desire and fantasy that he had ever entertained about women, embarking on a bold imaginative journey to connect with the feminine side of his soul. When he returned to his novel, he found that he could draw the female lead in vivid detail. Out of such stories I began to serve my literary apprenticeship.

In late August in Vermont there are hints of autumn at every turn—tall spikes of ripening mullein, opened pods of milkweed, reddening maple leaves—and when on the appointed day of our hike we set out after lunch, in broad sunshine, there was a chill in the air, which spurred our pace down the road. After some minutes we came to the driveway leading to the summer cabin of Robert Frost, Bread Loaf's tutelary spirit. It was Frost who in the 1920s had urged Middlebury to establish a writers' conference, and on the porch of his shuttered cabin, gazing at a meadow thick with mustard beyond which rose a mountain in bluish haze, it occurred to me that my ambivalent feelings about his poems had dissolved since college. His presence had been such a constant in my literature classes that in typically adolescent fashion I had rebelled against the entirety of his work only to discover that I had more of it by heart than that of any other poet.

This was a shock, which by a strange analogy brought to mind his poem "The Death of the Hired Man" and, specifically, the haunting exchange between a man and his wife about the unreliable employee who after a long absence has returned for his final hours:

> "Warren," she said, "he has come home to die:
> You needn't be afraid he'll leave you this time."
> "Home," he mocked gently.
>> "Yes, what else but home?
> It all depends on what you mean by home.
> Of course he's nothing to us, any more
> Than was the hound that came a stranger to us
> Out of the woods, worn out upon the trail."
> "Home is the place where, when you have to go there
>> They have to take you in."
>> "I should have called it
> Something you somehow haven't to deserve."[1]

How should we describe such a home? Where or what is that undeserved place or state of being? Is it the Kingdom of God promised by Jesus? But Heaven is reserved for the faithful, according to Christian theology, and there is nothing

---

[1] Robert Frost, *Frost: Collected Poems, Prose, & Plays* (New York, 1995), p. 43.

in the hired man's history to suggest that he believes in anything other than the pleasures of honest work—loading hay, clearing land—which may or may not be performed in a holy manner. Perhaps on Judgment Day it will be revealed that the hired man does not merit a place with the redeemed. What Frost suggests is dark indeed: that the good earth will take him in, as in fact it takes in everyone, sinners and saints alike.

There are some who find home in the Psalms and Proverbs, in Christ's parables, in the suras of the Qur'an and the sayings of the Prophet, in Hindu rituals and Zen koans, in prayer and song, in family and friends, customs and ceremonies, art and literature. Poets and writers may be most at home in their relationship to language—a recurring theme in my discussions with Tom, whose reverence for literary craftsmanship impressed upon me the need to revise every sentence, exploring to the limits of my ability the materials of my imagination. Only in revision, he said, in re + vision, does the writer have a chance to see clearly.

It was on his recommendation that I first applied to Bread Loaf. The dizzying selection of readings and lectures, the chance to talk shop with other writers, the exhilaration of meeting kindred spirits—I loved everything about the place except the workshop to which I was assigned. My instructor was a poet who seemed more interested in bedding his female students than in reading my work, and during my private conference with him I fell into despair, imagining that if I could not keep his attention for more than a minute—his eyes were darting around the barn in which students congregated, a bottle of vodka wedged under his arm—I could not hope to be a writer. This was a foolish conclusion to reach, but what young writer is not foolish? My mood soured steadily, and even now I do not understand how I summoned the courage, on the penultimate day of the conference, to approach the novelist John Gardner (the only faculty member who ever mingled with the students in the barn when he did not have to be there) and ask him to look at my work. He put aside the manuscript he was reading, motioned for me to sit down, and said, "I'll read until I get bored." Well, I thought, this won't take long.

My heart was pounding as he began to read a short story based on an old woman who had hired me at the age of 13 to work in her gardens, marking edits with his pencil, removing extra words. After going through a couple of pages he leaned back in his chair and looked at me, his long white hair covering his shoulders, his blue eyes boring into mine.

"You're a writer," he said—and for the next four and a half hours he talked to me about what that meant: the sacredness of the vocation, the technical exercises that must be mastered (he was about to publish a compilation of exercises and essays on the craft of writing, entitled *The Art of Fiction*, which he had written in his hospital bed after surgery for stomach cancer), the books to read in several languages, the endless revision, the daily work. It was a decisive encounter for me—one that changed my life. He was telling me to get serious. And I listened, as Tom had listened to him long before, when he was 125 pages into the writing of *Kingkill*. Gardner advised him to vary the rhythm of his sentences and the pacing of his story—counsel that I adapted to my own purpose, in poetry and prose. For

I was determined to make music, as Frost said, out of "the sound of sense," and this begins with listening—to the pulses in your blood, to the inflections of your surroundings, to the speech of everyone you meet.

Into the woods Tom and I marched, through a stand of Norway maples planted in long even rows, as if in imitation of what Frost called "strict iambics," the beauty of which depends upon rhythmic variation. And variation in the landscape was what we found when we left the tree farm behind, climbing uphill past the remnants of a stone wall, on a narrow path through thickening brush and hardwood forest. Our destination was a tumbledown farmhouse, whose deterioration we marked year by year. The roof had caved in, the windows were gone, and in a pit out back you could dig up pieces of old dishes. This scene of neglect was a living emblem of Gardner's last novel, *Mickelsson's Ghosts*, which chronicles the efforts of a brilliant philosophy professor to renovate a farmhouse in rural Pennsylvania. Peter Mickelsson, who bears more than a passing resemblance to the novelist (he teaches at SUNY-Binghamton, his finances are in disarray after a divorce settlement, he feels out of step with his contemporaries despite the fact that his writings on ethics have earned him wide acclaim), is a lost soul. And his effort to rebuild his life in a house haunted by his ghosts—his estranged wife and children; his colleagues and students; the philosophers responsible, in his view, for the lunacy of modern life—takes on a metaphysical aspect, his looming madness mirroring disturbing developments in society at large. But there is pleasure in the storytelling, and the novel reminds us of literature's healing power: in storytelling lies the possibility of redemption—the key to understanding Gardner's art.

The novel's autobiographical elements provided another level of interest for those, like Tom and me, who had profited from Gardner's generosity; circling the ruins of this homestead, we mourned Gardner's premature death in a motorcycle accident five years earlier, at the age of 49, a week before he was to wed for the third time. I recalled his erratic behavior at Bread Loaf that summer: his drunkenness, his arguments with other writers, his abbreviated lecture—"If you're not writing about political matters, you're not writing," he thundered, then marched out of the theater. Some thought that bad reviews of *Mickelsson's Ghosts* had sent him over the edge. But no one could explain why he had skidded off the road on a clear autumn day. Had an animal darted out in front of him? Had a car or truck veered into his lane? Had he killed himself?

I had a theory, derived from his *Paris Review* interview: that on the ride home from visiting his elderly father, a childhood memory—the death of his younger brother, in an accident on their family dairy farm—had welled up, causing him to lose control of his motorcycle. From the age of 12, Gardner blamed himself—he was driving the tractor that pulled the roller under which his brother somehow fell and was crushed—and his devotion to literature was a form of atonement: he wrote to make things whole, if only on the page, his powers of invention sufficient to bring to life a range of memorable characters in novels like *Grendel*, *The Sunlight Dialogues*, and *October Light*. "Redemption" is the autobiographical story of a farm boy whose inability to think clearly at a decisive moment results in his brother's death—an event which he will replay in his memory for the rest of his life. He stands aloof from his family, nursing his grief, his only solace the French horn, an instrument he will never master. Indeed, his realization that he lacks his teacher's gift is what frees the boy to find his way home. Gardner told *The Paris Review* that until he wrote "Redemption," the accident for which he bore responsibility (at least in his own mind) would flash before his eyes four or five times a day.

"I'd be driving down the highway," he said, "and I couldn't see what was coming because I'd have a memory flash."[2]

He claimed that the writing of this story freed him from that nightmare, and perhaps it did release him for a time, offering what Frost in his definition of poetry called "a momentary stay against confusion." "Redemption" provides a moment of bitter clarity in a life undone by chance. But it is only a moment. The fact is that grievous wounds never completely heal. Some thought that Gardner drove himself to write so much (he published more than 30 books of fiction, essays, poetry, and translations, not to mention a biography of Chaucer) to win back his parents' love, and I wondered if on the day of his death the recognition that his father's walk in the sun was nearly over triggered a recurrence of that memory trace.

Writers reckon with their demons in productive ways and otherwise, as Gardner showed in his short life. And since I was navigating a difficult passage of my own, having left academia to work as a caretaker of an estate in New Mexico, I took heart in Tom's revelation now that a personal crisis had informed the writing of each of his novels—a tenure debacle, a dissolving marriage, questions about the Church. This gave additional meaning to a lecture on faith which he had delivered in the chapel at Middlebury not long before he left to teach at the University of Rochester, the refrain of which was a sort of mantra for me. His subject was Kierkegaard's *Fear and Trembling*, Abraham's leap of faith being a constant in his meditations on the meaning of his time here below; his repetition of the prophet's answer to God's call on the mountain—"Here am I"—lodged in my memory as a token of our obligation to seek the divine at every turn. Literary writers are generally reluctant to speak about faith, especially in an academic setting, and Tom's willingness to lay bare his soul, his courage (there is no other word for it), made an impression on me. Whenever I approach that intersection of literature and belief, I hear his voice summoning from the depths of his being the words of Abraham: "Here am I."

We took another turn around the farmstead, our conversation drifting, as it often did when we came here, to Frost's magisterial poem "Directive," which is among other things a fine example of Freud's definition of the uncanny—"that class of the terrifying which leads back to something long known to us, once very familiar." It is also a splendid meditation on the idea of a homecoming, which never works out the way we imagine it will. He begins by encouraging the reader to "Back out of all this now too much for us, / Back in a time made simple by the

---

[2]   John Gardner, "The Art of Fiction No. 73," *The Paris Review*, Spring 1979.

loss" and thereby grants permission to retreat from a home filled with familiar cares. In its place, he grants the gift of a house that falls short of being a home, a universal and anonymous structure:

> There is a house that is no more a house
> Upon a farm that is no more a farm
> And in a town that is no more a town.

Weaving together descriptions of the age and heft of a place revealed by a guide who "only has at heart your getting lost" with a sense of the history of a town that one encounters through the sight of trees and moldering buildings, Frost reveals how even this place can inspire a sense of homecoming:

> And if you're lost enough to find yourself
> By now, pull in your ladder road behind you
> And put a sign up CLOSED to all but me.
> Then make yourself at home.

Within this space, the "children's home of make believe," a "house that is no more a house, / But only a belilaced cellar hole," Frost guides his reader to the possibility of a transformative homecoming, a homemaking established through time and space:

> I have kept hidden in the instep arch
> Of an old cedar at the waterside
> A broken drinking goblet like the grail
> Under a spell so the wrong ones can't find it,
> So can't get saved, as Saint Mark says they mustn't.
> (I stole the goblet from the children's playhouse.)
> Here are your waters and your watering place.
> Drink and be whole again beyond confusion.[3]

There is a story about Randall Jarrell diving into a quarry one day and surfacing to recite for his friend Richard Wilbur the whole of "Directive," which he was not aware he knew by heart until that very moment. This is how great poems work, rhythmically coursing through the blood in the time signature of our pulses (many note that the iambic foot—da-dum—sounds like a heartbeat), shaping our conduct in ways that cannot always be discerned.

"Directive" employs the imperative mode to instruct us how to read an illegible set of ruins; in other words, to grasp the significance of what has been lost—and what might be remembered, if not redeemed: a way of life. And the poem teems with uncanny homecomings, beginning with a metrical discovery: after all the

---

[3]   Frost, *Frost*, pp. 341–2.

stressed syllables in the first line (eight by my count) and then a pair of lines marked by spondees, Frost presents a run of relentlessly regular iambs, which have an odd effect on the ear: what in other circumstances might sound comforting reinforces the deadening effect of time and the weather, which ultimately wear everything down. The threefold repetition of the phrase "no more" adds yet more poignancy to the desolate scene. A house in earnest has vanished, its token of seriousness, its pledge to the future, now no more than the fantasy of "a guide who only has at heart your getting lost."

Who is this figure promising to lead us to the spring? A wise and impish man, schooled alike in the Book of Nature and the New Testament. What choice do we have but to trust him—even if he stole the goblet from the children's playhouse? Frost liked to say that his poetry was chiefly metaphorical, and in the last lines of the poem he invokes Mark 4:11–12 to sanctify the strategy: "And He said to them, "To you it has been given to know the mystery of the kingdom of God; but to those who are outside, all things come in parables, so that

> 'Seeing they may see and not perceive,
> And hearing they may hear and not understand;
> Lest they should turn,
> And their sins be forgiven them.'"

Frost told the poet Philip Booth that these verses summed up his view of Mark, the first Gospel in terms of composition, and in this fulfillment of Isaiah 6:8–10 (which, remember, begins with the prophet saying, "Here am I"), Christ explains that the Kingdom of God is closed off to the hard of heart—the same ones likely to miss the import of Frost's final metaphor: "These are your waters and your watering place," the poet says. "Drink and be whole again beyond confusion." Such is the promise of literature, which routinely falls on deaf ears.

We seek guides at every turn, though we may not recognize them at first. Tom Gavin and John Gardner made it possible for me to find a third guide in my apprenticeship, the poet David Wagoner, a remote figure to his graduate students who nonetheless gave me a crucial insight into the workings of the imagination when he passed along some advice from his teacher, Theodore Roethke: to abandon any semblance of control in generating the first draft of a poem, allowing the language to take you where it will, sometimes to very strange places. In his introduction to an edited selection of Roethke's notebooks Wagoner observed that the poet "apparently let his mind rove freely, moment by moment, in the early stages of composition, from the practical to the transcendental, from the lame and halting to the beautiful, from the comic to the terrible, from the literal to the surreal, seizing whatever he might from the language, but mulling over and taking soundings from every syllable." From this initial haul of words, phrases, and images, some containing seeds, some chaff, Roethke would then employ all the tricks of his trade, his craftsmanship, the technique that he had acquired by dint of hard work, the sum of his reading and reflection, to make a poem. It was a revelation to think of writing in this way, to explore the depths of the language in search of—what? That uncanny homecoming invoked by T.S. Eliot in *Four Quartets*: "to arrive where we started / And know the place for the first time."

I had not walked beyond the farmstead since college, but the vitality of our conversation and the growing warmth of the afternoon inspired me to suggest that we continue hiking. It was not long before we took the wrong fork at a juncture. The trail disappeared in a tangle of brush, and when we doubled back to the fork, we discovered that it had vanished. We walked uphill in search of the trail only to realize that we were lost, and now we made a series of bad decisions—taking a logging road for some distance before returning to another vanished trail; bushwhacking through thick underbrush; circling one clear-cut and then another, afraid that we were hiking deeper into the mountains; stopping and starting, calling out from time to time—in vain.

Hours passed. My rural childhood, my expeditions in the mountains and deserts of the West, my work as a caretaker—all suggested that I had a better feeling for nature than Tom, who grew up in the city. But the sun was lowering, I had begun to shiver in my sweaty clothes, and my mind was racing. I remembered a spring camping trip with my college girlfriend and another couple in the White Mountains: the daylong hike to a lean-to by a lake; the night of high spirits; the discovery in the morning, in the woods at the end of the lake, where the snow had not melted, of an airplane wing sheared off the fuselage, which, we decided, was in the water. The footprints leading away from the wing led us to speculate that the pilot had survived the crash, and these we followed down the other side of the mountain until they abruptly disappeared. By then the snow was up to our hips, our dungarees were soaked through, and it took all our strength to raise one foot out of the snow and place it in front of the other. This went on for hours. When at last we found a trail that led to a stream, we were too tired to say anything for some time, and indeed we had just resumed talking when we came around a bend and stopped in our tracks. There in the middle of the stream was a naked couple making love. We held our tongues until we were past them. I suspected that my adventure with Tom would not end on such a strange note.

Fortunately, he kept his wits about him. Staring at some felled trees on a mountain slope, debating whether to walk deeper into the woods on an overgrown path or to blaze a trail through the brambles, I looked to my friend for guidance, not trusting my instincts. Nor did I hesitate to follow his lead in searching for a new trail, my trust in his judgment a product of the kind of educational experience that can shape a life. Off we went, and it was still another hour and a half before we found our way to a path that led to the pond below the barn at Bread Loaf.

It was a close call—a night in the mountains, without food, water, or adequate clothing, would at the very least have been miserable, and quite possibly worse. For the next several days the woods inspired in me a dread that can only be described as existential, and upon my return to New Mexico I found myself dwelling on a pair of poems by David Wagoner, which must have guided my decision to defer to Tom at the crossroads. The first poem, "Staying Found," narrates an experience that Wagoner recounted one day in class. It begins with a line from Bradford Angier's *How to Stay Alive in the Woods* that reads, "We become lost not because of anything we do, but because of what we leave undone ... We stay found by knowing approximately where we are at every moment..." and concludes with the following lines:

> One moment he had been healed. He had forgotten
> The defeated trees, the flowers starving
> In poisonous wind and rain, the dead ground
> Where he had tried to grow. In another moment,
> He had learned a different way of dying
> Called Here and Now, called There and Where and Nowhere.
> When he stumbled onto the road again, his mind
> Had changed. He was no longer lost in the woods
> Or in cities as he had always been,
> Not knowing it. Now, he would stay found.[4]

This event took place not long after Roethke had invited Wagoner to leave the Midwest for a teaching position at the University of Washington, where his colleague, William Matthews, would later observe that the theme of being lost was central to his literary work. Indeed, it is the subject of Wagoner's most famous poem. "Lost" begins with a quiet imperative, "Stand still" and indicates how the relativity of location provides a magic capable of bestowing home: "Wherever you are is called Here, / And you must treat it as a powerful stranger, / Must ask permission to know it and be known." In the place of Here, harbored by the recognition of the world, there is no "lost." The poem ends just as powerfully, returning to the joy of recognizing that you are recognized in a quiet and solemn celebration of homecoming:

> If what a tree or a bush does is lost on you,
> You are surely lost. Stand still. The forest knows
> Where you are. You must let it find you.[5]

It might be said that Wagoner's body of work is an essay in letting the forest find him—a variation, if you will, on Christ's imperative in Luke 9:24: "For whoever desires to save his life will lose it, but whoever loses is life for My sake will save it." Orthodox Christians are counseled to find the right relationship to God, the right way to worship, and this is not unlike the relationship that Wagoner seeks in the natural order. His thinking may derive more from Native American cosmology than Christianity—he retold myths of the Pacific Coast Indians in his collection

---

[4]   David Wagoner, *Through the Forest: New and Selected Poems 1977–1987* (New York, 1987), p. 124.

[5]   David Wagoner, *Traveling Light: Collected and New Poems* (Urbana, 1999), p. 10.

Who Shall Be the Sun?—but his insistence on developing the right attitude of receptivity to nature is quite close to Paul's counsel to empty ourselves, *kenosis*, with the hope of being filled by God's presence. The spirit is the same. "Here am I," said Abraham. "Here are your waters and your watering place," said Frost. "Stand still," said Wagoner. What we find there, what finds us, forest or faith, will be our homecoming—uncanny and, perhaps, eternal.

References

Frost, Robert, *Frost: Collected Poems, Prose, & Plays* (New York: The Library of America, 1995).

Gardner, John, "The Art of Fiction No. 73," *The Paris Review*, Spring 1979.

Wagoner, David, *Through the Forest: New and Selected Poems 1977–1987* (New York: Atlantic Monthly Press, 1987).

Wagoner, David, *Traveling Light: Collected and New Poems* (Urbana and Chicago: University of Illinois Press, 1999).

PART II:
Unsettling Foundations of Homes

Chapter 3

Homecoming and the Half-Remembered: Environmental Amnesia, the Uncanny and the Path Home

Forrest Clingerman

What is an "uncanny homecoming"? In the following chapter, I wish to offer an *oblique definition* for the theme of this volume. My investigation is not an analysis of the terms "uncanny" and "homecoming." Rather, it is a meditation that attempts an unlikely theological journey homeward, in spite of a despatialized, disembodied age. By saying that this is a "meditation," I mean to suggest something particular about the following travels: what I seek is an interpretive movement, a chronicle of how we might glean meaning from the space between cultural works and our world. To make this strange journey, I use as conveyance a reflection on two works of art. Separately, Joseph Beuys' *Show Your Wound* and Rachel Whiteread's *House* clarify our sense of the uncanny and our sense of home. Together, they suggest a different sort of place is possible, and thereby propose the ethical and theological import that can be found by locating our need to undertake an uncanny homecoming.

Peering through these works, in other words, we understand our uncanny homecomings as an antidote for an ailment of contemporary existence: our environmental amnesia, that is, our inability to see where we are and who we are. As I have written elsewhere,[1] environmental amnesia is what characterizes the contemporary memory of place. But it is not an ordinary memory: it overwhelms our sense of place by manifesting the underside of our memory of the meaning of place. This underside threatens to become our platial memory itself and, as such, it is an absence of memory: environmental amnesia can be defined as our lack of awareness of natural and built environments. It is, as it were, the inability to

---

[1] Forrest Clingerman, "Environmental Amnesia or the Memory of Place? The Need for Local Ethics of Memory in a Philosophical Theology of Place," in Celia Deane-Drummond and Heinrich Bedford-Strohm (eds), *Religion and Ecology in the Public Sphere* (New York, 2011), pp. 141–59. The present paragraph follows the discussion on p. 150. These issues are further elaborated in Forrest Clingerman, "Memory, Imagination, and the Hermeneutics of Place," in Forrest Clingerman, Brian Treanor, Martin Drenthen, and David Utsler (eds), *Interpreting Nature: The Emerging Field of Environmental Hermeneutics* (New York, forthcoming).

remember where and who we are. This is not only a lack of scientific or theoretical knowledge, but equally a lack of embodied exposure to the environments that surround and intertwine with us. Environmental amnesia has been chronicled in discussions such as Marc Augé's "non-places"[2] and Richard Louv's "nature deficit disorder."[3] This problem has also been illustrated in a discussion of urban environments by Sigurd Bergmann. Bergmann notes that our erasure of the pastness of place is a characteristic of late modern urban space: "We need to account for the difference between what could be called good and bad amnesia. Or should we use two different terms? 'Natural oblivion' could circumscribe the process where spatial constructions must be demolished or left to decline naturally, while 'amnesia'—in accordance with the connotation in medicine—would describe the process where the intention to build something at a specific place displaces what is already there and violates the memories which are carried by the place."[4] Environmental amnesia is the diagnosis of our home in the contemporary world.

Placing environmental amnesia in the context of our homecoming, environmental amnesia is *a present that does not include the presence of the pastness of nature*. Home has become a forgotten place, a surrounding that is not deep within our memory. That is to say, we are lost, unable to pursue an act of homemaking, of discovering the meaning of our surroundings and thus our own self-identity. We are no longer concerned with the maintenance of a healing space or with the continual recognition of the temporal and spatial depths that are embodied as home. We have lost the way home and thus are left to wander aimlessly in environments bereft of their *place*. What, then, might serve to point us homeward?

Joseph Beuys' *Show Your Wound*

Our journey begins by an encounter with Joseph Beuys' *Show Your Wound*. It is an ideal place to uncover the uncanny: it is at once reassuringly methodical and the site of a disconcerting aberration. The entire work consists of doubles: two sets of two different tools, two framed fragments of an Italian newspaper, two blackboards, and two boxes affixed to the wall. Our eyes might gravitate toward two metal dissection tables from a morgue, placed in the corner of the installation. Sitting unused in the gallery space, these mortuary tables seem have been wheeled to the corner only temporarily, awaiting use once more. Underneath the tables are boxes filled with fat—a common substance in Beuys' work, malleable and evocative of life. Embedded in the fat are bird skulls and other objects. Rosenthal

---

2　　Marc Augé, *Non-Places: Introduction to an Anthropology of Supermodernity* (New York, 1995).

3　　Richard Louv, *Last Child in the Woods* (Chapel Hill, 2005).

4　　Sigurd Bergmann, "Making Oneself at Home in Environments of Urban Amnesia," *International Journal of Public Theology* 2 (2008): p. 84.

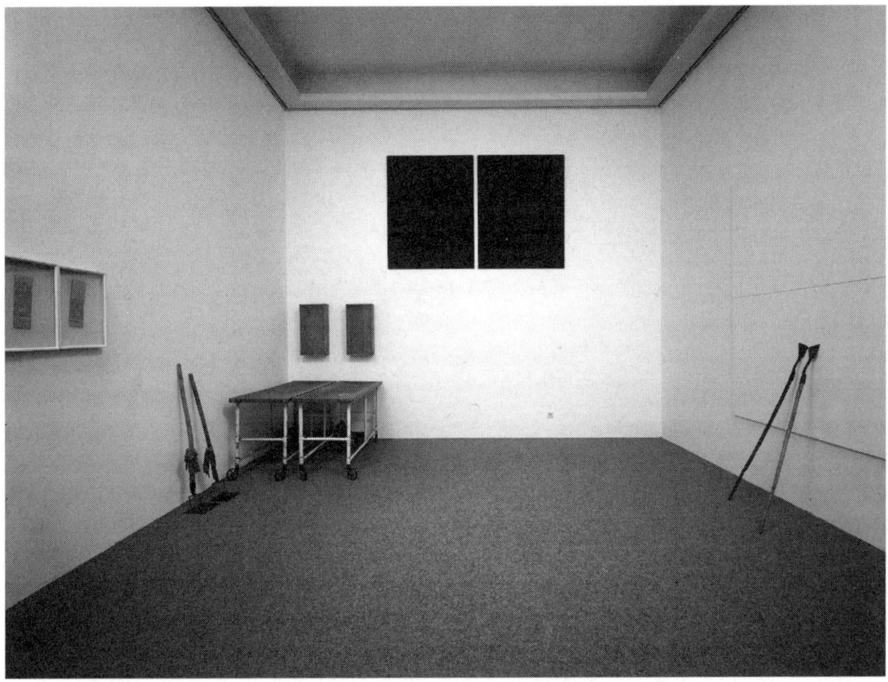

Figure 3.1   Joseph Beuys, *Zeige Deine Wunde* [*Show Your Wound*], 1974/1975, Mixed Media. Courtesy of Städtische Galerie im Lenbachhaus und Kunstbau, Munich. © 2012 Artists Rights Society (ARS), New York / VG Bild-Kunst, Bonn

suggests that: "With *Show Your Wound*, Beuys emphasized that one must look underground, beneath the sanitized veneer of contemporary life, to see reality and contemplate the 'wound.'"[5] Beuys creates a clearing, a dissonant space that purifies our fragmentation and seeks to heal us through the process of art itself. In Beuys' work, it seems, healing is completed at home; the task of healing is undertaken through the journey homeward.

Show Your Wound is one of the artist's later environments. It is concerned with themes common in Beuys' work: life and death, the artificial and the natural, wounds and healing, and finally the inevitable reimagination of space in our contemporary existence. In this work, Beuys brings us out of the gallery and into a *place*—a *somewhere*, an *environment*—which distills the play of meaning and possibility from our own everyday sense of things. *Show Your Wound* takes its name from two blackboards hanging on the wall of the environment. Beuys has instructed us, in white lettering on a black background, to "show our wound." By

---

[5]   Mark Rosenthal, *Joseph Beuys: Actions, Vitrines, Environments* (Houston, 2005), p. 72.

presenting such instructions, we are invited to respond to Beuys' configuration. In so doing, the work suggests the transcendent quality of art, for art moves beyond the visceral to open up a place to heal. Such healing takes place, so Beuys suggests, by forcing what is hidden to be uncovered. In other words, the work of art *accomplishes* its healing work through *an uncanny shock* of laying bare our wound. It creates a sense of dissonance that pries open what is closed. To heal, Beuys forcefully opens a wound, with our blessings. He gathers the injury of contemporary existence in a radical way: *he presences the uncanny*, not as an idea or a feeling, but *as an actual place in which we think, feel, and show our separation from wholeness*. To reach home—to return to wellness in the place of rest—means we encounter the hurtful space, the site that commands us to confront our present location as disorienting, uncanny distance.

The Uncanny and its Place

If *Show Your Wound* presences the uncanny, what *is* the "uncanny"? And why is it so closely tied to place? Freud's influential essay on the uncanny begins by noticing that "the 'uncanny' is that class of the terrifying which leads back to something long known to us, once very familiar."[6] For Freud, we almost immediately acknowledge that the "'uncanny'—*unheimlich*—is the opposite of *heimlich*, the "'familiar,' 'native', [and the] 'belonging to home'…"[7] Yet we cannot merely define the uncanny as the unfamiliar. By looking at the definitions of *heimlich* and *unheimlich* together, Freud explains that "the word *heimlich* is not unambiguous, but belongs to two sets of ideas, which without being contradictory are yet very different: on the one hand, it means that which is familiar and congenial, and on the other, that which is concealed and kept out of sight."[8] As a result, "What is *heimlich* thus comes to be *unheimlich*."[9] The uncanny is not the opposite of the homely, the familiar—it is a "subspecies" of it.[10] Furthermore, Freud reminds us of Schelling's definition: "everything that is uncanny that ought to have remained hidden and secret, and yet comes to light."[11]

Moving into a specific literary instance of the uncanny (E.T.A. Hoffmann's "The Sand-Man"), Freud suggests that a prominent feature that displays the uncanny is the "double." We have seen the double at work in Beuys' environment. In such an "involuntary return to a known situation," that is, when we are reminded of what Freud calls a "repetition-compulsion," we are left with the uncanny. To move

---

[6]   Sigmund Freud, "The Uncanny," in *Collected Papers*, vol. 4 (New York, 1959), pp. 369–70.

[7]   Ibid., p. 370.

[8]   Ibid, p. 375.

[9]   Ibid., p. 375.

[10]   Ibid., p. 377.

[11]   Ibid., p. 376.

further, Freud argues that the connection between the familiar and the uncanny, especially in light of doubling and repetition, becomes one of estrangement:

> among … cases of anxiety there must be a class in which the anxiety can be shown to come from something repressed which *recurs*. This class of morbid anxiety would then be no other than what is uncanny, irrespective of whether it originally aroused dread or some other affect … [I]f this is indeed the secret nature of the uncanny, we can understand why the usage of speech has extended *das Heimliche* into its opposite *das Unheimliche*; for this uncanny is in reality nothing new or foreign, but something familiar and old-established in the mind that has been estranged only by the process of repression. This reference to the factor of repression enables us, furthermore, to understand Schelling's definition of the uncanny as something which ought to have been kept concealed but which has nevertheless come to light.[12]

Thus, the uncanny is something that once was familiar, native, home-like, but has been *repressed* or *rendered forgotten*— "the uncanny is nothing else than a hidden, familiar thing that has undergone repression and then emerged from it..."[13] But then, this thing re-emerges—it is half-remembered, in shadows, distorted, much like Beuys' installation.

For Freud, the uncanny is associated with castration and sexual desire. But perhaps the uncanny has a more general, paradoxical location: the uncanny is *a site, which cleaves the home*. In other words, this site cleaves in both senses of the word, for in the uncanny we are separate from and tethered to home. *The uncanny is a half-remembered* place*, whose meaning arises from the inexplicable physical and temporal trace of purpose and design that—precisely in its meaning—cannot be understood as it once was.* It is illogical to assume that the uncanny resides in the realm of conceptual understanding. Rather, it is a wilderness, a clearing, where the most near is strange: in Beuys, such a place is manifested in the everyday of a newspaper, a tool, or death itself. As Anneleen Masschelein has commented, Freud sees the uncanny as an aesthetic experience, related to sentiment, feeling, and the subjective.[14] So the uncanny is not an intellectual abstraction, it is an experience that emerges from a place or environment like that created by Beuys. It is, quite literally, *the intimacy of one's home* when home sits radically askew and estranged. The uncanny is formed when a *place is outside itself.*

Although Beuys' environment is not home, it solidifies the movement homeward that is found only in the space of the uncanny. Thus, the uncanny *gathers meaning* only *as a response to what might be* home. From distance and

---

[12] Ibid., p. 394.

[13] Ibid., p. 399.

[14] Anneleen Masschelein, "A Homeless Concept: Shapes of the Uncanny in Twentieth-Century Theory and Culture," *Image and Narrative* 5 (2003), available at www.imageandnarrative.be [accessed July 25, 2012].

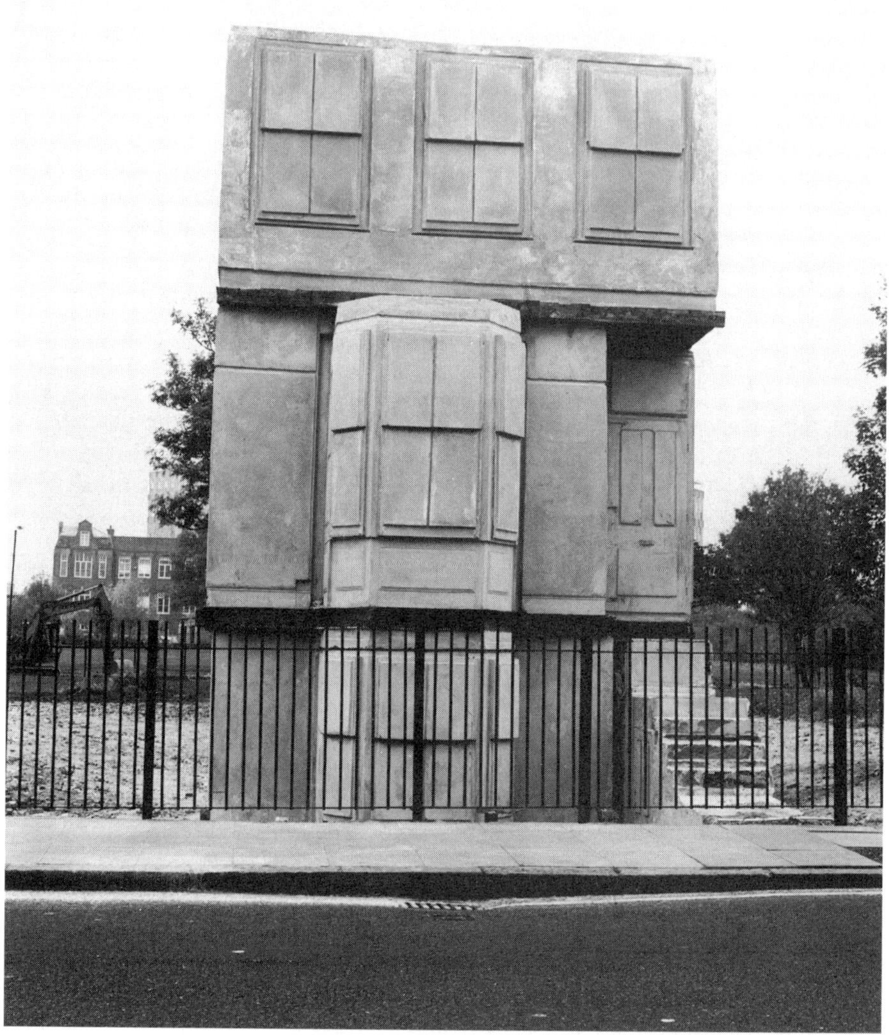

Figure 3.2   Rachel Whiteread, *House*, 1993, concrete. Photo, Sue Ormerod.
Courtesy of the artist, Luhring Augustine, New York, and Gagosian
Gallery

memory it points us to what is intimate, what is near, through a doubling: a
repetition and recollection. But the uncanny does not fulfill meaning; it stands
outside our home but within our memory, as it points us *homeward*. It challenges
us to remember meaning lost, and a hope of once more finding a place of depth to
which we might return. As such, *Show Your Wound* is a hurtful memory sculpted

of place, offering a map to the healing repetition of the homeward bound. The same might be said of Egon Schiele's landscapes, Van Gogh's famous *Wheatfield with Crows*, or several paintings of Edward Hopper such as *Groundswell*, to name a few other examples.

Rachel Whiteread's *House*

But then where are we going? Beuys' environment forms a place that seeks to heal our fragmented life. It is "unhomely," but through its uncanny shock, it offers us a trace of the path homeward. As we will see, the homeward journey ends with a homecoming, for the uncanny journey illuminates the depth of our homecoming and thus the reality of home: we find the uncanny homecoming in the unlikely wholeness of the fragmented, the inconceivable healing of the wound.

To achieve such an uncanny homecoming, what is necessary is a complement to the abstract medicine of Beuys. This we find in Rachel Whiteread's sculpture *House*, which forms a humble, radical embodiment of the space of home in its physical and temporal depth. In many respects, Whiteread's work is a prescient statement of our contemporary world: it is enigmatic without the excessive irony of postmodernity, concerned with the fullness of space created through physical absence. It is a work that locates our visions of habitat: as concrete, anonymous and substantial, it presents a fragility and ephemeral sense of who we are and where we dwell. *House* is a fossil; the shell-like calcification of human home that conveys the past into the present.

Whiteread's sculpture began as a nineteenth-century terraced house in an area of London being cleared of these older row houses. Choosing one archetypal structure, she created a concrete casting of the house with sprayed concrete and reinforcing steel in the interior of the house. This casting of the interior of the dwelling included its own foundation, and marked out windows, doors, stairwells, and the shapes of the rooms themselves. Finally, the original house itself was removed, leaving behind a trace of home, standing in the midst of a vacant space where a row of humble dwellings stood. Windows became opaque and impenetrable, doors became mere molds that did not allow entry.

Whiteread created a monument to space, dwelling, the past, and the humble foundation of the everyday. It is important to acknowledge the specific location of Whiteread's work: an urban redevelopment project that tore down a series of nineteenth-century row houses as part of a process of building something new. At the time, only Whiteread's concrete fossil was left where once a row of houses stood. In effect, her sculpture was an instantiation of the fleeting instant between demolition and renewal. And standing in the midst of vacancy, it reversed our sense of time itself: Rather than "developing" wilderness into human cultural space, Whiteread's sculpture is involved in the reversion of human inhabitation into the wildness underneath such dwelling places. In other words, not only did it stand as a monument to the previous uses of the space, but it also indirectly pointed our attention to the non-human, "empty" lots that these houses once covered. As with Beuys, we have an opening in the face of the covered. To do this, Whiteread's sculpture sought to narrow our experience to basic concerns:

> To solidify the interiors of a house may be to conceal them, to seal them off, but it is also to reveal how basic our needs and our lives have remained down the centuries. There is a kind of pathos in the revelation. Our houses tend to be places that we like to think of as containing the evidence of our own unique sensibilities, repositories where we store the evidence of our sophistication and impeccable tastefulness. *House*, being a house without furniture, a house reduced to the shape of the air that a house contains, serves as a reminder that we are all, on one level at least, utterly and primally the same: creatures that have always sought shelter, a roof over our heads.[15]

Whiteread's *House* was made from an anonymous row house. However, it is not simply a house; it is also an instantiation of the memory of human dwelling in all its imaginative variations. Providing an encapsulation of one house in one spatio-temporal location, we are offered an icon for encountering the possibility of human dwelling. *House*—in the way it captures the weight of the empty space in a humble, historical site of dwelling—concretizes our dreams of home. To reflect on *House* (as the basic, humble basis of what it means to be human) amounts to a homecoming.

This homecoming is not without its distance. Whiteread asks us to dwell *on House*, not to dwell *in* it. In so doing, she offers us the tools to reflexively rediscover the meaning of home in an uncanny world. We find the memories and dreams of human dwelling by contemplating the meaning of the work. After such contemplation, we do not then enter Whiteread's *House* and claim it as our own; instead, we become alienated from dwelling, which we have seen is the most basic meaning of human being in the world. This is not simply the opening of the uncanny, however, for the physical absence of any house (something at the heart of *House*) questions such simple alienation. This work finally serves to recall home, precisely because it is not *our* home or in fact any home at all—it is home because it creates a place to experience the radical distance from a more general sense of what it means to dwell. But only through such distance can the work tenderly open the place of home. Or we might say that Whiteread's *House* illuminates the trace of our own uncanny homecoming.

---

[15]   Andrew Graham-Dixon, "This is the House that Rachel Built" *The Independent*, 2 November 1993: http://www.independent.co.uk/arts-entertainment/art/this-is-the-house-that-rachel-built-rachel-whitereads-house-is-one-of-the-most-extraordinary-public-sculptures-to-have-been-created-by-any-english-artist-working-this-century-says-andrew-grahamdixon-here-he-examines-the-work-pictured-by-nicholas-turpin-and-below-whiteread-and-three-other-artists-nominated-for-the-turner-prize-describe-their-work-1501616.html [accessed July 25, 2012].

Dwelling and the Home

As we saw, the uncanny is a homeward stance, but with only a misaligned glimpse of that primordial place. Spying Whiteread's *House*, how can we envision this most intimate of spaces, to recollect the half-remembered, to stand before Whiteread's re-created home? What emerges is this: *home is our place to dwell* and thus *to be* in the sinewy physical and emotional folds of *who* and *where* we are. With the resonance of societal memory and the grittiness of embodied space, Whiteread takes us home. By stepping back from Whiteread's walls, we see that to face homeward is a turn toward the most primordial of places.

Home, Whiteread's work of art explains, situates us in a familiar location in spite of any perceived distance; *it is the place that extends into us as an* intrusion *on the self of our own innermost selves*. It is formative for our being, our wholeness as manifested in embodied space and lived time. This sentiment is at the heart of Gaston Bachelard's work *The Poetics of Space*. Bachelard writes: "For our house is our corner of the world. As has often been said, it is our first universe, a real cosmos in every sense of the word. If we look at it intimately, the humblest dwelling has beauty."[16] Home is a container of memory, frequently the memories that are imperative for our self-identity and our sense of being in the world. That is to say, *home is a key that, through its reach into our past, decodes who and where we are in the present*. Indeed, Bachelard writes that: "All great, simple images reveal a psychic state. The house, even more than the landscape, is a 'psychic state,' and even when reproduced as it appears from the outside, it bespeaks intimacy."[17] Home is not only a building, but a physical and emotional "where" that is closer to us than we are to ourselves. Bachelard's point is echoed in Whiteread's work: reflecting on what is left after the creation of *House*, we immediately acknowledge that Whiteread has dismantled the building. What has been left standing are the intimate traces of a specific "where," a physical object that allows us to contemplate the meaning of our emotional attachment to home.

A home is more than an objective, abstract built environment. It is part of an organic, intersubjective embodiment. Kirsten Jacobson writes that home is a "second body." Taking a cue from Bachelard, she argues that who we are is partly the result of our homes, especially our childhood home. According to Jacobson, "home" includes a passivity and an agency, as well as an inside and outside. "So, although 'to dwell' is inherent to our nature, 'how' to realize this nature is something learned."[18] *Home, we can say, is where we* learn *to dwell; it is a most basic place*. After all, place (Jacobson discusses this as "space") is:

---

[16]   Gaston Bachelard, *The Poetics of Space* (Boston, 1994), p. 4.

[17]   Ibid., p. 72.

[18]   Kirsten Jacobson, "A Developed Nature: A Phenomenological Account of the Experience of Home," *Continental Philosophy Review* 42 (2009): p. 356.

an extension of ourselves, not as a predetermined grid into which we are inserted … [Our] body extends into the things with which we are engaged—as if we were elastic spheres stretching and contracting as our attention moves from one project and one object to the next. In this way, we are neither isolated *I-heres* that orient ourselves with respect to independent *there-things* nor are we at the center of a rigid set of distant objects; rather, we *dwell* in the things for which we care, and this dwelling is constitutive of our existence.[19]

Or, as Janet Donohoe writes: "The house is where we develop a certain style of acting in the world. In many ways it reflects our character in the way in which it is decorated and arranged. But the house too arranges us, much as any building arranges us, but in a much more fundamental and determinate way."[20]

Therefore, using Heidegger's terms, home is where we dwell. Heidegger posits that *to be* human is *to dwell*. In "Building Dwelling Thinking," he writes that dwelling is the way in which humans as mortals are on the earth. For humans, dwelling gathers humans up into a site, a place where things can be true through the interaction of earth and sky, gods and mortals. Truth thereby occurs in the locales where humans poetically dwell. In other words, dwelling is who we are; and *dwelling occurs in place*: "Spaces open up by the fact that they are let into the dwelling of man. To say that mortals *are* is to say that *in dwelling* they persist through spaces by virtue of their stay among things and locales."[21] *Dwelling, then, brings us home.* Bachelard concurs with this spatio-temporal intimacy: "[Bachelard] recognizes that the dwelling place of home is intimately connected to memory. In fact, he understands the home as retaining our past and opening up an immemorial domain."[22] Thus:

> Heidegger's overall argument, as with Bachelard's, emphasizes the existential nature of home rather than the literal makeup of a house or house-like enclosure in which we may live. Heidegger maintains that we are the kind of being that is homely, and our way of being-at-home is principally one of developing and maintaining a place for ourselves, of securing a sense of our "own-ness."[23]

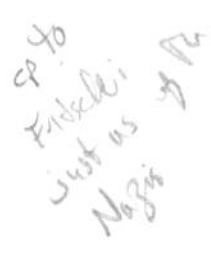

Whiteread's sculpture forces us to explicitly acknowledge what it might mean for us to dwell, to be at home. It does so by re-creating a house that exists before our past in unbending materials and alien space. Whiteread then strips away the

---

[19] Kirsten Jacobson, "Agoraphobia and Hypochondria," *International Studies in Philosophy* 36 (2004): p. 33.

[20] Janet Donohoe, "The Place of Home," *Environmental Philosophy* 8 (2011): p. 26.

[21] Martin Heidegger, "Building Dwelling Thinking," in *Poetry, Language, Thought* (New York, 1971), p. 159.

[22] Donohoe, "The Place of Home," p. 27.

[23] Kirsten Jacobson, "The Experience of Home and the Space of Citizenship," *Southern Journal of Philosophy* 48 (2010): p. 222.

unessential, the mundane bricks and mortar—leaving behind home, which remains after the removal of the impersonal and temporary. *House*, in other words, exists as a physical trace of home. It is what is left of home when home is all but gone. As a trace, and not as a physical place, it is precisely at the heart of home:

> Bachelard's analysis of our experience of home, and ultimately of space, extends beyond any tangible house-structure, addressing the very way in which we find ourselves existentially at-home in a world. Bachelard's argument suggests that, more than a physical structure, a home is a way of finding a certain world comportment, of finding one's own way of being-in-the-world. To be at-home is to have a developed and familiar way engaging with and in one's surroundings.[24]

Whiteread's sculpture—created from the cast of an actual house, once inhabited and then finally abandoned—thus offers us an experience to see the memory of home distanciated, manipulated, emplaced. By reflecting on this work, we follow a circuitous route to the ground upon which home stands: from what is other than our home to a fossil of home, from fossil to memory, from memory of home to a renewed meaning of place.

Place and the Uncanny Spirit of Home

Placed together, the works by Beuys and Whiteread offer an exchange that is characterized by the mutual dependency of intimate dwelling and distanced journeys, that is, by the passage of uncanny homecoming. Echoing this, Jacobson and Donohoe both argue that the home is possible only in light of the unhomely, and simultaneously the uncanny comes into being through a trace of home. As Donohoe writes: "The environment prescribes or calls forth a type or style of comportment towards it. This comportment becomes, then, not simply one's comportment towards this particular place, but simply one's comportment. It is one's way of being, living, engaging in the place that is home, but also in the place that is alien."[25] In other words, both home and the uncanny are embedded, embodied in place. Just as Beuys motions us homeward, Whiteread beckons us to be at home. Together, we find an uncanny homecoming to the half-remembered place that grounds who and where we are.

In all this, the present reflections on Beuys and Whiteread join together to create a new pathway from our homecoming to another question – apart from its manifestation in works of art, where has home gone? This is the question of a homemaking, a healing existence, and in many respects it is a topic that both artists seek to address: the problem of our own lack of place, our lack of wholeness. Both Beuys and Whiteread suggest the importance of returning to that elemental human

---

24   Ibid., p. 221.
25   Donohoe, "The Place of Home," p. 31.

desire for home, for a meaningful environment. They show us that *who we are* is grounded in *where we are*, and vice versa. Whiteread's sculpture did not mark its space for long; it was torn down a few years after its creation. But through this temporary work, Whiteread created a presence that rendered a new somewhere; it became a marker of time and space through being named and given a meaning. *House* was human work that reflexively stood as the stolid, corporeal memory of everyday human dwelling, as an impenetrable physical boundary that blocked us from returning to the now-empty space of home. It was an audacious inversion of space: it was a mold of the empty space between its dismantled walls and floors. In its radical inversion, *House* filled the empty, absented what it portrayed. Just as we can imagine the shape of the mold by looking at what has been created by it, *House* beckons us to conceive what once stood as container to this space. It thereby called us to re-create its place, to remember the home that once stood. In sum, *House* is a work of memory and locale, the interpretation of place, and the meaning of dwelling within space and time. Uniquely, it forces us to confront the intimacy of home amidst the anonymity of destruction. Whiteread's work materially solidifies private space, but at the cost of forcing us to acknowledge this home is now displaced—out of time, out of space.

Similarly, Beuys' work opens up the rarified world of the gallery and vanquishes it, throwing us into the midst of everyday items pregnant with reflexive meaning. The separation between the purified space of art and the messy space of the mundane is found in the enigmatic, curious placement of objects—objects that are neither completely ordinary nor intricately made to complement space. Beuys' work, too, is a work that confronts our fragile life inside time and space, a gathering of the everyday in a way that beckons us to search for meaning. As its theme, its place suggests the need to account for our own embodied temporality, our finitude, our death. Beuys invites us to complete the work—it is only when we enter into a dialogue with this environment that the fragile human body completes the work. Thus, like Whiteread's *House*, Beuys' work presents us with memory, place, physical presence, and the everyday.

These works challenge us, beckon us with absences and paradoxes, thus hiding some meanings and opening others. I would like to suggest that these two works give us examples of our interpretation of place, for both leave us with a sense of an uncertain darkness, of a "disquieting strangeness," toward the meaning of the places of our existence. In both cases, the dark uncertainty of these works serves as certain illumination: *in the struggle to remind ourselves of how we encounter who and where we are, Beuys and Whiteread uncover our environmental amnesia, which troubles how meaning flows through our interpretations of place.*

Environmental amnesia is the dis-ease, and the work of an *uncanny* homecoming is the cure. If our experience of Beuys and Whiteread re-places us— renews our need to be emplaced—how can we move past the non-place? This is not merely an ethical question, but is also a spiritual one. It returns us to the desire of Beuys, namely, human wholeness and healing. In contrast to such wholeness, we are homeless. As Heidegger writes in a discussion of Nietzsche: "Having become God-less and world-less, the modern human is home-less. Indeed, in the absence of the God and the ruin of the world, homelessness is especially expected of the modern historical human. Therefore, modern humans do not feel at home, and especially the case when they flee to that which makes them forget the failed home and what should replace it."[26] Thus, how might the half-remembered aid in overcoming our own forgetful homelessness?

It is no accident that both artists seek to reinvest place with meaning in light of the "non-place" of contemporary existence. These works, in fact, remind us of the temporal, bodily space of the ambiguity of healing (in the case of Beuys) or dwelling (in the case of Whiteread)—if healing and dwelling are in fact separate things. But this means that each work plays on the half-remembered: the meaning of the works is grounded on what vanishes within time, within space, within our sense of self and the absolute. Furthermore, the reason that these works speak to our sense of place is that, through their concern with portraying the paradoxical time of embodiment—through the memorializing the everyday and the radically shifting sense of time—they exemplify the problem of place in our contemporary world.

In conclusion, Beuys and Whiteread open our wounds, re-place us in home, and offer us an uncanny homecoming. More than a shallow experience of returning to a house or neighborhood, an uncanny homecoming is a confrontation with the overwhelming depth of the surroundings that make us who we are. In other words, an uncanny homecoming is defined as the movement from the unknowable non-place to the infinite depths of the *where* that makes us who we are. Such homecomings finally push us beyond the half-remembered, toward the possibility of a new place, a healing environment. We might take note of Bachelard's claim: "And what is more, the imagination, by virtue of its freshness and its own peculiar activity, can make what is familiar into what is strange. With a single poetic detail, the imagination confronts us with a new world."[27] Uncanny homecomings finally present an imagination of how we might return home—and with such a journey we build heaven in presence of the mundane.

References

Augé, Marc, *Non-Places: Introduction to an Anthropology of Supermodernity* (New York: Verso, 1995).

Bachelard, Gaston, *The Poetics of Space* (Boston: Beacon Press, 1994).

Bergmann, Sigurd, "Making Oneself at Home in Environments of Urban Amnesia," *International Journal of Public Theology* 2 (2008): 70–97.

Clingerman, Forrest, "Environmental Amnesia or the Memory of Place? The Need for Local Ethics of Memory in a Philosophical Theology of Place," in Celia

---

[26] Martin Heidegger, *Introduction to Philosophy—Thinking and Poetizing* (Bloomington, 2011), 24.

[27] Bachelard, *The Poetics of Space*, p. 134.

Deane-Drummond and Heinrich Bedford-Strohm (eds), *Religion and Ecology in the Public Sphere* (New York: T&T Clark, 2011).

Clingerman, Forrest, "Memory, Imagination, and the Hermeneutics of Place," in Forrest Clingerman, Brian Treanor, Martin Drenthen, and David Utsler (eds), *Interpreting Nature: The Emerging Field of Environmental Hermeneutics* (New York: Fordham University Press, forthcoming).

Donohoe, Janet, "The Place of Home," *Environmental Philosophy* 8 (2011): 25–40.

Freud, Sigmund, "The Uncanny," in *Collected Papers*, vol. 4 (New York: Basic Books, 1959).

Graham-Dixon, Andrew, "This is the House that Rachel Built," *The Independent*, 2 November 1993: www.independent.co.uk/arts-entertainment/art/this-is-the-house-that-rachel-built-rachel-whitereads-house-is-one-of-the-most-extraordinary-public-sculptures-to-have-been-created-by-any-english-artist-working-this-century-says-andrew-grahamdixon-here-he-examines-the-work-pictured-by-nicholas-turpin-and-below-whiteread-and-three-other-artist-s-nominated-for-the-turner-prize-describe-their-work-1501616.html [accessed July 25, 2012].

Heidegger, Martin, "Building Dwelling Thinking," in *Poetry, Language, Thought* (New York: Harper, 1971).

Heidegger, Martin, *Introduction to Philosophy—Thinking and Poetizing* (Bloomington: Indiana University Press, 2011).

Jacobson, Kirsten, "Agoraphobia and Hypochondria," *International Studies in Philosophy* 36 (2004): 31–44.

Jacobson, Kirsten, "A Developed Nature: A Phenomenological Account of the Experience of Home," *Continental Philosophy Review* 42 (2009): 355–73.

Jacobson, Kirsten, "The Experience of Home and the Space of Citizenship," *Southern Journal of Philosophy* 48 (2010): 219–45.

Louv, Richard, *Last Child in the Woods* (Chapel Hill, NC: Algonquin Books, 2005).

Masschelein, Anneleen, "A Homeless Concept: Shapes of the Uncanny in Twentieth-Century Theory and Culture," *Image and Narrative* 5 (2003), available at www.imageandnarrative.be [accessed July 25, 2012].

Rosenthal, Mark, *Joseph Beuys: Actions, Vitrines, Environments* (Houston: Menil Collection/Yale University Press, 2005).

Chapter 4
Dwelling Beyond Poetry: The Uncanny Houses of Hawthorne and Poe

Daniel Boscaljon

Making Home through Poetic Dwelling

The spatial dimensions of a house—the square feet that provide us with a shelter and a place to rest—provide strangers with an abstract or universal understanding of what a house entails. The value of a house, measured in terms of lumber and labor, provides another objective measurement. As is often true, however, such quantifiable and objective standards do not account for what is most important to us: in a house, we require a temporal relationship with a space. It is only in time that we convert space into a place, a home.

The process of moving into a new home—whether rented room or mansion—is usually attended by moving one's things. Relics of this sort provide us with tangible points of continuity: allowing an unfamiliar space to contain concrete reminders of our past helps to transform it into something familiar. Practically speaking, moving our things with us minimizes the effort it takes to preserve our habits. The continuity allowed by the goods we have collected reinforces the trajectory by which we measure progress in our lives. Lest this be misunderstood as a celebration of consumerism, it is worth noting that the most important possessions are not the newest things purchased, but the random objects—old teddy bears, a trophy earned long ago, a favorite shirt with an unfortunate hole—that have become priceless reminders of our histories. This has been a constant in the human experience: for example, the Hebrew Bible emphasizes the role that one's things—from household gods to silver cups—played in mediating a character's identity.

Just as our things each gather a memory or a story, so too do the spaces themselves begin to accrue a history as they transition from house to home. Each room shapes and holds time as well as possessions, gathering and collecting different people over months and years. For both places and things, humans depend on language to measure the passage of time from the potential futures of dreams into the personal archives of memory. Dwellings are places that accrue time as narratives: we use language to tell these narratives, which become a bond that anchors us to the land and gathers the things surrounding us into a home.

The genius of Heidegger's interpretation of Holderlin's line "poetically man dwells" in his later essays occurs in his acknowledging and emphasizing the mutual coalescing that gives us a world.[1] For Heidegger, poetic dwelling occurs once we are intentional in co-creating a world and requires that we co-respond with the things that we assemble around us. Our interaction with things creates what he calls *Das Geviert*, or the Fourfold of earth and sky, mortals and divinities. Unlike objects, which are quantifiable, objective entities, Heidegger argues that each thing gathers earth and sky, mortals and divinities in a unique fashion.[2] As a concrete example, a house exists as an object when it is constructed as an anonymous shelter in a series of similar shelters, defined only in terms of utility and economy. It becomes a thing when it gathers a person or family within it, people who use language in order to appropriate the space through the stories that gather in the memory.

Dwelling and poetry blend together nicely in Heidegger's thinking: in part, this is because both dwelling and poetry are conservative in nature. Dwelling, according to the *Oxford English Dictionary*, is a verb whose earliest meanings involve "to tarry, delay; to desist from action" and "to abide or continue for a time, in a place, state or condition."[3] Dwelling involves an experience of time without change, prolonged moments that become difficult to differentiate quantitatively from each other. Further, although dwelling requires a history, its focus remains on presence—the task of continually co-creating one's world in tandem with one's things. In dwelling, we follow the example of our things and gather our goods and memories around us, preserving tangible goods as anchors of a prolonged "now." The thinglike "now" of dwelling slows our experience of time and change, causing us to attend more frequently to what persists than to what is lost. Focusing on the presence of things from our past relieves the things of the weight of accumulated time; doing so means we no longer experience time as marching forward imperiously toward change and difference, but instead rejoice in its prolonged gift of continued presence.

Poetry does something similar: a poem draws the reader into its space, often providing a variety of entrances into its center. The poem is an occasion and a site for particularized reflection: it reveals a distilled essence or thought, enabling a time for the reader to pause and be stilled within the poem's space. This frequently occurs within a poem's structure, as the vast majority of poems are governed by an internal center of gravity, causing the poem's language and the reader's attention to be pulled inward. As Ricoeur notes in *Interpretation Theory*, poetry operates centripetally as an impertinent attribution collapses back upon a word.[4] Thus, when Emily Dickinson begins a poem with "I dwell

---

[1]   Martin Heidegger, "… Poetically Man Dwells," in A. Hofstadter (ed.), *Poetry, Language, Thought* (New York, 1971), p. 215.

[2]   Martin Heidegger, "The Thing," in Hofstadter (ed.), *Poetry, Language, Thought*, pp. 179–81.

[3]   *Oxford English Dictionary*. Entry: "Dwelling."

[4]   Paul Ricoeur, *Interpretation Theory: Discourse and the Surplus of Meaning* (Fort Worth, 1976), pp. 67–8.

in Possibility— /A fairer House than Prose /,"[5] the noun "House" is altered, transformed from an objectively certain structure to a poetic and futural "possibility," something neither certain nor present at all.

While we spend most of our lives co-creating our worlds in a synthesis of language and the material world around us, certain spaces prohibit our dwelling. Not all spaces are conducive for our dwelling because not all spaces are receptive to our appropriation in time. Spaces that promote the management and regulation of human bodies as abstracted objects, such as classrooms or lobbies, discourage dwelling and are intended only for very short-term use. These are zones of diminished possibilities, limiting its user to existing as a physical object in space. Other spaces allow us to live in them for slightly longer periods—hotel rooms or a rental apartment or house. Hostile to the idiom of any one particular life in the interest of remaining potentially open to all, such spaces strangle our attempts to co-respond. While possible to re-appropriate such spaces, such a process would require far more time than what one generally is permitted. Being gathered into such spaces does violence to our capacity to imagine possibilities, just as it displaces us from the narratives of our pasts.

Literature cannot generate a full world because texts lack an objective or material component. As Dickinson's poem indicates, dwelling in language occurs in subjectively accessible realms of possibility. Anchored in our subjective conviction, the realm of future possibilities is as personal to us as memory. Other unreal worlds also beckon to us, such as the language worlds of narrative, relating us to fictive pasts and unknowable futures. But even these extremes—earthly spaces that limit dwelling by encouraging sheer objectivity, and worldly domains that limit dwelling by displacing us from physical reality—still depend upon the intermingling of earth and language as the two extremes.[6] Both the activity of dwelling poetically and the dwellings whose spaces enfold us depend on the complete and mutual interpenetration of language and earth. We dwell poetically as we, with our things, appropriate and gather language and earth.[7] Doing this intentionally—reflecting on our narratives and how they relate to our things— allows us to find ourselves at home in a structural or ontological way. Instead of assuming our world as a habit, idly, we understand our home to be the connections between our stories and our things.

---

[5]   Emily Dickinson, "466," in R.W. Frankling (ed.), *The Poems of Emily Dickinson* (Cambridge, MA, 1999).

[6]   Although near to Heidegger's terms, I use "earth" here to connote the objective and material component of our world, while "language" refers to the subjective, narrative, and poetic components.

[7]   The intentional work of appropriation and gathering occurs in the creation of works of art when we are displaced in light of a new truth, and occurs as dwelling relative to truths omnipresent within our world. While Heidegger indicates that one might need to construct a temple or painting to preserve a new truth, he also indicates that fashioning jugs and chalices—and thinking about their use—constitutes poetic dwelling.

Homecomings occur, then, when humans are gathered into spaces that they have worked to appropriate to themselves. On a concrete or objective level, these spaces often feature a collection of tangible things that provide instant physical anchors to concrete memories. In terms of the past, such spaces are ones that have imprinted certain habits (making them seem like "natural" places) and memories of past events that one can recollect through language. Because homes have the structural property of gathering, we do not think of their possibilities as boundless: instead, we naively anticipate that the futures of our homes will occur as repetitions of their pasts. These assumptions about our home cause us to experience inevitable changes as an unsettling combination of the familiar and the unfamiliar, as uncanny.

The *Unheimlich* of Language

In his essay *The Uncanny*, Freud returns to Schelling's definition of the uncanny, claiming that it occurs when something that was secret comes into the open. Although the harbinger of the uncanny initially appears as new or unfamiliar, Freud finds that this is due to its having been estranged through repression.[8] Other qualities that frequently generate an experience of the uncanny include doubles or *doppelgangers*, times when we are intellectually uncertain as to "whether something is animate or inanimate,"[9] and also when we are faced with "the reality of what had originally been considered imaginary, when a symbol takes on the full function and significance of what it symbolizes."[10] Freud's conclusion is also telling: he finds that the uncanny element "arises either when repressed childhood complexes are revived by some impression, or when primitive beliefs that have been *surmounted* appear to be at once again confirmed," although he cautions that these two sides of the uncanny are difficult to separate.[11]

Put otherwise, Freud anchors our experiences of the uncanny in moments of uncertain identity, when the normal experience of life as a given becomes impossibly disrupted, bifurcated in terms of space (a single image that inhabits two spaces at the same time) or time (a re-presentation of an entity from the past shown, again, in the present). My point here is not merely to repeat Freud's psychological interpretations of the uncanny; instead, I wish to explore the ontological preconditions that enable uncanny encounters, especially as these preconditions are intertwined with the gathering localizations of home. The uncanny both requires and unsettles the sense of unity and completeness acquired in a general or normal sense of poetic dwelling.

---

[8]   Sigmund Freud, "The Uncanny," in David McLintock (trans. and ed.), *The Uncanny* (New York, 2003), p. 132.

[9]   Ibid., pp. 141–2.

[10]   Ibid., p. 150.

[11]   Ibid., p. 155.

The first way that an uncanny moment can haunt our poetic dwelling, our intentional appropriation and gathering of land and language, occurs when an experience of the uncanny causes an evacuation of language that, in turn, sunders us from the world. Uncanny disruptions occur as a doubling of the "identity" of subject or object: in such moments, our ability to use language to "identify" our experience fails. I either cannot use language to articulate what it is that I see, or I lack a sense of who the one is that is seeing in a displacement of my sense of self—effects similar to those generated by the sublime. Bereft of language, the uncanny separates us from our home, the normally seamless conjunction of word and earth that provides us with our world. We are used to grasping world as a whole while we dwell, but the experience of the uncanny divides our use of language from the earth that generally accepts it. Even without the arrival of a literal ghost, soldiers returning from a distant war might well experience the uncanny revelation that one's home—recognizable, as it has not changed—is also *unfamiliar* as a relic that no longer speaks to one's present circumstances. The moment of first return is too often without a story that allows the soldier to solder the two worlds together, to gather life lived both here and there, then and now. This might also occur in the first night one spends at home after having buried a beloved spouse, or in the absence of a favored friend without whom one has not experienced one's town. I am stunned. Speechless. Homeless.

Wordless and worldless, we view familiar vistas in foreign ways as we struggle to return to home. Although such experiences might unsettle us, the uncanny is valuable in the revelation of a new world.[12] The truth of this new world conflicts with the surrounding world, displacing both the recipient of the revelation and the thing that originally brought it into the shared world. Preserving this truth requires living in a conflict between rival claims on the being of the same thing, as one sees the world as an echo of itself, recreating Freud's uncanny struggle of plurality within identity. Agonizing, these moments of uncanny existence disclose the powerful connection between language and earth lost in our everyday struggles and cares.

The second and more insidious way that our poetic dwelling may become disrupted is through an experience of the uncanny that is *caused* by language. Language is at its most uncanny when the perfect symmetry of word and thing fractures *incompletely*. Although the sublime experience of wordlessness may disorient us, it also ushers in a space for awe that overpowers our despair. Thus, more troubling than the absence of language—not knowing what to call something—is when our words say either more or less than what we desire and therefore produce the uncanny. A difference appears between the concrete, earthly dimension and the language world that usually combines with it for a perfect presentation of dwelling. Freud's slips of the tongue, which expose the deep ways that words work, presents the most familiar way that we find a doubled world in

---

[12]   Martin Heidegger, "Origin of the Work of Art," in Hofstadter (ed.), *Poetry, Language, Thought*. See especially pp. 66–78.

a single word.[13] We laugh, and the laughter disguises the twinge of anxiety that such slips elicit.

The third way that our poetic dwellings can be disrupted is through the unsettling possibilities that persist at the ontological or structural level of narrative. Narrative structures do not usually produce uncanny disruptions because the utter absence of the earthly taken up into narratives makes the type of doubling produced in the suddenness of a revelation or the incompleteness caused by a slip of the tongue unlikely. We are not normally troubled when interrupted while reading a book or watching a movie, because most narrative worlds are ephemeral in nature. The production of a truly uncanny narrative dwelling (examples of which follow below) requires that a self-enclosing plot, serving as an analog of the earthly, come into conflict with its linguistic background. This tension would necessarily be incomplete (and thus more disturbing), as the "earthly" correlate is more truly based in language. For maximal effect, an author can incorporate pools of the uncanny—slips of the tongue, revelations of otherworldly possibilities—as ontic instances within the self-referential structure that provides us with the opportunity for an uncanny homecoming.

The Distinction of Narrative Dwellings

Before exploring the ways that narratives might invite an uncanny homecoming, it is first necessary to clarify what a narrative dwelling might entail. While Heidegger never comments on the possibility of dwelling in unpresent domains, the amount of time we spend in fictional worlds invites an exploration of the meaning of these worlds and our ability to inhabit them. When we hearken to a narrative, the relation of the tale displaces us from the physical space around us and from the Fourfold that inheres within things. Movies and books transport us into a narrative space: we cease sensing signifiers and instead enter an unreal world as the words that convey a story are displaced by an emphasis on the relationship between words. Unlike poetry, which juxtaposes present words to make them meaningful, the narrative impulse pushes away from the presence of words toward the ungiven *connections* we imagine and remember between them. Words in narratives are important as they form boundaries that are less a limitation than what allows for a defined space to come into being. Words guide us through narrative as a type of marker, ensuring that we gain knowledge of a whole that gathers through a net total of associations. Thus, even though we can be immersed in a narrative, the narrative itself only ever appears indirectly, through the combined efforts of memory and the imagination. As an activity, narrations ex-ist in a trajectory that cannot be anchored into any one moment of presence. Unlike the poetic function, where words serve as a verbal analog to things, gathering and merging until they

---

[13] Sigmund Freud, *The Psychopathology of Everyday Life* (New York, 1965). See especially Chapters 5 and 6.

become more than what they are, words in narratives sacrifice themselves to highlight that which they themselves are not.

On an existential level, narrative dwelling does not require being part of an audience: when we relate to unpresent people, spaces, or times, we inhabit objectively uncertain worlds that cause us to be instantly displaced. Remembering, imagining, and dreaming also allow us access to the unreal. Spending time in narrative worlds, we learn to inhabit spaces that lack objective correlates. Unlike occupying merely functional spaces that reduce us to the bare life of our bodies, narrative worlds require time and language, memory and imagination, and thus provide us with an unreal space that we can inhabit uncannily.

Despite the time we spend in such spaces, these inhabitations fall short of a dwelling because narratives gesture away from themselves instead of coalescing inward. Not only do narrative worlds lack the gathering necessary for the experience of dwelling, but their forward propulsion is antithetical toward the permanent pastness we long for in a home. Exceptions to this rule occur when a narrative creates a closed space within itself as an isolated and separate sphere. Although the narrative maintains many points of access and, like all narratives, allows for a variety of voices to mix and stir within it, the structure of these stories does not permit a profusion of exits. This is the textual basis for a narrative dwelling.

Uncanny Dwellings in Nineteenth-Century American Literature

I provide two examples of narrative dwellings, which provide different ways for creating a self-enclosing plot that creates the effect of an "earth" with which the language of the plot can conflict. A common feature of Gothic literature in the US, dwellings in the narratives produce uncanny spaces able to contain the reader. In particular, Nathaniel Hawthorne's *The House of the Seven Gables* incorporates a narrative dwelling that invites the reader to preserve the tension between land and language through three displacements undertaken throughout the time it takes to read the book.

The initial work of displacement occurs in the prologue, which defines Romance as resting in the "attempt to connect a by-gone time with the very Present that is flitting away from us. It is a Legend, prolonging itself, from an epoch now gray in the distance." Hawthorne figures his temporal gathering as light, stating that the distant gray Legend will come "into our own broad daylight, and bringing along with it some of its legendary mist." These mists of time might be discarded or "float almost imperceptibly about the characters and events, for the sake of a picturesque effect."[14] The temporal juxtaposition is twofold: on one level, the "very Present" that Hawthorne references, with its "broad daylight," exists as past relative to the reader. On a second level, the past within the story filters our way of understanding the novel's diegetic present, and this past presents itself as a

---

[14]   Nathaniel Hawthorne, *The House of the Seven Gables* (New York, 1986), p. 2.

time sustained into the reader's present in a way analogous to how we think of our homes. Reading the book mediates our awareness of the present as it summons us to the temporal depth that contextualizes every present that we see. Language, like a spider's web, provides a slight, sticky thickness that forces us to reflect on the differences separating language, time, and space.

The second displacement in the novel is spatial. Hawthorne grants his reader permission "to assign an actual locality to the imaginary events of this narrative." He blames this on "the historical connection," which reveals his awareness of the objective quality of time. In other words, his refusal of a "real" setting requires readers to localize the story in geographic spaces they find familiar. The next sentence differentiates the reader's work from the author's. In it, Hawthorne clarifies that the author's work exists in defining boundaries within the realms of language and time, writing that he wants to avoid offense "by laying out a street that infringes upon nobody's private rights, and appropriating a lot of land which had no visible owner, and building a house, of materials long in use for constructing castles in the air".[15] Hawthorne thus emphasizes both that the space of literature requires neither settlers nor violence and that reading transforms imagined spaces into actual ones. Further, despite his claim to "be glad … if … the book may be read strictly as a Romance, having a great deal more to do with the clouds overhead, than with any portion of the actual soil of the County of Essex,"[16] the concluding suggestion of *actual* soil in a material space pushes the reader toward an uncanny actualization of plot. After reading the statement, in other words, readers familiar with the area would find it difficult to *not* visualize the County of Essex.

Third, the book temporally displaces its reader as its plot features an ontological ground that induces readers to filter the experience of an objectively certain world through a linguistically mediated temporality. Hawthorne explicitly expresses this temporality through his character Clifford, who states:

> that all human progress is in a circle; or, to use a more accurate and beautiful figure, in an ascending spiral curve. While we fancy ourselves going straight forward, and attaining, at every step, an entirely new position of affairs, we do actually return to something long ago tried and abandoned, but which we now find etherealized, refined, and perfected to its ideal.[17]

The book reinforces the notion of a spiral consistently in the plot. One finds it in the seemingly eternal return of the Pyncheons, in face, figure, and situation, to the House that thereby becomes their uncanny home. Additionally, the spiral proleptically signals that Hawthorne's faux-attempt at a "new beginning" at the novel's end, where love between two characters "transfigured the earth, and made

---

[15]   Ibid., p. 3.

[16]   Ibid.

[17]   Ibid., p. 260.

it Eden again, and themselves the two first dwellers in it,"[18] is less a new beginning than yet another turn of the screw.

Structurally, Hawthorne's story provides a self-enclosing space, one that curves the reader's inclination to move forward, such that progress is always a return to the past. The plot's pairing of a house with an explicit focus on the present as a prolonged past provides us with a very human conception of home: twisted by Gothic excesses on the surface of the text, the "world" of the story is put at odds with its "earth." This is figured in the Pyncheons' attempted flight from the House by railroad: the temporary nature of their liberation, a freedom that the reader wants for their characters, undermines the human sense of home that serves as the book's "earth" or foundation.

Another moment of disruption is found at an existential level, based on the reader's appropriation of the structure of the text (made possible through the hours one has spent living in Hawthorne's *House*). The spiral sublates simple interpretations of similarity (the circle) or difference (time's arrow) into its structure, mediating the reader's non-textual awareness through its possibility. Framed by the spiral, the reader's return to a shared, objective world remains obscured by images of ghosts future and present. We see beyond the spaces of the present that coalesce through a poetic dwelling, as the narrative dwelling draws attention to how time relates space and language. The attention to the space of relation, magnified by Hawthorne's emphasis on temporality, disrupts a poetic focus on presence—especially a homely presence as elongated past. Dwelling narratively, we include the relations of time that let us better see the mists of has-beens and will-becomes that surround us. Hawthorne's mediation of our normal mode of being makes foreign what is most familiar, such that our return to a poetic dwelling apart from the novel becomes an uncanny experience.

Like Hawthorne's *House*, Edgar Allan Poe's "The Fall of the House of Usher" builds an edifice whose roots are sunk into time and language instead of space. Also like Hawthorne, Poe creates a textual world from an exaggerated account of normal homemaking behaviors and frames it in terms of Gothic conventions in order to render uncanny the reader's return to his or her poetic dwelling. Unlike Hawthorne, who focused on the gathering and conservative tendencies of homemaking, Poe concentrates on the importance of identity as a central ingredient of normal modes of poetic dwelling. This shows that the foundations of an uncanny dwelling can be built on different grounds.

Poe's plot draws the reader's attention to the problems caused by attending to presence at the expense of absence. Criticizing the hope of a "complete" world, one that would lack absence, Poe indirectly draws attention to the need for the *space* of relating, for the absences and differences that emerge in narrative dwelling. Poe constructs his "House" without spaces, providing details that emphasize its internal congruity, its absolute nature, its undifferentiated sense of identity. Thus, the "House of Usher" itself includes "both the family and the family mansion."

---

[18] Ibid., p. 307.

Poe mentions that the family has grown "with very trifling and very temporary variation," and the narrator mentions that "about the whole mansion and domain there hung an atmosphere peculiar to themselves and their immediate vicinity" and sees "fungi overspread the whole exterior."[19] Further, the narrator notes a "striking similitude between the brother and sister," and Usher confirms that they "had been twins, and that sympathies of a scarcely intelligible nature had always existed between them."[20] Building, family, past and present are all merged together within a fog of an identity so absolute that the uncanny itself is suppressed for want of something external to serve as a double.

The care with which Poe reveals undifferentiation allows for an implosive ending, in which the House of Usher falls under the weight of its own identity. First, Poe draws attention to the lingering fracture in identity, figured as a "barely-discernible fissure," which widens until the narrator sees "the mighty walls rushing asunder." The sundering then collects all remaining possible differences before gathering both building and family into a wholly undifferentiated mass of brute presence—which subsequently disappears. This spectacle is announced with a series of overstimulating sensory explosions: a "wild light" issuing from "the full, setting, and blood-red moon" accompanied by "a long tumultuous shouting sound like the voice of a thousand waters" before "the deep and dank tarn at my feet closed sullenly and silently over the fragments of the '*House of Usher.*'"[21] As a last gesture of closing the "House's" absolute self-identity, the final fragment of the House of Usher is textually contained by the final period and quotation mark: building, people, and text terminate at the same moment.

Unlike Hawthorne's concretization of his tale in a New England landscape, Poe places his tale fully in the world of language, remaining in Hawthorne's clouds while refusing the County of Essex. The first words of the story displaces its events into a space outside of the shared, certain world. Poe writes: "DURING the whole of a dull, dark, and soundless day in the autumn of the year, when the clouds hung oppressively low in the heavens, I had been passing alone, on horseback, through a singularly dreary tract of country; and at length found myself, as the shades of the evening drew on, within view of the melancholy House of Usher." The temporal markers—day, autumn, year, and evening—engulf the anonymous "singularly dreary tract of country," whose spatial importance is undermined. The alliteration of the "d" sound keeps the reader's focus on the linguistic formation of the house as well, accentuated by the fact that the House inflicts a "depression of the soul" that "can compare to no earthly sensation more properly than to the after-dream of the reveler upon opium."[22] The warning against dwelling wholly in language, as Roderick Usher did in his world of words, comes with the collapse of the language

---

[19]   Edgar Allan Poe, "The Fall of the House of Usher," in *Sixty-Seven Tales* (New York, 1985), p. 200.

[20]   Ibid., p. 207.

[21]   Ibid., p. 212.

[22]   Ibid, p. 200.

world under its own weight. There can be no return to the House of Usher, which vanishes behind the final period of the story: ejected from a narrative dwelling, the reader returns to a world where land and language combine to provide a newly awakened demand for difference. This difference presents itself as an uncanny lens over one's home: trained by the text, one desires to make *unfamiliar* that which otherwise would have been taken for granted.

Both texts thus present uncanny visions of homes and push readers into experiencing the return to a world that merges language and land as an uncanny homecoming. The spaces the stories produce haunt the reader, forcing him or her to consider "the reality of what had originally been considered imaginary" as the houses, a symbol, have taken on "the full function and significance of what it symbolizes."[23] The temporal form of Hawthorne's novel takes on a reality just as it alters the reader's perception, just as the collapse of the House of Usher destroys the desirability of identity in the world beyond the text.

Each narrative gathers the reader into an unpresent space of relation that feels oddly closed and restricted: Hawthorne's insistence on the spiral of time negates the difference implied in futural progression, just as Poe's isolated word world collapses in on itself. The uncomfortable claustrophobic feeling produced in these texts lingers as we see how many of our poetic dwellings, collapsing land and language, run a similar risk. These narrative dwellings make returning to shared worlds an uncanny experience, and thereby empower us to seek out moments of difference in the localized spaces of our world. Unsettled from nonchalant appropriations of a gathered world, we can examine the spaces of relation for moments of difference. Instead of dwelling in a way that Heidegger advises, sparing and preserving in a frozen present of sheer *identity* in "the simple *oneness* of the four,"[24] a narrative dwelling allows us to free things into the dynamic world of time, a world of becoming and emerging.

Dwelling Beyond Poetry

The awareness of being and presence awakened in dwelling poetically allows us to engage in the intentional co-creation of our worlds, gathering things and time into spaces that subsequently become our homes. Conservative in nature, the poetic world coalesces its disparate elements into a homogenized sense of "home," which eschews difference in its appetite for localized preservation. At best, a poetic dwellings threaten to keep the gods isolated: measuring the span of distance from what is alien, it collects and gathers what is most familiar to us. This sense of familiarity is not a bad thing and it provides a sense of world that feels both full and fulfilling: it is, however, not enough. It is only when we dwell

---

[23]   Freud, *The Uncanny*, p. 150.

[24]   Martin Heidegger. "Building, Dwelling, Thinking," in Hofstadter (ed.), *Poetry, Language, Thought*, p. 150.

narratively and risk focusing on the uncanny nature of our homecomings that we allow a space that can be measured, where we can enjoy what is different without fear—and without converting it into a mirror of ourselves.

The haunts of Gothic fiction produce uncanny homecomings, and thereby unsettle our tendencies to dwell poetically and open new spaces. Dwelling narratively—not to be confused with the narrative dwellings that cover the Gothic spaces of certain texts—is a comportment that focuses on spaces, on differences, on futures. Rather than building our homes in the safety of a prolonged past, dwelling beyond poetry pushes us to embrace uncertain possibilities. When we arrive at home, we search for what is unfamiliar and cling to what distinguishes it from what we can recall, and thus avoid the totalizing nature of an absolute present. Dwelling beyond poetry, we can recognize our distance from our homes and embrace a habit of uncanny homecomings that reminds us of the bliss of absence and the joy of the unknown.

References

Chandler, Marilyn R., *Dwelling in the Text: Houses in American Fiction* (Berkeley: University of California Press, 1991).

Crow, Charles, *History of the Gothic: American Gothic* (Cardiff: University of Wales Press, 2009).

Franklin, R.W., *The Poems of Emily Dickinson* (Cambridge, MA: Harvard University Press, 1999).

Freud, Sigmund, *The Psychopathology of Everyday Life*, trans. and ed. J. Strachey (New York: W.W. Norton & Company, 1965).

Freud, Sigmund, "The Uncanny," in David McLintock (trans. and ed.), *The Uncanny* (New York: Penguin, 2003).

Garrett, Peter K., *Gothic Reflections: Narrative Force in 19th Century Fiction* (Ithaca: Cornell University Press, 2003).

Goddu, Teresa A., *Gothic America: Narrative, History, and Nation* (New York: Columbia University Press, 1997).

Hawthorne, Nathaniel, *The House of the Seven Gables* (New York: Penguin Classics, 1986).

Heidegger, Martin, "Building, Dwelling, Thinking," in A. Hofstadter (trans. and ed.), *Poetry, Language, Thought* (New York: Harper & Row, 1971).

Heidegger, Martin, "Poetically Man Dwells," in A. Hofstadter (trans. and ed.), *Poetry, Language, Thought* (New York: Harper & Row, 1971).

Heidegger, Martin, "The Thing," in A. Hofstadter (trans. and ed.), *Poetry, Language, Thought* (New York: Harper & Row, 1971).

Lloyd Smith, Allan, *American Gothic Fiction: An Introduction* (New York: Continuum, 2004).

Martin, Robert K., *American Gothic: New Interventions in a National Narrative* (Iowa City: University of Iowa Press, 2009).

Poe, Edgar Allen, "The Fall of the House of Usher," in *Sixty-Seven Tales* (New York: Gramercy Books, 1985).

Ricoeur, Paul, *Interpretation Theory* (Fort Worth: Texas Christian University Press, 1976).

Ricoeur, Paul, *Time and Narrative, Vols. 1–3*, trans. Kathleen Blamey, David Pellauer and Kathleen McLaughlin (Chicago: University of Chicago Press, 1990).

Ringe, Donald, *American Gothic: Imagination and Reason in Nineteenth-Century Fiction* (Lexington: University of Kentucky Press, 1982).

Schrimeister, Pamela, *The Consolation of Space: The Place of Romance in Hawthorne, Melville and James* (Palo Alto: Stanford University Press, 1990).

Sedgwick, Eve Kosofsky, *The Coherence of Gothic Conventions* (New York: Methuen, 1986).

Wardrop, Daneen, *Emily Dickinson's Gothic: Goblin with a Gauge* (Iowa City: University of Iowa Press, 1996).

Williams, Anne. *Art of Darkness: A Poetics of Gothic* (Chicago: University of Chicago Press, 1995).

Chapter 5

The Paradox of Homecoming: Home is Where the Haunt is

Kimberly Carfore

The world is in crisis. The crisis involves a proliferation of complex and uncertain phenomena like global financial instability, poverty, immigration, climate change, species extinction, water scarcity, ethnic and cultural conflict, etc. Some people respond to such phenomena by attempting to save the world from its critical condition. However, as Jacques Derrida observes, "the convulsive effort to save a 'world'" is itself a symptom of the crisis, for the crisis is precisely that there is no single "world" in crisis, no common home or dwelling to save, "no more *oikos*, economy, ecology, livable site in which we are 'at home.'"[1] The very idea of home (coming home, being at home, etc.) is cracked open by all that which is not at home, all that which is away, uncanny, and other.

To respond to the crisis of the world today, what is called for is not more efforts to save our common home. What is called for is participation in the deconstruction of home, participation in the opening up of home to the coming of that which is strange, foreign, unexpected, and impossible. Only then will a just world arrive. This is the work of deconstruction: opening up the home to the impossible conditions of its own reality, opening up the home so that something wholly other can come. Derrida continues:

> The deconstruction of logocentrism, of linguisticism, of economism (of the proper, of the at-home [*chez-soi*], *oikos*, of the same), etc., as well as the affirmation of the impossible are always put forward *in the name of the real*, of the irreducible reality of the real—not of the real as the attribute of the objective, present, perceptible or intelligible *thing* (*res*), but of the real as the coming or event of the other.[2]

What follows is an elaboration on the deconstruction of home, particularly in light of the sense of the messianic conveyed in Derrida's *Specters of Marx*. The

---

[1] Jacques Derrida, *Negotiations: Interviews and Interventions 1971–2001*, ed. Elizabeth Rottenberg (Stanford, 2002), p. 70.

[2] Ibid., p. 367. Translation modified by Pheng Cheah, "Non-Dialectical Materialism," in Diana Coole and Samantha Frost (eds), *New Materialisms: Ontology, Agency, and Politics* (Durham, 2010), p. 76.

deconstruction of home, for Derrida, affirms a messianic call for the arrival of an event of justice, yet his messianic affirmation takes place without a determinate messiah and without a determinate messianism, whether Jewish, Christian, or otherwise. The arrival of the event of justice is always to come, infinitely exceeding the limits of presence. Accordingly, the messianic call for justice is a call for something or someone to come that displaces place, exceeding the limits of every home. In other words, welcoming the other, the wholly other, foreigner or stranger into one's home is a welcoming of an impossible event—a justice that exceeds the coordinates of what we currently understand to be possible. To welcome home the *arrivant* is to practice what could be called a postsecular "religion without religion," opening up to the otherness or "alterity" that overflows the proper boundaries that mark the home apart from its other (believers from non-believers, saints from sinners, the saved from the damned, the sacred from profane, etc.). Welcoming the stranger into one's home marks the arrival of an event of justice, an event that implodes these otherwise neatly categorized boundaries—sacred/profane, religious/secular, familiar/foreign, self/other—opening to the paradoxical space of the uncanny homecoming. When the stranger comes home, that home becomes uncanny, and the paradoxical space of this uncanny homecoming marks the arrival of an event of justice.

This chapter is divided into four parts: 1) I articulate Derrida's understanding of the messianic without a messianism, including an account of the incalculability and otherness that marks the messianic; 2) I discuss the injustices that haunt the dwelling spaces of global society and prevent anyone from being at home; 3) I express an invitation to respond to injustice by welcoming the singular otherness of every other (human and non-human), such that the ghosts of our history are welcomed as newcomers and given places at our homes, although it renders strange what would otherwise be familiar to us; 4) finally, I give an overview of similar responses to otherness that can be found in the humanities, specifically in feminism and eco-feminism.

In the impossible event of welcoming the other, what shows up is a ghost—an absent presence, a haunting that calls for justice. Accordingly, for homecoming to be a just practice, it must be a matter of coming home to a haunting—a haunted house—and preparing for a messianic event of justice with no hope of the presence of a determinate Messiah. The messianic call for justice is a call to exorcise the ghosts of history by respecting the wholly otherness of their arrival. Preparing for this event, a messianic event without a determinate Messiah demands a radical openness that brings justice to those others who have been excluded or otherwise rendered invisible throughout history.

Messianic

Every messianic call for justice happens somewhere, in some historical context, wherein the justice that is called for takes a particular form and is thus implicated in a particular messianism—a particular understanding of how justice is determined. A Jewish call for justice and a Christian call for justice are not unsituated messianic structures, but are situated in the messianisms of Judaism and Christianity. Furthermore, a call for justice is situated in a messianism even if the call is not expressed in explicitly religious terms. Thus, Derrida notices that Marx's seemingly atheistic call for justice involves its own messianism reflected in Marx's understanding of the dialectical movement of history.

It is not possible to live in the messianic in general, stripped of all contexts or all messianisms. Yet, in Derrida's *Specters of Marx*, what is proposed is precisely a messianic without a historical messianism or determinate Messiah. But how is this possible? How can one "remove a biblical surface from a messianic structure?"[3] How do we practice a messianic justice without a messianism? How do we practice a religion without religion? We must welcome the arrival of the messianic without knowing or having a determinate expectation of what the messianic is. Therefore, the arrival of justice would not necessarily be the second coming of Jesus Christ, but it also does not rule out the possibility of Christ as the Messiah.

Similar to the Jewish custom of setting an extra place at the Passover table, Derrida performs a "messianic opening to what is coming ... to the event as the foreigner itself, to her or him for whom one must leave an empty place, always, in memory of the hope ... nothing and no one would arrive otherwise."[4] This movement is filled with anxiety, "since it involves the operation of taking into one's home the *unheimlich*, the one who is not part of the home, the stranger."[5] It is uncanny, such that a home opens a space for discomfort and unfamiliarity rather than comfort and the familiar. Therefore, the ethics of a home calls for radical openness, or openness toward that which is foreign. What would happen if a stranger actually arrived to claim his or her seat at the table? Who would this stranger be and how might we react?

The space at one's table is a constant reminder of the uncanniness of home. Welcoming the stranger, the newcomer, the messianic without a determinate Messiah is the impossible task at hand. It is the task of justice—"a welcoming that is a little uneasy about what is to come, a little spooked. For welcoming is unnerving."[6] It is unnerving in the sense that radical openness demands radical uncertainty, which is rightfully anxiety producing. The uncanny home is both descriptive and prescriptive. It is descriptive in that justice requires welcoming, and welcoming the other happens to be unnerving. In another sense, Derrida conveys a prescriptive tone, as if to say that one *should* become unnerved. However, it is ultimately neither prescriptive nor descriptive—any prescription telling you what to do and any description of what is are parts of the familiar home that the

---

[3]   John D. Caputo, *The Prayers and Tears of Jacques Derrida: Religion Without Religion* (Bloomington, 1997), p. 135.

[4]   Jacques Derrida, *Specters of Marx: The State of the Debt, the Work of Mourning, and the New International*, trans. Peggy Kamuf (New York, 1994), p. 65.

[5]   Caputo, *Prayers*, p. 145.

[6]   Ibid., p. 144.

stranger disrupts. Upon arrival, the stranger states "Deal with me in my alterity" (an imperative), which means dealing with the other without assimilating them into your horizon of de-, pre-, and pro-scriptions. Uncanniness *should* trouble the is/ought dichotomy, opening to the unnerved welcome.

To be unnerved or unsure of what one is waiting for, what one is opening to or welcoming, is to be living at the boundary of what is livable or habitable. Derrida uses the image of a desert to express such an uninhabitable habitation. This desert implies an emptiness or barrenness. It is only in this barren space that we can encounter a messianic openness that makes tremble the borders, structures, and expectations that determine what or who the Messiah is, what or who justice looks like. The barren space of the desert is the space of the wholly other, a wholly other that is so radically other that it resists identification with any particular name, for example, God. Leaving this space open, untouched—a paradox—is maintaining a space to make possible the impossible. Practicing radical openness within the boundaries of our own homes extends outside of our homes, opening up the possibility of a more just future.

That which is wholly other may or may not imply God. If the Messiah were definable, it would lose its uncanniness or radical alterity. If one could predict its arrival, one could prepare for its coming, making it no longer wholly other, or an event to come. In short, for the wholly other to be wholly other, it cannot be present. The arrival of the wholly other is, in this sense, strictly impossible. The wholly other must arrive in a rupture within the possible, a rupture that opens a space for justice to come. As John Caputo says:

> The passion for the impossible is precisely not to be quenched. The one who is coming … the *tout autre*, can never be present. He must always function as a breach of the present, opening up the present to something new, to something impossible. Were the horizon of possibility to close over, it would erase the trace of justice, for justice is the trace of what is to come beyond the possible.[7]

This space beyond-the-possible is the space of the messianic, and the trace of one to come. Welcoming the messianic into our homes is a great place to enter these remarkable spaces—cultivating a passion and promise for justice to come.

The messianic without a Messiah is messianic because it is always calling for the arrival of justice, yet there is no being that would possibly bring this justice— no Messiah—insofar as justice is an impossible task. Justice is always to come, never fully present. Moreover, lest those who hear Derrida's messianic call feel disempowered, it is important to mention that this call for the impossible does not imply inaction. It implies an ongoing vigilance in maintaining an ethical obligation towards bringing justice. The disjointed or impossible condition of bringing about justice is precisely what makes justice possible. Without this impossibility, justice "rests on the good conscience of having done one's duty, it loses the chance of the

---

7   Ibid., p. xxiv.

future."[8] Losing the chance of a future means losing the chance for inheritance. This does not imply making a home in an unrealizable future instead of a past, but rather to remain open to a future and past that are not present or (re)presentable, but wholly other.

The absolute alterity of the other must remain ineffaceable in the name of justice, the impossible, and the future to come. Furthermore, it is not only the alterity of some others that evokes Derrida's concern; it is the alterity of every single other. Derrida writes: "Every other is altogether other." In French, this is palindromic: "tout autre est tout autre," where its translation is both "every other is altogether other," and "altogether other is every other."[9] Maintaining the ineffaceable mark of the other, of every other, calls for a respect for the absolute singularity of every other. It does not mean that one would indiscriminately open up his or her borders to welcoming any other, nor would they indiscriminately close their door upon the arrival of the other. What it does mean is that respecting the absolute alterity of every other would be responding to the unique imperatives of each, breaking open the limits of the possible, welcoming the impossible, and responding to the singular call of justice issuing from the otherness of every other.

When entering into a relationship with any other, that other is translated or assimilated into one's own horizon of perception or meaning. Therefore, upon the arrival of that which is other, the other loses its sense of otherness because it is now in relation to a self or non-other. Real hospitality implies an impossible openness that cannot be fulfilled. In other words, hospitality toward the other is always already contaminated by hostility toward the other. Derrida expresses this paradox with the term "hostipitality"—a portmanteau term combining hospitality and hostility.[10] To put this another way, there is no way of relating to the other without also narcissistically appropriating its alterity. "There is not narcissism and non-narcissism; there are narcissisms that are more or less comprehensive, generous, open, extended."[11] As I have mentioned already, this is not meant to discourage action. Rather, the ontological impossibility of fully welcoming the other compels us toward ethical and political obligations characterized by ongoing encounters with the imperatives of all others—a commitment to responding to the call of justice.

This is the ethics and politics of deconstruction. "To prepare oneself for this coming [*venue*] of the other is what can be called deconstruction."[12] Deconstruction is a practice of welcoming the alterity of every other, which could also be described as a practice of welcoming the other. This is likewise the task of doing justice to the other. Remember Derrida's provocative phrase: "*Deconstruction is justice.*"[13]

---

8   Derrida, *Specters*, p. 28.

9   Ibid., p. 195n37.

10   Jacques Derrida, *Acts of Religion*, ed. Gil Anidjar (New York, 2002), p. 358.

11   Jacques Derrida, *Points: Interviews, 1974–1994* (Stanford, 1995), p. 199.

12   Caputo, *Prayers*, p. 73.

13   Derrida, *Acts*, p. 243.

If deconstruction is justice, then deconstruction is a practice of an uncanny homecoming. Deconstructing the demarcations of home and opening one's home to include strangers, ghosts, the unexpected, and the impossible is the task at hand, the task of justice. Practicing this impossible task in our own homes—in mind and body—opens us to the messianic structure, therefore welcoming the embodiment of new structures of reality. This messianic call for justice, although not to be quenched, is the ongoing call for new ways of welcoming the other.

Haunting

The call for justice emerges in the disjunction of time—a paradoxical space of non-resolution or impossibility, a gap that opens to invite the ongoing call for justice to arrive and remains open for what is to come. Derrida opens his *Specters of Marx* with the words of Shakespeare's Hamlet, who decries, "The time is out of joint. O cursèd spite, / That ever I was born to set it right!"[14] The time is out of joint indeed. Ecological, economic, social, psychological, and spiritual problems plague us, and never has the crisis been so extensive, so multifaceted. In these difficult times we face difficult issues. The call for justice is communicated through the voices of subjugated, oppressed others— women, children, racial minorities, animals, and the environment, to name a few. The one who bears witness to injustices present in the other, the stranger, the foreigner inherits the responsibility as one's duty to set things right. We may not want it and may curse its presence, nagging memory, or haunting voice, which is very much the case. Derrida's idea of *haunting* is exactly this—a nagging memory, obsession or voice. That which haunts is the return of those subjugated, oppressed others that have been excluded in history.

The call for justice in the presence of the other is a *haunting*—"A certain revisitation of the present by a ghost from the past."[15] The haunting other is a ghost, a *revenant*. Its constant presence and relationship to us through time is Derrida's *hauntology*.[16] To exorcise ghosts is to "grant [ghosts] the right," even if it is "making them come back alive."[17] To exorcise is not to chase them away, but to give them a place at one's table and a hospitable welcome. The visible other, which has been made invisible through violence, oppression, or injustice, is kept alive as the *revenant*, the ghost, and calls for justice through its haunting apparitions. It calls for your attention or, more appropriately, demands your attention, through the glance, the touch, the voice—it *haunts*.[18]

---

[14]   Derrida, *Specters*, p. 21.

[15]   Caputo, *Prayers*, p. 135.

[16]   For more on *hauntology*, see Derrida, *Specters*, pp. 10, 51.

[17]   Ibid., p. 175.

[18]   Ibid., p. 177n2.

Living one's life means living in the impossible space of a justice to come, the space of haunting. One dwells in one's haunts. "To live, by definition, is not something one learns ... from oneself," but "only from the other and by death."[19] "What happens between ... life and death, can only *maintain itself* with some ghost."[20] These ghostly apparitions, these fuzzy boundaries are representative of the vagueness and openness to ambiguity necessary in cultivating justice. In our ongoing interactions with one another, it is important to practice muddying boundaries or opening these liminal spaces. In these liminal spaces between life and death, sacred and secular, self and other, foreign and familiar lies an ontological space for new development, a space for new possibilities—for the future. Injustices from the past can be reconciled through the haunting presence of the ghost. Attending to these nagging memories or obsessions, whatever they might be, exorcises these ghosts, and creates a more just past, present, and future.

Derrida writes that "haunting is historical,"[21] expressing the lives and deaths of past others, calling for justice to bring about the future. This implies an ongoing process of encountering alterity, uncomfortable spaces despite apprehension, disinterest, or fear. In relation to the home, this implies an ongoing openness to the other, the stranger, the guest. Maintaining that open place at one's table demonstrates the importance of remaining open to the possibility that all one's comforts could be shattered by the arrival of the other. This is not to say that one allows every stranger, guest, or foreigner into one's home. What it does imply is accepting responsibility and practicing discernment—a responsibility and commitment to our haunts—our uncanny homecomings.

"Given that a *revenant* is always called upon to come and to come back, the thinking of the specter, contrary to what good sense leads us to believe, signals toward the future. It is a thinking of the past, a legacy that can come only from that which has not yet arrived—from the *arrivant* itself."[22] As haunting is historical, the thinking of the specter is reminding oneself of the imperatives it speaks. When thinking of the specter—one's haunts, obsessions, nagging presences—that which shows up is the *arrivant*.

Arrivant

Where the *revenant* is a ghost, the *arrivant* is a guest or newcomer, not a determinate Messiah. Derrida describes the welcoming of the *arrivant* as always to come, in the future (*avenir*, translated literally as "the future"). *Revenant* means "a coming back" or "return" where *revenir* literally means "to come back." Where *arrivant* is the messianic future and the coming of justice, what shows up as the *revenant* is

---

19 Ibid., p. xviii.
20 Ibid.
21 Ibid., p. 4.
22 Ibid., p. 196n39.

always a ghost. The thinking of the ghost "is a thinking of the past, a legacy that can come only from that which has not yet arrived—from the *arrivant* itself."[23]

The *arrivant* is always "to come" (*à-venir*), in "the future" (*l'avenir*), such that when the *arrivant* haunts, it marks the coming of a past that calls for a more just future.[24] In the hope and promise of one day bringing about justice, the *arrivant* continues to arrive, as an unpredictable force that haunts us with its compelling alterity. Deconstruction is the practice of welcoming the alterity of the *arrivant* as it shows up in the haunting calls for justice issuing from all others. Dwelling in the space of haunting, deconstruction welcomes every ghost as a newcomer.

Injustice plagues so many beings right now. It is impossible to keep track of all the others calling for justice. As haunting is historical, injustices show up as ghosts—fuzzy representations of past events, which should be set right. The thinking of the specter is an impossible task, indeed. Taking on this impossible task, Derrida lists 10 "plagues" of the current global civilization (the "new world order"): unemployment (or social inactivity); exclusion of the homeless and stateless; economic war; contradictions of the free market; national debt; the arms industry; nuclear proliferation; interethnic wars; mafia and drug cartels (phantom states); and the limits of the concept and practice of international law.[25] This list does not include the injustices I mentioned earlier—the ecological crisis, social, spiritual, and psychological problems, etc. As humans become more aware of their interconnection among and within species, it is important to begin including the injustices of non-human others in our lists. As Derrida's list focuses primarily on injustices done to human beings, it raises the question as to whether Derrida really honors the compelling alterity of *every* other.

What about non-human others? David Wood (2007) responds to this question in his attempt to propose an ecological deconstruction or "econstruction—a living, developing, and materially informed deconstruction."[26] According to Wood, deconstruction can and does indeed respond to the alterity of the natural environment. "Environmental destruction gives us a wake-up call of epic proportion, and is surely a candidate for the status of *arrivant*."[27] Accordingly, Wood suggests that Derrida's list of plagues should be extended to include the environmental crisis.[28] Furthermore, when Wood made this suggestion to Derrida in conversation, Derrida "quickly accepted this suggestion."[29] Dwelling in the space of haunting, deconstruction is a messianic practice of welcoming every

---

[23]	Ibid.

[24]	Ibid.

[25]	Ibid., pp. 81–4.

[26]	David Wood, "Specters of Derrida: On the Way to Econstruction," in Laurel Kearns and Catherine Keller (eds), *Ecospirit: Religions and Philosophies for the Earth* (New York, 2007), p. 267.

[27]	Ibid.

[28]	Ibid., p. 266.

[29]	Ibid., p. 588.

ghost as a newcomer, even animals, plants, and ecosystems. Moreover, Wood is not alone in his ecological approach to the *arrivant*. This is also the argument that Timothy Morton makes in *The Ecological Thought*, where he suggests that we should welcome all beings as strange strangers, where the phrase "strange stranger" is his translation of Derrida's *arrivant*.[30]

As *oikos* (Greek for home) translates to the English prefix eco of ecology (as well as economy), it is important to extend our conception of home to include earth as home—an uncanny move indeed. The multifaceted crisis we face demands an expansion of worldviews, including an extension of our ideas of history and inheritance. Did we inherit the earth? What is our responsibility towards non-human others? Where did we come from? Where are we going? What *is* a homecoming? This expansion forces humans to think on an evolutionary scale rather than through closed conceptions of self and other, familiar and foreign, sacred and profane. We open ourselves to different implications of these questions of home, deconstructing our notions of home for a just world to arrive—not a world to be saved, but rather a world to be questioned.

Animals, plants, trees, ecosystems—these certainly are strange strangers. How do we welcome the alterity of these creatures? What are the ethics of a home that includes trees, plants, animals, and ecosystems? Following the trends of the eco-humanities, we can observe how others have already extended the concept of uncanny homecomings to include non-human others. Exemplified by David Wood's ecological contribution to deconstruction, we can also see such an extension occurring in another philosophical movement with which deconstruction is closely affiliated—feminism. Like Wood's transformation of deconstruction into ecological deconstruction, feminism has entered ecological expression as eco-feminism.

Feminist Others

As quoted earlier, obligations towards the familiar, the at-home are "always put forward *in the name of the real*." Attending to alterity is a way to respect the singularity of all others, including non-human others. Feminist theorists have accomplished much by way of bringing more attention to alterity, specifically in relationship to the otherness of gender and sexuality. Many feminists articulate ways in which the patriarchal structures of Western civilization objectify the alterity of women, subjugating and subordinating women to the subjective agency of men. To attend to this alterity and welcome it on its own terms is to subvert the domination of women that has marked the history of patriarchy. In *The Second Sex*, Simone de Beauvoir recognizes this subversive power in her

---

[30] "I develop the concept of the strange stranger from Derrida's *arrivant*, the ultimate arrival to whom one must extend ultimate hospitality." Timothy Morton, *The Ecological Thought* (Cambridge, MA, 2010), p. 140n39.

classic work of feminist philosophy when suggesting that "the very fact that woman is *Other* challenges all the justification that men have ever given" for assimilating women into their own identity.[31]

Eco-feminist theorists extend feminist concerns with the domination of the alterity of women to address the domination of all others, human and non-human. In other words, eco-feminism addresses the domination of women while also addressing the underlying logic whereby oppressive hierarchies and asymmetries facilitate the domination of women as well as the domination of nature, the poor, and racial and ethnic minorities. This follows the definition of eco-feminism set forth by Karen Warren, for whom eco-feminism focuses on overcoming the "logic of domination," which underlies multiple forms of domination (sexism, naturism, racism, classism, ethnocentrism).[32] All of the oppressive hierarchies and asymmetries of globalization are thus folded together with feminism.

Respecting the alterity of human and earth others does not call for differences and otherness to be incorporated so that everybody is the same. That would be what the eco-feminist philosopher Val Plumwood calls an "uncritical reversal," and it is this behavior that reinforces the very structure we are working to do away with.[33] For Plumwood, the answer in resolving this dualism is to cultivate continuity with difference, where we recognize both the interconnectedness of things as well as their alterity. In Morton's terms, this means recognizing every being as part of the interconnected "mesh" (continuity) and as a strange stranger (difference).[34] This also resonates with the work of the feminist theorist Donna Haraway, particularly her category of "companion species," which figures the coevolutionary interconnectedness between species while also affirming the "significant otherness" of species.[35]

Feminists' work with alterity deconstructs the conceptual framework that keeps us "at home." Recognizing the coevolutionary interconnection between species, specifically the human to non-human relationship, is welcoming these strange strangers into our homes. Overcoming the logic of domination opens space for recognizing our ongoing obligations towards these others. The coevolutionary relationship is articulated in Haraway's discussion of the human-to-lab-animal relationship: "Response ... grows with the capacity to respond, that is, responsibility. Such a capacity can be shaped only in and for multidirectional

---

[31]   Simone de Beauvoir, *The Second Sex*, trans. Constance Borde and Sheila Malovany-Chevallier (New York, 2009), p. 10.

[32]   Karen Warren, "The Power and Promise of Ecological Feminism: Revisited," in Louis Pojman and Paul Pojman (eds), *Environmental Ethics Readings in Theory and Application*, 5th edn (Belmont, 2008), pp. 33–48.

[33]   Val Plumwood, *Feminism and the Mastery of Nature* (New York, 1993), p. 31.

[34]   Morton, *The Ecological Thought*, p. 15.

[35]   Donna J. Haraway, *When Species Meet* (Minneapolis, 2008), pp. 90, 97, 165.

relationships."[36] We are enmeshed in these multidirectional relationships. It is therefore our inheritance and responsibility as humans to include non-human others into our homes, ethics, and politics. This is not to be taken literally, however. It would be ridiculous to allow all animals into our homes. What this does mean is that species extinction is our responsibility. What it calls for is the deconstruction of one's assumption of home as well as one's haunts. This might mean developing a more comprehensive environmental ethic, as well as recognizing what it means to share a common home—the earth. As the global crisis extends to ecological proportions, it is our duty to respond to the singular call of justice issuing from these creatures and, in this, welcoming their alterity.

Conclusion

Trends in feminism and eco-feminism show that Derrida's messianic sense of justice is situated amidst other philosophical movements that aim to welcome the alterity of human and earth others. One need not adhere to Derrida's work or to any determinate form of deconstruction to participate in the messianic without a messianism. One only needs to come home: to dwell in one's haunts and welcome ghosts in ways that respect them as arriving newcomers and also let them come home.

To come to one's haunted home, to one's impossible place, one is called to make the boundaries and borders of home more just, more open and amenable to strangers, newcomers, and other others. One is called to recognize that one's home is only home when haunted by all the ghosts who could not be present, by all the strangers rendered invisible throughout history. This includes non-human others who have been oppressed under current structures of home.

As one's home is pervaded with things familiar, common, and domestic, it might appear questionable that a home is a just home insofar as it is haunted by that which is uncanny, alien, foreign, strange, and absent. The hip hop artist Sean "Diddy" Combs asks this question in his recently released song "Coming Home": "Is a house really a home when your loved ones are gone?"[37] Derrida would answer that this is precisely when a house is really a home. Participating in the deconstruction of home, it is evident that a home is really a home precisely insofar as it is haunted by the absence of loved ones and other others that call for our concern and compassion, for welcome, and for a place at home. A home is really a home precisely insofar as it is impossible. Opening up all possibilities and every determinate Messiah and messianism, we can come home, strangely coming back to our old haunts and preparing vigilantly for justice to come.

---

[36]   Ibid., p. 71.
[37]   Sean J. Combs, "Coming Home," in *Last Train to Paris* (Bad Boy Records, 2010).

References

Caputo, John D., *The Prayers and Tears of Jacques Derrida: Religion Without Religion* (Bloomington: Indiana University Press, 1997).

Cheah, Pheng, "Non-Dialectical Materialism," in Diana Coole and Samantha Frost (eds), *New Materialisms: Ontology, Agency, and Politics* (Durham: Duke University Press, 2010).

Combs, Sean J., "Coming Home," in *Last Train to Paris* (Bad Boy Records, 2010).

De Beauvoir, Simone, *The Second Sex*, trans. Constance Borde and Sheila Malovany-Chevallier (New York: Random House, 2009).

Derrida, Jacques, *Specters of Marx: The State of the Debt, the Work of Mourning, and the New International*, trans. Peggy Kamuf (New York: Routledge, 1994).

Derrida, Jacques, *Points: Interviews, 1974–1994* (Stanford: Stanford University Press, 1995).

Derrida, Jacques, *Acts of Religion*, ed. Gil Anidjar (New York: Routledge, 2002).

Derrida, Jacques, *Negotiations: Interviews and Interventions 1971–2001*, ed. Elizabeth Rottenberg (Stanford: Stanford University Press, 2002).

Haraway, Donna, *When Species Meet* (Minneapolis: University of Minnesota Press, 2008).

Morton, Timothy, *The Ecological Thought* (Cambridge, MA: Harvard University Press, 2010).

Plumwood, Val, *Feminism and the Mastery of Nature* (New York: Routledge, 1993).

Warren, Karen, "The Power and Promise of Ecological Feminism: Revisited," in Louis Pojman and Paul Pojman (eds), *Environmental Ethics Readings in Theory and Application*, 5th edn (Belmont: Thomson, 2008).

Wood, David, "Specters of Derrida: On the Way to Econstruction," in Laurel Kearns and Catherine Keller (eds), *Ecospirit: Religions and Philosophies for the Earth* (New York: Fordham University Press, 2007).

Chapter 6
Uncanny Courage and Theological Home

Verna Marina Ehret

The idea of theological homecoming places us before a mystery that we are immediately drawn to in its ability to center our lives. At the same time, we are unsettled by this home because it places us before an abyss of the unknown we can never fully grasp. In the process of narrating home, some find themselves attempting to encompass all aspects of theological home in a single, all-embracing narrative, eliminating the unknown abyss. Others embrace difference by claiming there is no over-arching narrative of home. There are multiple, incomplete narratives because human understanding cannot fully grasp theological home – if it can be grasped at all. In the dialectical tension of these two ways of narrating theological home, there is tremendous exclusion. Those who seek a single narrative find no place in the ever-shifting world of multiple narratives, while those who diverge from an over-arching narrative are cast out, finding no home. Theological home is uncanny because it presents what is both familiar and unknown. An over-arching narrative sacrifices the uncanny, to the detriment of a person's ability to return home. At the same time, multiple disconnected narratives embrace the uncanniness at the expense of a sense of belonging.

The purpose of this chapter is to propose a path of integration, a way that people can be gathered into a home that both is and is not one's own, an uncanny home, through the recognition and acceptance of the multiple voices of sacred history. To construct this path, this chapter builds the notion of the transcontextual narrative as a narrative of mediation within religious communities, thereby enabling the creation of integration within difference.

Sacred Space and Courage: Foundations of Uncanny Theological Homecoming

What makes theological homecoming uncanny? The uncanniness comes in the mystery of the sacred – the sacred is a place of simultaneous belonging and uncertainty. One feels at home in the sacred and at the same time aware that one cannot fully grasp this sacred in human language and knowing. Theological homecoming can be tied to space, but what makes the space a theological home is not the space itself, but rather one's interpretation of it and one's narrative of how one fits into the space. The significance of the space is the home to which it points and of which it is a symbol. Theological homecoming points toward the idea of finding oneself at home in the sacred,[1] the center of one's personality in one's ultimate concern,[2] and the holy that is *mysterium tremendum et fascinans*.[3] In Tillich's language, theological homecoming is a kind of reunion with that with which we are essentially united but from which we are existentially estranged.[4]

In beginning an exploration of the question about uncanny theological homecoming, one can turn to Mircea Eliade and his discussion of sacred space. Eliade famously describes sacred space as a place where we find orientation, a focal point or center for our lives. Sacred space, unlike profane space, has an ordering principle created by an in-breaking of the holy. It is the space where we encounter the divine. Sacred space is non-homogeneous, different from all other space around it, and therefore stands out in such a way as to give a center or focus. Profane space, in contrast, is chaos.[5] Yet space is sacred not because one simply declares it to be, but rather because the experience of the in-breaking of the sacred founds and is incorporated into the narrative of the individual or community. In order to live in the world, one seeks the sacred in space. Space in this sense encompasses both physical space—where one feels oneself in the presence of the holy—and intellectual space—feeling at home in language, the narrative of one's life in relationship to the holy.

Eliade goes on to discuss sacred time as the way the community continually lives its relationship to the divine through ritual activities throughout the year. These activities become incorporated into the collective narrative or sacred history of the community. Eliade divides human experience into the sacred and the profane. The profane is undifferentiated chaos, and what gives a sense of order is the experience of the sacred that breaks up the homogeneity of space and time by giving a focal point. These ways of encountering the sacred reveal what is uncanny about theological homecoming: on the one hand, the experience of the sacred puts one in touch with that which focuses the chaos, but, on the other hand, it does so by disrupting the homogeneity of space and time.[6] Undifferentiated sameness is made different, and differences unsettle us.

Because sacred space suggests an uncanny homecoming, to find oneself at home in light of the sacred requires a sense of belonging or inclusion. At the same time, our belonging to the sacred stands out from the rest of the world, indicating difference, that something unknown and powerful has broken in. In response, I wish to argue, there is a need for courage. Tillich's discussion of courage arises out of his understanding that human experience is fraught with anxiety. At its most basic, courage is the courage to be in spite of the threat of non-being. In

---

[1]   Mircea Eliade, *The Sacred and the Profane: The Nature of Religion*, trans. W.R. Trask (Orlando, 1959).

[2]   Paul Tillich, *The Dynamics of Faith* (New York, 1957).

[3]   Rudolf Otto, *The Idea of the Holy*, trans. J.W. Harvey (London, 1923).

[4]   Paul Tillich, *Systematic Theology* (3 vols, Chicago, 1957), vol. 2.

[5]   Eliade, *The Sacred and the Profane*, pp. 20ff.

[6]   Ibid., p. 27.

The Courage to Be, Tillich identifies two basic types of courage: the courage to be as a part and the courage to be as oneself. Life is a blending of these two types of courage.[7] To these I will add a third, the courage of the uncanny, to live in the tension of belonging and difference—the courage to live in or with uncertainty.

Theological homecoming requires courage as the basic mood between joy (the awareness of being-itself) and anxiety (the awareness of non-being), and the capacity to live in that tension between belonging and difference created by the tensions of life as a constant flux of joy and anxiety. Belonging is the courage to be as a part, while difference is the courage to be as oneself. Moreover, courage is made manifest through the narratives we tell. Our identity and belonging are dependent upon narrative. I know who I am and feel at home because of the narrative I have created that emplaces me in time, space, and community.[8] Through this emplacement, I build my understanding of the world and overcome anxiety. Through those narratives, communities grow and change as people find belonging in them.

Courage as expressed in narrative is not only the courage to be a part, but also the courage to be as oneself, to be aware that life is not simply joy, but the tension of joy and anxiety, where anxiety can be seen as the awareness of difference and uncertainty. What makes theological homecoming as faith an act of courage is the uncertainty of it. Doubt, for Tillich, is an essential part of faith, where faith contains both the experience of being grasped by an ultimate concern and the concrete content, the beliefs that make the human side of the relationship possible. Doubt is the awareness of the uncanniness of theological homecoming as awareness of the mystery that is ultimate reality. One comes home through narrative because the unfolding of identity through story opens up the human side of the relationship for some level of understanding and relationship. But this narrative expresses and embodies the courage of theological homecoming, in being a part and being oneself. To live in both of these requires the courage of the uncanny.

Perhaps the best example within the Christian tradition of speaking theologically about the relationship between courage and narrative is Augustine in the *Confessions*. In the autobiographical books of the *Confessions*, Augustine is calling out to God in search of what he does not know and yet for that which he always already has:

> Grant me to know and understand, Lord, which comes first: to call upon you or to praise you? To know you or to call upon you? Must we know you before we can call upon you? Anyone who invokes what is still unknown may be making

---

[7] Tillich identifies a third type of courage at the end in relation to the God above God. In offering my own third option, I am seeking to move into a different area from that which shaped *The Courage to Be*.

[8] Forrest Clingerman, "Reading the Book of Nature: A Hermeneutical Account of Nature for Philosophical Theology," *Worldviews* 13 (2009): pp. 72–91.

a mistake. Or should you be invoked first, so that we may then come to know you?[9]

There are three levels to this narrative. First, Augustine is telling his story to God. On a second level, he is telling his story to himself, coming to terms with his past in order to understand himself better as a member of the Christian community. He reimagines his own story, reading the presence of God into every aspect of his wild youth when God appeared to be absent. Finally, he is narrating his life in order to be a model for others so that they might see the courage it took for him simultaneously to stand against the call of fame and with those on another path.[10] In the process, he is narrating his own uncanny homecoming. The home he seeks is unfamiliar and yet draws him in. It is a mystery that fascinates and terrifies. These levels correspond inversely to the three levels of courage. The third level of narrative is the courage to be as a part, to create community. The second level of narrative in Augustine is the courage to be as oneself, to come to grips with what focuses his life. The first level of the narrative is, then, the courage of the uncanny, the relationship with the mystery that is God that pre-exists his understanding of it, even his awareness of it, and yet that he always already has in order to seek it. Even in retelling the story, he remains a seeker, always trying to grasp the home in the divine that he already has. In the process of the autobiographical books, then, Augustine exemplifies the union of narrative and courage.

Meta-narrative and the Courage to be as a Part

The courage to be as a part is the courage of belonging, being a part of a community. It comes with the uncanny theological homecoming of the weirdly familiar, when one finds oneself at home where one did not know before that one belonged. At the same time, this feeling of being at home is an overwhelming sense of belonging, being a part of the whole. In many ways, this experience of courage is the homecoming of Augustine at the end of the autobiographical books of the *Confessions*, because the journey to Christianity takes tremendous courage and wrestling with doubt, but his arrival, though painful, erases his doubts about where he belongs.[11] The courage to be as a part affirms one's own being by participation in the world to which one belongs through participation in a particular community. People become who they are meant to be by being in community, in relationship with others. In the courage to be as a part, Tillich draws on Buber's I-Thou relationship, where people realize their full humanity in relationship with others in the others' full humanity, made possible through the relating power of

<hr>

[9]   Augustine, *Confessions*, trans. M. Boulding (New York, 1997), p. 3.

[10]   Ibid., p. 54.

[11]   Augustine, *Confessions*, pp. 120–45.

being of the Eternal Thou.[12] "Only in the continuous encounter with other persons does the person become and remain a person. The place of this encounter is the community."[13] Communities exist through a shared language.

Narrative brings one to this point of community, but the nature of the narrative requires one to think carefully about how a narrative is constructed. One cannot eliminate uncertainty simply because one seeks the comfort and belonging of certainty: Augustine does not eliminate doubt. He does not eliminate the uncanny completely, finding that a complex emotional and spiritual life elevated his understanding. The risk of belonging is the temptation to eliminate uncertainty in all ways. Meta-narrative is the narrative of belonging, but a belonging that problematically erases all sense of the uncanny, of uncertainty. It is an all-embracing narrative of absolute Truth that raises the beliefs of the community to ultimacy, becoming idolatrous in Tillich's language.[14]

The meta-narrative has long been the standard in Christian theology, where the attempt to narrate the sacred history of a community is given distinct parameters. Divergent narratives exist, but are at best marginalized for the sake of the dominant narrative. In meta-narrative, to be Christian is to hold to the creeds and councils of the church; the Chalcedonian definition of Jesus as the Christ is one example of ways in which a dominant position was determined to be orthodox and all others considered heterodox or even dangerous and needing to be destroyed.[15] Taking Jesus' claim to be "The Way, the Truth, and the Life" (John 14:6) as an absolute statement of the nature of reality has led Christians for centuries to persecute non-Christians as those among the damned who threaten the faithful and their narrative. Any storyline that interferes with the meta quality of this narrative is a threat to the lives of those who belong.

This courage to be as a part is seen in contemporary religious narratives of theological home in the realm of religious fundamentalism such as Worldview Weekend and its founder Brannon House, Christian Reconstruction, or the New Apostolic Reformation. These groups have developed a narrative of Christian belonging that is at once universal and highly exclusivistic. The narratives are an attempt to eliminate the uncertainty of theological home by erasing doubt and replacing it with certainty. But the certainty is placed in the language of belief, raising finite beliefs to ultimate status. In the process, an insider-outsider problem is created. People are driven away from theological home because their voices of difference, diverging from the dominant narrative, are excluded. Key examples of this activity include Worldview Weekend and others who promote "right" Christianity by establishing battle lines with secularism, progressivism, feminist and queer theologies, as well as the "false" prophets of the Emerging Church.[16]

---

[12]   Martin Buber, *I and Thou*, trans. W. Kaufmann (New York, 1970), p. 127.

[13]   Paul Tillich, *The Courage to Be* (New York, 1952), p. 91.

[14]   Tillich, *Dynamics of Faith*, p. 13.

[15]   *The Christological Controversy*, trans. and ed. R.A. Norris, Jr. (Philadelphia, 1980).

[16]   http://www.worldviewweekend.com [accessed July 30, 2012].

Marty and Appleby define fundamentalism through what I describe as an attitude of withdrawal-dominance, expressed by them as fighting back:

> *Fighting Back.* It is no insult to fundamentalism to see them as militant, whether in the use of words and ideas or ballots or, in extreme cases, bullets. Fundamentalists see themselves as militant. This means that the first word to employ in respect to them is that they are reactive (though not always reactionary) … fundamentalists begin as traditionalists who perceive some challenge or threat to their core identity, both social and personal. They are not frivolous, nor do they deal with peripheral assaults. If they lose on the central issues, they believe they lose everything. They react; they fight back with great innovative power.[17]

The work of the community to protect the theological home is to globalize not only the message but also the collectivist society. One's participation in evangelism at home and abroad, in one's family, neighborhood, or work, is the process of saving souls. In saving souls, one increases the strength of one's church community by increasing the number of committed members. At the same time, one is living out one's responsibility as a saved person. Failure, humiliation, and suffering at the hands of one's detractors are all incorporated into the salvation narrative through the idea that one suffers *because* one has the right understanding of theological home, having removed its uncanniness. Believers in the meta-narrative are mocked because the devil's supporters cannot understand the language of faith.[18] Therefore, failure does not lead to despair but rather to courage. In that courage is the power of being of the community as a whole. This is a power of being that sees the other as *threat* to power of being. Removing the uncanny from homecoming requires one to become absorbed in the *beliefs* of the community, to have the courage to be as a part that does not question, losing the courage to be as oneself. It is joy without anxiety.

Contextual Narrative and the Courage to be as Oneself

In contrast to the meta-narrative, postmodern sensibilities have led to the development of what can be called the contextual narrative. The contextual narrative is a narrative that recognizes the contextual limitations of any person's or community's understanding of the sacred. The contextual narrative is a little narrative, recognizing that it exists in a cornucopia of narratives. As a result, it

---

[17]   Martin Marty and Scott Appleby, "The Fundamentalism Project: A User's Guide," in M. Marty and S. Appleby (eds), *The Fundamentalism Project: Fundamentalisms Observed* (Chicago, 1991), p. ix.

[18]   Tim and Beverly LaHaye, "Christian Children Persecuted in America," *Fundamentalist Journal* 8 (1989): p. 51.

makes space for the uncanny by allowing that there is more to the sacred than can be put into words. In Tillich's sense, all such narratives are symbols that point toward or even participate in ultimate reality—but cannot wholly contain it. Thinkers such as Taylor and Sartwell have challenged the very notion of narrative, but at a minimum can recognize the unity in diversity of descriptions of theological home, that each person has a point of view, but these points of view also intersect in various ways.[19] And while the traditional form of narrative may have been deconstructed, I would argue that there is still a story being told of the contextual yet intersecting ways in which people describe their understanding of themselves in relation to others. There is a dialectic at work, where contextual narrative challenges the authority of meta-narrative, threatening the unity of that narrative. Contextual narrative, then, expresses the courage to be as oneself.

Theological home (as a place of belonging and uncertainty in the divine that is a familiar and yet unknown abyss) in contextual narrative qua contextual narrative is found in the acceptance of this world as it is given, a tension of joy and anxiety, of belonging and uncertainty. We create the place of eternity in which we can project our own possibilities to be. The willingness of contextual narrative to embrace the interconnection of human life after breaking down the singularity of doctrine is the courage to be as oneself, to explore one's possibilities to be.[20] The courage to be as oneself, then, is the courage of difference. Challenging meta-narrative is an act of courage because what one risks is belonging.

An emphasis on contextual narrative where focus is placed on the dialogue of differing voices can be seen in the work of people such as Farley and Carbine, as they turn to the marginalized and disenfranchised.[21] Turning to those who are "driven away" in terms of meta-narrative, courage is an expression of individualization. This courage is exhibited in postmodernism, but not in exactly the way that Tillich describes. The courage to be as oneself rises out of the modern notion of the self as a distinct and centered entity. Courage to be as oneself expressed in contextual narrative is the courage to accept the possibility that there is no *distinct* self as well as no *distinct* community of which one is a part. This is the courage of doubt, to take doubt about the divine, about the community, and about the nature of truth into the self. The self is a relation, not of itself to itself, but rather of itself to the other in itself. The courage to be as an individual is the courage to stand at a critical distance from the community, in the world, but with no place in the world.

---

[19] See Mark C. Taylor, *Erring: A Postmodern A/Theology* (Chicago, 1984); and Crispin Sartwell, *End of Story: Toward an Annihilation of Language and History* (New York, 2000).

[20] Mark C. Taylor, "Denegating God," in *About Religion: Economies of Faith in Virtual Culture* (Chicago, 1999).

[21] See Wendy Farley, *Gathering Those Driven Away: A Theology of Incarnation* (Louisville, 2011); and Rosemary Carbine, "Turning to Narrative: Toward a Feminist Theological Interpretation of Political Participation and Personhood" *Journal of the American Academy of Religion* 78/2 (2010): pp. 375–412.

In radical critique, the innocence of community-belonging is gone as a naïve understanding of the world at best and at worst a hostile takeover of it. Resisting either aspect of collectivism is the courage to be as oneself.

In a sense, the only difference between the meta-narrative and the contextual narrative is that a meta-narrative is presented as universal whereas the same narrative could be expressed in contextual form, recognizing its own limitations. Meta-narrative creates belonging for some at the expense of the reality and belonging of others. The contextual narrative, on the other hand, recognizes the multiplicity of voices that have come together to create the meta-narrative and sees the meta-narrative paradigm as shutting down the dynamic quality of narrative. In *Gathering Those Driven Away: A Theology of the Incarnation*, Wendy Farley focuses on how Christian theology has over centuries systematically excluded multiplicity, marginalizing and even silencing the voices of those who offered an alternative perspective. In particular, she is concerned with the voices of women and homosexuals who, finding their voices actively attacked by the churches, have simply been driven away from the community. They challenge the meta-narrative by claiming the value of contextual narrative and as a result are often actively ostracized.

Contextual narratives can run counter to a meta-narrative within a particular community. For example, Farley's narrative embraces the multiple voices of difference found within the Christian tradition, but doing so means breaking apart the meta-narrative. In the process, those who cling to meta-narrative in order to feel at home lose a sense of theological home. Home is no longer familiar because of all the differences it expresses. At the same time, the force of meta-narrative toward courage to be as a part can lead to the expulsion of individual counter-voices, either by actively pushing them out as a threat to the community or because the individuals no longer feel at home when their voices are denied.

The postmodern critique of meta-narrative leading to recognition of contextual narrative highlights the danger of the courage to be as a part. The danger of such courage is that it will push out the self and become simple collectivism. The loss of doubt is a significant loss because it is the attempt simply to eradicate anxiety rather than continually to overcome anxiety with the power of self-affirmation. The inability to ask questions is the inability to engage an ever-changing, kaleidoscopic world. This protection of community robs the self of its autonomy. The collectivist protection of doctrine as Absolute Answer against the forces of multiculturalism limits the prophetic voices of particular community to critiques, to make home open to all. But prophets speak *within* a community *to* the community as the voices of doubt and awareness of fallibility.

Theological home is uncanny because it is uncertain. In turn, this uncertainty requires a third kind of courage that will embrace the uncanny. In contextual narrative, what develops is a drive to belonging that embraces differences and uncertainty to belonging that is not simple collectivism. Are we at an impasse, having to choose between the courage to be as a part and the courage to be as oneself?

Transcontextual Narrative and the Courage of the Uncanny

In the contemporary world there has been a bifurcation between those fighting for a meta-narrative and those fighting against it. As a result, theological home is lost both for those who are driven away and for those who do not recognize their home in the multiplicity of voices. Is homecoming possible in a way that theological home can embrace all of these voices? Perhaps. What is needed is a transcontextual narrative of theological home with the courage to embrace the uncanny, the mediation of belonging and difference in the uncertainty of the divine.

A transcontextual narrative is a mediating narrative, one that recognizes both the desire behind the meta-narrative for belonging *and* the reality of uncertainty and contextual emplacement found in contextual narrative. The work of the transcontextual narrative is to build a bridge between a sense of belonging and a sense of difference, where neither is obliterated by the other and yet both can feel at home. But it does require the courage of the uncanny. By the courage of the uncanny, what I mean is the courage to embrace uncertainty, accepting that one belongs to the sacred but will never fully know the sacred without intellectual remainder. The courage of the uncanny is the courage both to recognize the value of the symbols of narrative to put one into relationship with the divine and to bring one home – as it does for Augustine. At the same time, it is the courage always to recognize the limitations of those symbols as pointing toward – even participating in – the sacred while not being identical with it. This courage is exemplified in Augustine when, through the help of Ambrose, he learns to read the sacred history of scripture in a figurative rather than literal way.[22] And it is this courage that must be regained in the meta-narrative camp in order to avoid idolatry and make room for contextual narrative and difference, to live in both anxiety and joy.

In his essay "Interpreting Heaven and Earth: The Theological Construction of Nature, Place, and the Built Environment," Forrest Clingerman asks if it is possible to build heaven. In short, he asks how the sacred is encountered in environments, how sacred space is built, and if it is even possible to do so. Through his analysis of nature as text, he explains that sacred space is built through the reinterpretation of space. This building of sacred space builds home through the narrative interpretation of place. In other words, we find ourselves "at home" when we are emplaced. What is it to be emplaced? Drawing from Ricoeur's notion of emplotment, emplacement is the particular reinterpretation of a place through narrative that expresses its meaningfulness *for me*. In a sense, we narrate ourselves into existence. In narrating ourselves into existence, we create the foundation story, that which is essentially "home-base." Home is not simply a place; home is an interpretive claim.

Home as theological home is where one experiences the divine as the dimension of depth in all aspects of life, as Tillich has shown.[23] To be at home is to belong, but

---

22 Augustine, *Confessions*, pp. 75–95.
23 Tillich, *Systematic Theology*, vols 1–3.

to belong *as oneself*. The dialectical engagement of meta-narrative and contextual narrative reveals the need for the transcontextual narrative. Each is responding in opposing ways to the anxieties created by each other, and in so doing is in danger of distorted courage leading to a loss of theological home. On the side of meta-narrative, a theological home is lost because the sacred is replaced by narrative itself. On the side of contextual narrative, a theological home can be lost by the power of exclusion created by meta-narrative. Being oneself without belonging is incomplete being. The other to which each struggles to respond is the needs of the world in its multiculturality. Meta-narrative requires active denouncing of otherness that steadfastly refuses to become sameness. Postmodernism embraces otherness as a part of self, but bears the risk of lack of belonging.

So how do we mediate between these conflicting voices in order to create an integrated transcontextual narrative? What is required is not the elimination of difference of perspective, but rather a recognition that theological home is dynamic and that the give and take of the courage to be as a part with the courage to be as oneself strengthens rather than threatens home through the courage of the uncanny. Through this recognition, it may be possible to begin to gather in those driven away[24] by building home anew. This transcontextual narrative is aided, then, by recognizing the importance of discourse in sacred history as the theological narrative of home. Discourse, as understood by Ricoeur, is an exchange that also changes those engaged in the conversation. Understanding is built through the dialectic of discourse. In relation to a text, discourse comes through the hermeneutical process, the unfolding of the meaning of the text. In relation to space, discourse comes in the unfolding of the story of the space as different voices contribute to that story.[25]

The dialectical process finally becomes clear. The courage to be as a part grounds the individual and is at the heart of feeling at home, theologically speaking. The courage to be as oneself is both counterpoint and the possibility for forward movement, to live within the diversity of the world, the uncertainty of the sacred, and the tension of anxiety and joy. Meta-narratives are not really meta. They are contextual narratives, and these narratives are dynamic. A transcontextual narrative sees the importance of both the courage to be as a part and the courage to be as oneself. These two ways of being are the living dynamic of the narrative of theological home.

The Emerging Church movement may provide an example of the move toward transcontextual narrative and the courage of the uncanny. This emergent movement embraces a postmodern, deconstructionist perspective of narrative. Doubt, difference, and uncertainty are not necessarily excluded. At the same time, the power of narrative to emplace one in theological home is also embraced. Members of this movement actively reject meta-narrative in order to hear the

---

[24]   Farley, *Gathering*.

[25]   Paul Ricoeur, "The Task of Hermeneutics," trans. J.B. Thompson, in James M. Edie (ed.), *From Text to Action: Essays in Hermeneutics, II* (Evanston, 1991), pp. 53–74.

voices of the marginalized and focus on social justice in the here and now. Yet they are grounded in community, in creating belonging. Scot McKnight summarizes the goals of the Emergent Church through Gibbs and Bolger, who have described this movement in terms of participation:[26]

> Emerging churches are communities that practice the way of Jesus within postmodern cultures. This definition encompasses nine practices. Emerging churches (1) identify with the life of Jesus, (2) transform the secular realm, and (3) live highly communal lives. Because of these three activities, they (4) welcome the stranger, (5) serve with generosity, (6) participate as producers, (7) create as created beings, (8) lead as a body, and (9) take part in spiritual activities.

Scot McKnight, as an evangelical and self-proclaimed Emergent Churcher, adds to this description the claim that emergent churches are prophetic or provocative, postmodern, praxis-oriented, post-evangelical (in particular, post-systematic theology), and political (particularly in terms of social justice).[27] But this movement faces challenges. For example, Brannon House of Worldview Weekend has described the Emerging Church as the "Emerging Apostasy," finding it to be a bigger threat to Christianity than the "secular left."[28]

Where, on the one hand, then, the Emerging Church is an example of the recognition of contextual narrative, on the other hand, it is also the movement toward transcontextual narrative. Emerging Churches speak from within Christianity. They are beginning to create a meeting ground between traditional and postmodern Christianity. But the opposition to this movement is intense. To move more fully toward a transcontextual narrative that integrates these poles will require enhancing the value of discourse within the meta-narrative camp, such that the courage to be as a part joins with but does not absorb the courage to be as oneself – in short, the courage of the uncanny.

Theological home is more than place. It is resting in and, in a sense, simultaneously wrestling with the sacred. This uncanny homecoming unfolds in Augustine's own narrative. Home implies a kind of ownership, security, and stability in an otherwise unsettling world. When we long for home, it is not simply the place we long for, but the belonging to that place through how the place fits into our story. "Home is where the heart is" may be an unimaginative way to sell plaques, but it resonates for people because a place becomes home when

---

[26] See also Eddie Gibbs and Ryan Bolger, *Emerging Churches: Creating Christian Community in Postmodern Cultures* (Grand Rapids, 2005).

[27] Scot McKnight, "Five Streams of the Emerging Church," *Christianity Today*, February, 2007, http://www.christianitytoday.com/ct/2007/february/11.35.html [accessed July 30, 2012].

[28] http://www.worldviewweekendfoundation.com/article.php?id=1535 [accessed July 30, 2012].

one feels one belongs in it. A theological home becomes home because one finds oneself in relation to the sacred, through space as concrete and through belief as the expression of the relationship with the sacred. Home is built through the building of narrative, and heaven is built through the interpretive process of place and narration in light of the relationship to the sacred.

Yet this description of the relationship between reading a place and narrating home is not necessarily theological. What makes a theological home is the way we think about how we think about home. Clingerman states:

> The depth of nature – the divine manifested in being – can be recognized in two complementary ways. On the simplest level, a meditative reading of nature occurs when we allow contradictory understandings of nature to remain in a fruitful and productive tension, and thereby open ourselves to the transcending dimension that shows the underlying identity that holds together identity and difference.[29]

Clingerman is pushing toward a transcontextual narrative of sacred space that expresses the courage of the uncanny. Transcontextual narratives will be successful as mediating narratives if they recognize the mystery of life, its uncertainty, and therefore remain fluid in that uncertainty rather than becoming rigid and speaking from a single point of view. While emplacement as described by Clingerman is tied to a place, it is not limited by place or, rather, place need not be just a place. Home understood theologically is not only place, it is also the narrative of how an individual and a community both belong to and are in relationship with the divine. The story is not static. We do not build theological home in a vacuum, but in a cacophony of voices, each with a particular perspective on what home means. This multiplicity keeps theological home alive as the narrative is continually engaged by individuals and groups. Theological home is uncanny because of its uncertainty. Belonging to that home requires developing the ability to live within that uncertainty by reimagining the nature of theological narrative.[30]

References

Augustine, *Confessions* (New York: Vintage Books, 1997).
Buber, Martin, *I and Thou* (New York: Simon & Schuster, 1970).
Carbine, Rosemary, "Turning to Narrative: Toward a Feminist Theological Interpretation of Political Participation and Personhood," *Journal of the American Academy of Religion* 78/2 (2010): 375–412.

---

[29]   Clingerman, "Reading the Book of Nature."

[30]   A special thank you to Dr. Forrest Clingerman and Dr. Robert von Thaden Jr. for their patience and insights.

Clingerman, Forrest, "Interpreting Heaven and Earth: The Theological Construction of Nature, Place, and the Built Environment," in Sigurd Bergmann, Peter Scott, Heinrich Bedford Strohm and Maria Jansdotter (eds), *Nature, Space and the Sacred* (Aldershot: Ashgate Publishing, 2009).

Clingerman, Forrest, "Reading the Book of Nature: A Hermeneutical Account of Nature for Philosophical Theology," *Worldviews* 13 (2009): 72–91.

Eliade, Mircea, *The Sacred and the Profane: The Nature of Religion* (Orlando: Harcourt, 1959).

Farley, Wendy, *Gathering Those Driven Away: A Theology of Incarnation* (Louisville: Westminster John Knox Press, 2011).

Gibbs, Eddie and Bolger, Ryan K., *Emerging Churches: Creating Community in Postmodern Cultures* (Grand Rapids: Baker Academic, 2005).

LaHaye, Tim and LaHaye, Beverly, "Christian Children Persecuted in America," *Fundamentalist Journal* 8 (1989): 51.

Marty, Martin and Appleby, Scott (eds), "The Fundamentalism Project: A User's Guide," in *The Fundamentalism Project: Fundamentalisms Observed* (Chicago: University of Chicago Press, 1991).

McKnight, Scot, 'Five Streams of the Emerging Church', http://www.christianitytoday.com/ct/2007/february/11.35.html [accessed July 30, 2012].

Norris, Richard A. (ed.), *The Christological Controversy* (Philadelphia: Fortress Press, 1980).

Otto, Rudolf, *The Idea of the Holy* (Oxford: Oxford University Press, 1923).

Ricoeur, Paul, *From Text to Action: Essays in Hermeneutics, II* (Evanston: Northwestern University Press, 1991).

Sartwell, Crispin, *End of Story: Toward an Annihilation of Language and History* (New York: State University of New York Press, 2000).

Taylor, Mark C., *Erring: A Postmodern A/theology* (Chicago: University of Chicago Press, 1984).

Taylor, Mark C., *About Religion: Economies of Faith in Virtual Culture* (Chicago: University of Chicago Press, 1999).

Tillich, Paul, *The Courage to Be* (New Haven: Yale University Press, 1952).

Tillich, Paul, *Systematic Theology* (3 vols, Chicago: University of Chicago Press, 1957).

Tillich, Paul, *The Dynamics of Faith* (New York: Perennial Classics, 2001).

Chapter 7

ALT + HOME: Digital Homecomings

Rachel Wagner

The home key we are familiar with from the very first computer keyboards had a very specific function. Using the home key was often the easiest way to reorient, to see the beginning of a linear document and move through it in a forward motion. Today, however, the home key is an anachronism, absent from most laptop keyboards altogether. A digital sense of "home" may still involve walls (firewalls) and keys (codes), spaces (webpages) and objects (for programming), but we are less likely to have just one home, and there are likely to be several versions of ourselves in any digital "home" at any given time. Increasingly, home has become less a physical site of inhabitation than a marker of movement, a trail of pixels, a trace of where we have been and a longing to find the beginning of things—an impossible but oddly powerful compulsion.

William Mitchell notes that the increasing ubiquity of wireless technology alongside expanding network infrastructure and handheld electronic devices has "radically refashioned the relationships of individuals to their constructed environments and to one another".[1] Arjun Appadurai agrees, using the term "technoscape" to refer to "the global configuration … ever fluid, of technology and …. the fact that technology, both high and low, both mechanical and informational, now moves at high speeds across various kinds of previously impervious boundaries".[2] For Mitchell, this has resulted in "a shift from a world structured by boundaries and enclosures to a world increasingly dominated, at every scale, by connections, networks, and flows".[3] Home, too, is increasingly fluid, networked to other places, and in motion. This emerging sense of home hovers uncannily around a traditional sense of home as a stable center that organizes our lives.

Home as Navigation Hub

When we look online, the most common place we will find the idea of home is as home *page*, the place from which we begin a search, and the menu to which

---

[1]   William Mitchell, *Me++: The Cyborg Self and the Networked City* (Cambridge, 2003), p. 2.

[2]   Arjun Appadurai, *Modernity at Large: Cultural Dimensions of Globalization*. Public Worlds Series (Minneapolis, 1996), p. 34.

[3]   Mitchell, *Me++*, p. 5.

we return when lost. With such a view of home, everywhere is on the way to somewhere else. Even home is in motion—and it is personalized and different for everyone. Home is, as home page, a self-generated selection of possibilities for going elsewhere. It is unbounded choice; it has no particular *telos* and is largely driven toward self-fulfillment. And we arrive at what appears to be an oxymoron: home as journey. As one web designer at Carnegie Mellon advises: "There's no place like home! A Home Page link should be always be placed in the Section or Utilities, so that it remains in sight at all times ... [so that] the user can navigate back to the Homepage easily whenever he/she wants!"[4] Home lets us begin again, but it seldom invites us to linger. Home as home page is threshold, portal, gateway, and invitation. As Gary Shelly and Denise Woods advise would-be web designers:

> A Web site home page should identify the *purpose* of the Web site by briefly stating what content, services, or features it provides. The home page also should indicate clearly what *links* the visitor should click to move from one page on the site to another. A Web developer should design the Web site in such a way that the links from one Web page to another are apparent and the navigation is clear. The Web site home page also should include an e-mail link, so visitors can find contact information for the individual or organization.[5]

Home defines purpose; it offers connections (links); its navigation system is clear; and it is a portal to real people elsewhere. Today, we are "visitors" to most homes online.

The marketing potential of self-designated home pages for individuals who are not business owners was recognized as early as 1997, when hopeful registrants patented a "device" to make it easier for users to circumvent popular web browsers' default settings to their own company's determination of the home page. For these creators, "home" became something you *do*, as their "Hom*er*" device allowed users to "automatically change the home page of a Web Browser" to a site that you select (an astonishing prospect in 1997). The creators suggested that the ability to change one's home page "maximizes potential consumer exposure to a company's products and/or services by causing individuals to start each and every browsing session at that company's Web Site."[6] Home, they had discovered, could be bought and sold, and changed at will.

---

4   Website for the CarnegieMellon Computer Club, http://www.contrib.andrew.cmu.edu/~htasnim/example1.html [accessed August 1, 2011].

5   Gary B. Shelly and Denise M. Woods, *HTML: Complete Concepts and Techniques.* (Boston, 2009), p. 91, emphasis added.

6   Robert Domine and Fred Abaroa, "Web Browser Detection and Default Home Page Modification Device," Patent Number 5,949,419, http://patft.uspto.gov [accessed March 29, 2012].

Today, such freedom is taken for granted and we have many, many home pages, all directed increasingly toward our individual desires. When you join Facebook, for example, a local home page is created "just for you" with specialized links, a unique news feed, and information about upcoming events. A recent Vista user guide explains that users "are not stuck" with pre-designated home pages and might instead prefer to "use a search site so that you start with tools for finding information."[7] This impulse—to have the home page be a search tool—suggests even more strongly the notion that home, in its contemporary digital forms, is not a place at all, but is rather an orienting motion, a search, a quest—for information, for belonging, for perfection, answers, and hope. In other words, home as navigational hub is also home as portal, promise, and desire.

Our physical homes today are as deeply transformed as online versions of home. We are always connected, even when alone in our houses. As Pramod Nayar observes, the interior of the home is being transformed by digital devices: "Workstations enable the user to link to the workplace, shop online from home, and debate a community matter on an email." Our homes are personified and become breachable via digital lines:

> "Smart" homes, wired and networked, enable children to "leave" home without really leaving it, just as information exiting the home through social networking sites can cause a possible invasion of the space by strangers ... [also] crucial information, such as credit card details or webcam telecasts of intimate moments, may leave it.[8]

Home today is no longer a place where we reside—it is a place from which we *decide* where to go next. Our "beginnings" are all repeatable, changeable, open.

The notion of home as defined by quest rather than origin, movement rather than fixedness, also applies to popular emerging notions of constructed identity— what Wade Clark Roof calls "seeker" activity. Lorne Dawson, drawing on Anthony Giddens, asserts that we are increasingly exercising a kind of heightened reflexivity in identity construction as "the local and traditional social order, the source of identity in the past, is being displaced by global influences and points of reference, as mediated and fostered by social networks in general and more specifically the Internet."[9] We, like our iPods, are collections of programs (or beliefs, or habits)

---

[7]   Shelley O'Hara, *Absolute Beginner's Guide to Microsoft Windows Vista* (Indianapolis, 2007), p. 118.

[8]   Pramod Nayar, "Augmented Spaces: Virtual Worlds, 'New' Territories, and the Politics of Cyberculture," in Bed P. Girir and Prafulla C. Kar (eds), *Thinking Territory: Some Reflections* (New Delhi, 2009), p. 156.

[9]   Lorne Dawson, "Religion and the Quest for Virtual Community," in Lorne Dawson and Douglas Cowan (eds), *Religion Online: Finding Faith on the Internet* (New York, 2009), p. 86.

that define us only insofar as we integrate them into our larger sense of self—our hardware, if you will. Elsewhere I call this phenomenon the "ipod self."[10]

The individual apps we run on ourselves need not be compatible. Like so many "home pages" on so many different websites, we can be scattered and still feel unitary through our singular bodies, our singular streaming emergent lives. In this sense, then, the individual self *as* home—or the body as home, if you will—is subject to the same strictures as the larger metaphorical sense of home. As Braziel and Mannur explain, identity is deeply affected by the fragmentations of contemporary life: "Diasporic traversals question the rigidities of identity itself—religious, ethnic, gendered, national; yet this diasporic movement marks not a postmodern turn from history, but a nomadic turn in which the very parameters of specific historical moments are embodied and—as diaspora itself suggests—are scattered and regrouped into new points of becoming."[11] Our individual "selves" or "identities" are also hubs, quests, subjects in motion, fragmented, seeking, surfing.

And yet we still long for home as an orienting performance. Despite the home key's disappearance from laptop keyboards, some devices still retain some sort of "home" button and afford it immense responsibility. For example, the iPhone's home button enables you to reorient under any conditions. Even if you feel lost exploring the functionality of apps, says one fan, "The joy of the iPhone's home button is that no matter where you are, or what confusing app you've got into, you can always escape."[12] Similarly, if users hit the home button on a Wii (a video game console), it takes them to the home screen, where they can access a number of channels for games, weather, surfing, etc. As one Wii reviewer explains:

> Home is what you press when you want to *pause* a Wii game, quit back to the main Wii *Menu*, check your Remote's *battery level* or … consult the Operations *Guide* … Many Virtual Console titles also employ Home to trigger their *Save States*—if you stop playing your game by pressing Home to back out, your progress is recorded and you can jump directly back to that *same point* in the adventure the next time you click on it … So Home's a versatile little button— understated, but packed with useful functionality.[13]

Home is navigational. Home allows you to pause; to check a menu of options; to see how much energy is available; to access a guide; and to set a checkpoint of

---

[10]   Rachel Wagner, *Godwired: Religion, Ritual and Virtual Reality* (New York, 2012), p. 99.

[11]   Jana Evans Braziel and Anita Mannur, "Nation, Migration, Globalization: Points of Contention in Diaspora Studies," in Jana Evans Braziel and Anita Mannur (eds), *Theorizing Diaspora* (Boston, 2007), p. 3.

[12]   Aza Raskin, "The Problem with Home," Professional Blog Post, http://www. azarask.in/blog/post/the-problem-with-home [accessed July 30, 2012].

[13]   Lucas M. Thomas, "The 3DS Has a Home," IGN, June 16, 2010, http://ds.ign.com/ articles/109/1098833p1.html [accessed July 30, 2012]. Emphasis added.

progress. One of the most compelling features of home buttons, however, is their ability to facilitate *escape*. Video game designer Scott Rogers explains that games should offer players a "home base" that they can return to, a "permanent location in the game ... where they can store their items."[14] Designer Ernest Adams agrees, explaining that the trope used is often of the teleporter, "available at the end of a long period of exploration, so the player can simply jump back to a previous location (such as a home base or camp) without having to walk all the way back."[15]

This is a nearly universal feature of home buttons, allowing the return to a familiar place, even as they symbolically insist that return happens again and again, and in idiosyncratic, individualized ways. Yet if "home" means that we may "escape," the question becomes: escape from what? If entry into a gameworld or Internet quest is in some ways itself an escape from reality, what does it mean to escape from a gameworld? It suggests, at least, that the world itself had some salience, was in some sense a *place* to which people could *go*, a generalized Other that I designate simply as elsewhere from wherever we are. In other words, the desire generated by our entry into online spaces and the orienting function of "home" keys and buttons and features suggest that despite our rhizomatic wandering therein, we are in fact some*where* when we surf, or perhaps some*wheres*. The home key on a keyboard only took us back to the beginning of an existing linear text. Home buttons and features in games and browsers call us back from journeys to other places and encourage us to embark again as soon as possible. The lingering echo of what had once been home haunts digital realities as something simultaneously familiar and strange, as something uncanny.

So the new model of home (the "model home?") is neither purely linear (like a printed book or edited film) nor exactly looping (like a seasonal myth retelling or a repeated ritual). Instead, it is an escape portal, a navigational menu with no single beginning and no end, and with no possibility of completion. It is a collection of links, sometimes exceedingly idiosyncratic. We can return "home," but only to our own personal home page or to one preset for us by a browser, and this page may likely just be a search engine itself. We can return "home" to millions of different "homes," all of which invite us to "visit," but never to live. 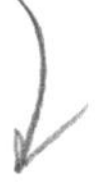

In his account of internment at the Shantung Compound in China during the Second World War, Langdon Gilkey describes his sense of home: "Somehow each self needs a 'place' in order to be a self, in order to feel on a deep level that it really exists. We are, apparently, rootless beings at bottom. Unless we can establish roots somewhere in a place where we are at home, which we possess to ourselves and where our things are, we feel that we float, that we are barely there at all."[16] This sense of rootlessness is symbolically present in the devices we use every day.

---

[14]   Scott Rogers, *Level Up! The Guide to Great Video Game Design* (Hoboken, 2010), p. 175.

[15]   Ernest Adams, *Fundamentals of Game Design* (Indianapolis, 2010), p. 404.

[16]   Langdon Gilkey, *Shantung Compound: The Story of Men and Women under Pressure* (New York, 1975), p. 80.

Home is becoming increasingly personalized, increasingly fluid, less of a place than an expression of desire, a quest always beginning.

Describing what he sees to be a common contemporary metaphysical orientation toward home, Peter Berger describes the "secularizing forces in modern society" and laments that humanity "has suffered from a deepening condition of 'homelessness.' The correlate of the migratory character of [humanity's] experience of society and of self has been what might be called a metaphysical loss of 'home.' It goes without saying that this condition is psychologically hard to bear."[17] Our devices and the technology that we have programmed to drive them echo in their function and their design the same symptoms that pervade society at large—features that in some ways match contemporary discussions of diasporic identity, but practised to such a degree as to become a nearly universal human experience.

Diaspora

The kind of rootless, restless movement that characterizes our movement online resembles in some remarkable ways how we commonly think of what it means to live in "diaspora." We "visit" websites, we do not "reside" in them. We have many "home pages" and we can choose what they will be and change them at any time. We have many selves that inhabit many different online spaces, some two-dimensional web pages and others three-dimensional virtual places like *Second Life* or *World of Warcraft*. We are hybrid, fragmented, present in multiple places at once, and redefine ourselves through uncanny connections that are global in scope and often disorienting.

James Clifford calls diaspora a "traveling term, in changing global conditions," pointing out the tendency of scholars to use it in imprecise and conflicting ways.[18] Most generally, though, "diaspora refers specifically to the movement—forced or voluntary—of people from one or more nation-states to another."[19] The most typical notion of diaspora, as Brian Keith Axel explains, tends to focus on the aftermath of colonialism when:

> large populations of people were torn away from their birthplaces or ancestral villages and transported as slaves or indentured servants to new lands where they labored and from where other generations departed for the metropoles of former colonial states. Within such descriptions, the lost context of diaspora takes on an originary value, as a place of origin, a homeland. Therefore, in our quest to define diaspora, to find its defining center in a proliferating domain of

---

[17]   Peter Berger, Brigitte Berger, and Hansfried Kellner, *The Homeless Mind* (New York, 1974), p. 82.

[18]   James Clifford, "Diasporas," *Cultural Anthropology* 9/3 (1994): p. 302.

[19]   Braziel and Mannur, "Nation," p. 8.

margins and to distinguish one diaspora from another, we employ well-worn anthropological tools—genealogy, for example. We trace a diasporic people back through the generations to what is presumed to be their defining locality—the homeland—where we discover the determining features of, for example, language and race.[20]

Many of these elements simply do not apply to online life. Whereas online community may indeed offer a sense of belonging, any sense of genealogy is fictional, and digital localities are imagined fantasy.

Nonetheless, some see the sense of rootlessness as a more general feature of contemporary life even for those not dislocated from familiar physical geography. We all live today, says Arjun Appadurai, in a state of diaspora. Certainly, not everyone lives in a physical state of forced displacement from their homeland, but more and more people can be described by their movements: "tourists, immigrants, refugees, exiles, guestworkers." People living in such a state can, of course, develop "stable communities and networks, of kinship, of friendship, of work and of leisure," but, cautions Appadurai, everywhere these "stabilities" are "shot through with the woof of human motion, as more and more persons and groups deal with the realities of having to move or the fantasies of wanting to move."[21] For those of us who move increasingly in wired spaces, is there any way in which we, too, are rootless?

Our fascination with online worlds like *World of Warcraft* or *Second Life* may represent privileged version of Appadurai's "fantasy of wanting to move," the easy and low-risk experiences of desire for habitation elsewhere—perhaps not a literal return to a lost homeland, but instead a familiar religious trope of "return" as symbolic of desired entry into an ideal space where wealth, beauty, strength, and victory are possible (and sometimes purchasable). For theologian Douglas Burton-Christie, "[t]he sense of having been banished from paradise, of being homeless wanderers, is deeply etched into modern and contemporary experience."[22] Braziel and Mannur might see such broad claims going too far, arguing that diaspora is "often used as a catch-all phrase to speak of and for all movements, however privileged, and for all dislocations, even symbolic ones."[23] For them, the most specific use of diaspora is to "denote communities of people dislocated from their native homelands through migration, immigration, or exile as a consequence of colonial expansion."[24] As more people move to more places around the globe, we

---

[20]   Brian Keith Axel, "The Context of Diaspora," *Cultural Anthropology* 19/1 (2004): p. 28.

[21]   Arjun Appadurai, "Disjuncture and Difference in the Global Cultural Economy," *Theory, Culture & Society* 7 (1990): p. 297.

[22]   Douglas Burton-Christie, "Place-Making as Contemplative Practice," *Anglican Theological Review* 91/3 (Summer 2009): p. 355.

[23]   Braziel and Mannur, "Nation," p. 3.

[24]   Ibid., p. 4.

all engage in increasing cultural exchange. Stanley Tambiah observes that "all societies are becoming increasingly multicultural while at the same time becoming more porous" or "open to multinational migration" with people in diaspora who identify with a home that is elsewhere.[25]

Braziel and Mannur point to the Greek origins of the term diaspora as *dia* for "across" and *spieren* for "to sow or scatter seeds." They suggest that diaspora "can perhaps be seen as a naming of the other which has historically referred to displaced communities of people who have been dislocated from their native homeland through the movements of migration, immigration, or exile."[26] Our presence online manifests as so many "nodes" or potential points of contact, what we might aptly consider a digital scattering of seeds across a host of digital contexts. The "self" is a single node in multiple networks, interacting in vast and complex relationships, connections, and conversations with others in a digital environment.

So is drawing connections between virtual engagement and diasporic existence a misnomer or, worse, a gesture of disrespect to those who live in real physical diaspora from their geographical homes? Or is it an apt description of the way that we now live in a world in which every homecoming has become uncanny? A comparison of virtual diaspora with real-life diaspora reveals a more nuanced perspective.

Virtual Diaspora?

We can consider some of the components of "diaspora" by looking at the online game and world *Uru*, produced by Ubisoft and active for much of 2004 in beta form. For inhabitants of *Uru*, the forced "diaspora" when the online game closed down drew a number of them to seek out other online worlds where familiar aspects of *Uru* could be reinstantiated. Some chose to recreate familiar "space" in *Second Life*, using pre-existing scripting software to visually replicate familiar architecture and landscape, and agreeing to follow cultural rules established in the original game, even if these same rules are not reinforced by *Second Life*'s software.[27] Others interacted via forums alone, while still others created new enclaves in online host worlds like *There.com* and *World of Warcraft*.

Pierce notes in the loss of *Uru* and subsequent search for a new home what she sees to be classic feelings associated with diaspora. As one longtime resident put it, the residents were "bound and determined to stay together in any way we could."[28]

---

[25]   Stanley J. Tambiah, "Transnational Movements, Diaspora, and Multiple Modernities," *Daedalus* 129/1 (Winter 2000): p. 169.

[26]   Braziel and Mannur, "Nation," p. 1.

[27]   Celia Pearce, *Communities of Play: Emergent Cultures in Multiplayer Games and Virtual Worlds* (Cambridge, MA: MIT Press, 2009), p. 94.

[28]   Quoted in ibid., p. 86.

Using self-designated language of being "refugees," the displaced members of *Uru* saw themselves as "dispersed" among different online environments, and experience intense longing and grief for their lost "homeland." Key ideas like memory, loss, identity, grief, nostalgia, alienation, attachment, disorientation, and an intense hope for "return" all crop up repeatedly for these players. The "shared trauma" serves as a bond between members of the dispersed community, and "many continue to cite this shared trauma as a factor in their deep emotional connection to one another."[29] As digital "refugees," they "wander" from one game environment to another. William Safran's definition of diaspora includes six components, all of which apply to the *Uru* players' self-described experiences. Clifford summarizes Safran's definition of diasporas as:

> expatriate minority communities (1) that are dispersed from an original "center" to at least two "peripheral" places; (2) that maintain a memory, vision, or myth about their original homeland; (3) that believe they are not—and perhaps cannot be—fully accepted by their host country; (4) that see the ancestral home as a place of eventual return, when the time is right: (5) that are committed to the maintenance or restoration of this homeland; and (6) of which group's consciousness and solidarity are importantly defined by this continuing relationship with the homeland.[30]

Indeed, for the past residents of *Uru*, it is precisely the identity-making properties of community and self that the original "place" provided that are the greatest markers of loss and the greatest glue for continuing to be connected to one another in whatever way possible. For *Uru* players, it was the loss itself that clearly defined what the place *had been* and that provided an ongoing sense of social adhesion that gave players an orientation in the chaotic online world. The loss of *Uru* is in some ways even more acute than real-life diasporas, since *Uru* was not simply left: it was shut down. In a ritually momentous act in February 2004, the servers were shut off and avatars deleted. Places disappeared, and the entire world became impossible to inhabit. As Pearce explains: "For members of the *Uru* Diaspora, this longing transposes itself into a kind of nostalgia for an entirely fictitious, imaginary world in which the experiences were real, emotional, and immediate."[31] But they were also ephemeral, non-binding on real-life resources, and, as it turned out, remediable. In 2004, *Uru* fans succeeded in reverse-engineering the world to re-create their homeland, now called *Until Uru*. Digital diaspora can be ended by simply programming a replica homeland.

Elements of racism and the on-the-ground difficulties of living in an unfamiliar and sometimes hostile culture simply cannot be replicated in full

---

[29]   Ibid., p. 89.

[30]   James Clifford, *Routes: Travel and Translation in the Late Twentieth Century* (Boston, 1997), pp. 304–5.

[31]   Pearce, *Communities*, p. 158.

force online, if for no other reason than the obvious fact that online, you can often depict yourself in any way you please. In *World of Warcraft*, for example, players can select one of a number of different "races" with which to identify their avatar. The descriptions are far from flattering for some of them and certainly seem grossly racist. For example, Blizzard's *World of Warcraft Game Manual* describes "the voodoo-practicing 'Barbarous and superstitious' trolls [who] come from islands renowned for their cruelty and dark mysticism [who] speak in a seeming African American vernacular." Douglas also points out the *Manual*'s explanation that the "Tauren race" take their qualities from "Native Americans of the Mix-n-Match tribe. Environmentally conscious citizens of the plains, they live in both tipis and longhouses, and carve totem poles. And their signature greeting is 'How!'"[32] As horrific as these racist statements are, the people experiencing these stereotypes in an online context may or may not in real life identify with the targeted groups. Clearly, players can choose to be whomever they want and can select their own race before play. Because people living in real-life diaspora are and must be present only in their born bodies, the ability to simply log off or change one's physical appearance is not an option. In *World of Warcraft*, race is a fashion statement and it is disposable. For real-life people living in hostile host cultures, the loss of homeland is hardly a game and racism cannot be remedied by simply designing a new avatar. Perhaps the persistence of racism in an online world serves as an uncanny echo and reminder of the struggles in the offline world.

Diaspora and Desire

Yet those living in diaspora are, according to a number of studies, increasingly utilizing wired technologies to keep in touch with their homeland. Tambiah observes that today's "migrants and immigrants" may be "distributed," but "they are interconnected especially by modern media and travel in a transnational transactional arena focused on their own preoccupations and interests."[33] Clifford remarks that "dispersed peoples, once separated from homelands by vast oceans and political barriers, increasingly find themselves in border relations with the old country thanks to a to-and-fro made possible by modern technologies of transport, communication, and labor migration."[34] Globalization has produced "enormous transnational movements of people," some of whom move for vocational reasons, others unwillingly as a result of civil wars, genocide, and other forms of unrest. As Tambiah notes, "there is an intensification in the creation of diverse diaspora

---

[32]   Christopher Douglas, "Multiculturalism in World of Warcraft," *Electronic Book Review* (June 4, 2010), http://www.electronicbookreview.com/thread/firstperson/intrinsically [accessed July 30, 2012].

[33]   Tambiah, "Transnational Movements," p. 172.

[34]   Clifford, "Diasporas," p. 304.

populations ... who are engaged in complex interpersonal and intercultural relationships with their host societies and their societies of origin." Instead of being "deterritorialized," says Tambiah, they "in fact experience and live in dual locations and manifest dual consciousness."[35] The ability to connect via communications technologies has a lot to do with the successful maintenance of relationships with people and things back "home," an uncanny place that remains both strange and familiar.

For example, in her analysis of Ethiopian diaspora, Nancy Hafkin describes how in recent decades communication technologies have "render[ed] commonplace diaspora contact with the homeland that was previously impossible."[36] Ananda Mitra looks at the status of Ethiopians who lived abroad before 1980 and compares them with those living in the post-1980 American diaspora, noting that the latter have "maintained continuous and close communication with the homeland" via contemporary communications technologies and arguing that:

> [Much of] what is lost through physical immigration (e.g., community solidarity) can now be recovered in the cybernetic space of the internet as more immigrants find and produce these spaces. In this discursive comfort zone the immigrants [began] to find connections with a place they left behind.[37]

Bernal says something similar when she argues that "the Internet is the quintessential diasporic medium, ideally suited to allowing migrants in diverse locations to connect, share information and analyses, and coordinate their activities."[38]

But is the Ethiopia that people living in diaspora experience online the same one that their family back home reside in? Appadurai uses the language of "imagined worlds" to think about diaspora, and suggests that memory and desire play a role in constructing how we view places from which we are absent, even if we can learn things about them from afar. He describes such worlds as "the multiple worlds which are constituted by the historically situated imaginations of persons and groups spread around the globe." Furthermore, he argues, such imagined worlds can provide a sense of identity, whether or not they accurately replicate real-life worlds of culture or community: "Many persons on the globe live in such imagined worlds ... and thus are able to contest and sometimes even subvert the imagined worlds of the official mind and of the entrepreneurial

---

35   Tambiah, "Transnational Movements," p. 163.

36   Nancy J. Hafkin, "'Whatsupoch' on the Net: The Role of Information and Communication Technology in the Shaping of Transnational Ethiopian Identity," *Diaspora* 15/2–3 (2006): p. 222.

37   Ananda Mitra, "Creating Immigrant Identities in Cybernetic Space: Examples from a Non- resident Indian Website," *Media, Culture and Society* 27 (2005): p. 385.

38   Victoria Bernal, "Diaspora, Cyberspace and Political Imagination: The Eritrean Diaspora Online," *Global Networks* 6/2 (2006): p. 175.

mentality that surrounds them."[39] Yet if such persons are learning about "home" through websites, forums, videos, and other snippets of life while they reside in other places, how could the screen of the computer not become a sort of dreaming fetish—an emblem of what they wish to see or at least a mirror that reflects those images they choose to retrieve?

It seems entirely possible that for those who know the homeland *only* through memory and via screens, desire and imagination can trump reality, since all they see of their homeland is what is *represented* to them digitally via textual conversations, photographs, videos, and websites. The imagination must fill in the rest. "Home" becomes, at least indirectly, associated with the *desire* for home that the screen represents.

In recent years, a number of scholars have similarly argued for the ability of virtual reality—in the form of computerized spaces in particular—to hierophantically represent an "other," a spirited imagining of our deepest dreams. As Jennifer Cobb puts it, virtual reality is "a place that feels removed from the physical world."[40] One enters a virtual world. One leaves a virtual world. One shifts one's "appearance" when one enacts one's avatar in a given virtual world. Furthermore, within such virtual worlds, there is no eating, no sleeping, and no aging. Some have even considered the experience of inhabiting virtual space as a sort of digital heaven or, perhaps, as Cobb describes it, "the Platonic realm incarnate."[41] Such a realm naturally invites our wish to inhabit it.

Miroslaw Filiciak says that the experience of interacting with virtual reality is characterized by intense desire: "We make the screen a fetish; we desire it, not only do we want to watch the screen but also to 'be seen' on it."[42] Ken Hillis expresses a similar sentiment about virtual reality's ability to induce our sense of desire and transcendence:

> There is a widespread belief that space (understood variously as distance, extension, or orientation) constitutes something elemental, and VR reflects support for a belief that because light illuminates space it may therefore produce space a priori. As a result, VR users may experience desire or even something akin to a moral imperative to enter into virtuality where space and light ... have become one immaterial "wherein." The ability to experience a sense of entry into the image and illumination enabled by VR's design, coupled with both esoteric and pragmatic desires to view the technology as a "transcendence machine" or subjectivity enhancer, works to collapse distinctions between the conceptions

---

[39]   Appadurai, "Disjuncture," pp. 296–7.

[40]   Jennifer Cobb, *Cybergrace: The Search for God in a Digital World* (New York, 1998), p. 31.

[41]   Ibid.

[42]   Miraslaw Filiciak, "Hyperidentities," in *The Video Game Theory Reader* (New York, 2003), p. 100.

built into virtual environments by their developers and the perceptive faculties of users.[43]

Brenda Brasher observes in cyberspace what she calls "omnitemporality," that is, "the religious idea of eternity as perpetual persistence." Using traditional religious language of the sacred, Brasher says that cyberspace is:

> [c]ontinuously accessible and ostensibly disconnected from the cycles of the earth … [It] appeared to its first Western consumers to be a concrete expression or materialization of the monks' concept of eternity … It is always present. Whatever exists within it never decays. Whatever is expressed in cyberspace, as long as it remains in cyberspace, is perpetually expressed … the quasi-mystical appeal that cyberspace exudes stems from this taste of eternity that it imparts to those who interact with it.[44]

The desire the screen represents is particularly enchanting since the "Internet" is itself a symbol of connection, the possibility of unity. Hillis has noted what he calls a "cosmopolitan Web dynamic" which is simultaneously "a culture of networks" and "a culture of individualism." The ennui implied by such identity "surfing" is what Hillis dubs "everyday manifestations of a desire for a worldwide *oikos* or *ecumene*," a term borrowed from the original form of Christian evangelism and the hope for a unified world under Christ.[45] The nearly mystical ability of programs to offer us meaning is recognized by advertisers, who have offered us (among others) things like Oracle (a corporation that produces databases and programs to manage them), Windows (into which we peer), a computer actually *called* a Gateway, and of course the iconic Mac "Apple" icon that some see as a riff on Edenic mythology.

Gracia Grindal may be saying something symbolically similar in a very different context when he argues that heaven (as home) may "appear more attractive to those suffering unrelieved horror on earth."[46] Heaven's promises of abundance may be especially comforting to those suffering as slaves, as expressed for example in African-American spirituals of the nineteenth century where "Zion" is not in contemporary Israel but rather consists of "the heav'nly fields" and "golden streets" of "the beautiful city of God" toward which they "march" with hope, from this life and into the next.[47] In all of these cases, the desire for "home" is a form of the desire for peace and for belonging, expressed in a hunger for Elsewhere

---

[43]   Ken Hillis, "Modes of Digital Identification: Virtual Technologies and Webcam Cultures," in W.H.K. Chun and T. Keenan (eds), *New Media, Old Media: A History and Theory Reader* (New York, 2006), p. 349.

[44]   Brenda Brasher, *Give Me That Online Religion* (San Francisco, 2001), p. 52.

[45]   Ken Hillis, *Online a Lot of the Time: Ritual, Fetish, Sign* (Durham, 2009), p. 2.

[46]   Gracia Grindal, "Heaven and Hell in Hymnody," *Word & World* 31/1 (Winter 2011): p. 50.

[47]   Ibid., p. 51.

and at times a wish to "return," increasingly expressed via desire attached to the screen as a dream of hope and possibility. The promises of the Internet generate in us a nostalgia for a perfection we never knew, a hope for fulfillment of all of our dreams, a desire for imaginary places we have never been and even symbolic habitation in them, and expansive imaginative promises of fulfillment that may or may not ever be met.

Alt + Home

"Alt" on a keyboard is a modifier key. This means that pressing it at the same time as you press something else "alters" how that something else works. "Alt" plus "Home" suggests symbolically how our sense of home is being shaped by our digital encounters, with the metaphorical and quite literal loss of the "home" key on many keyboards and, I am suggesting, an uncanny renegotiation of how we think of home in our flesh and blood, brick and mortar lives. "The world we live in," says Appadurai, "now seems rhizomic, even schizophrenic, calling for theories of rootlessness, alienation, and psychological distance between individuals and groups, on the one hand, and fantasies (or nightmares) of electronic propinquity on the other. Here we are close to the central problematic of cultural processes in today's world."[48] In other words, we are all alienated and we are all connected. And if we are honest, we may find that this diasporic component is both chosen by us *and* foisted upon us by contemporary life. To be wired is to be hybrid, to be connected and to be displaced, to be near and to be very far apart. It is to be fully represented as we have always wished but also to be deceptive and reductive in representation of ourselves. It is to reduce home to a thing always in motion. It is to make home into a home page, a search engine, a waypoint.

References

Adams, Ernest, *Fundamentals of Game Design* (Indianapolis: New Riders Press, 2010).

Appadurai, Arjun. *Modernity at Large: Cultural Dimensions of Globalization.* Public Worlds Series (Minneapolis: University of Minnesota Press, 1996).

Appadurai, Arjun. "Disjuncture and Difference in the Global Cultural Economy," *Theory, Culture & Society* 7 (1990): 295–310.

Axel, Brian Keith, "The Context of Diaspora," *Cultural Anthropology* 19/1 (2004): 26–60.

Berger, Peter, Berger, Brigitte, and Kellner, Hansfried, *The Homeless Mind* (New York: Vintage, 1974).

---

[48]   Appadurai, *Modernity*, p. 29.

Bernal, Victoria, "Diaspora, Cyberspace and Political Imagination: The Eritrean Diaspora Online," *Global Networks* 6/2 (2006): 161–79.

Brasher, Brenda, *Give Me That Online Religion* (San Francisco: Jossey-Bass, 2001).

Braziel, Jana Evans and Mannur, Anita, "Nation, Migration, Globalization: Points of Contention in Diaspora Studies," in Jana Evans Braziel and Anita Mannur (eds), *Theorizing Diaspora* (Boston: Blackwell Publishing, 2007), pp. 1–22.

Burton-Christie, Douglas, "Place-Making as Contemplative Practice," *Anglican Theological Review* 91/3 (Summer 2009): 347–71.

CarnegieMellon Computer Club, Website, http://www.contrib.andrew.cmu.edu/~htasnim/example1.html [accessed August 1, 2011] (link no longer active).

Clifford, James, "Diasporas," *Cultural Anthropology* 9/3 (1994): 302–38.

Clifford, James, *Routes: Travel and Translation in the Late Twentieth Century* (Boston: Harvard University Press, 1997).

Cobb, Jennifer, *Cybergrace: The Search for God in a Digital World* (New York: Crown Publishing, 1998).

Dawson, Lorne, "Religion and the Quest for Virtual Community," in Lorne Dawson and Douglas Cowan (eds), *Religion Online: Finding Faith on the Internet* (New York: Taylor & Francis, 2009), pp. 69–84.

Domine, Robert and Abaroa, Fred, "Web Browser Detection and Default Home Page Modification Device," Patent Number 5,949,419, http://patft.uspto.gov [accessed March 29, 2012].

Douglas, Christopher, "Multiculturalism in World of Warcraft," *Electronic Book Review*, (June 4, 2010), http://www.electronicbookreview.com/thread/firstperson/intrinsically [accessed July 30, 2012].

Filiciak, Miraslaw. "Hyperidentities," in *The Video Game Theory Reader* (New York: Routledge, 2003).

Gilkey, Langdon, *Shantung Compound: The Story of Men and Women under Pressure.* (New York: HarperOne, 1975).

Grindal, Gracia, "Heaven and Hell in Hymnody." *Word & World* 31/1 (Winter 2011): 57–64.

Hafkin, Nancy, "'Whatsupoch' on the Net: The Role of Information and Communication Technology in the Shaping of Transnational Ethiopian Identity," *Diaspora* 15/2–3 (2006): 221–45.

Hillis, Ken, "Modes of Digital Identification: Virtual Technologies and Webcam Cultures," in W.H.K. Chun and T. Keenan (eds), *New Media, Old Media: A History and Theory Reader* (New York: Routledge, 2006), pp. 347–58.

Hillis, Ken, *Online a Lot of the Time: Ritual, Fetish, Sign* (Durham: Duke University Press, 2009).

Mitchell, William, *Me++: The Cyborg Self and the Networked City* (Cambridge, MA: MIT Press, 2003).

Mitra, Ananda, "Creating Immigrant Identities in Cybernetic Space: Examples from a Non-resident Indian Website," *Media, Culture and Society* 27 (2005): 371–90.

Nayar, Pramod, "Augmented Spaces: Virtual Worlds, 'New' Territories, and the Politics of Cyberculture," in Bed P. Girir and Prafulla C. Kar (eds), *Thinking Territory: Some Reflections* (New Delhi: Pencraft International, 2009), pp. 152–70.

O'Hara, Shelley, *Absolute Beginner's Guide to Microsoft Windows Vista* (Indianapolis: Que Press, 2007).

Pearce, Celia, *Communities of Play: Emergent Cultures in Multiplayer Games and Virtual Worlds* (Cambridge, MA: MIT Press, 2009).

Raskin, Aza, "The Problem with Home," Professional Blog Post, http://www. azarask.in/blog/post/the-problem-with-home [accessed July 30, 2012].

Rogers, Scott, *Level Up! The Guide to Great Video Game Design* (Hoboken: John Wiley & Sons, 2010).

Shelly, Gary B. and Woods, Denise M., *HTML: Complete Concepts and Techniques* (Boston: Course Technology Publishing, 2009).

Tambiah, Stanley J., "Transnational Movements, Diaspora, and Multiple Modernities," *Daedalus* 129/1 (Winter 2000): 163–94.

Thomas, Lucas M, "The 3DS Has a Home," IGN, June 16, 2010, http://ds.ign. com/articles/109/1098833p1.html [accessed July 30, 2012].

Wagner, Rachel, *Godwired: Religion, Ritual and Virtual Reality* (New York: Routledge, 2012).

Chapter 8

Faith or Friendship: On Integrating Dimensions of Self-realization in Kierkegaard and Aristotle

Nathan Eric Dickman

Hard Choice or Opportunity?

Individualization and participation are primary ontological dimensions of human being.[1] Conditions of existence, however, variously pressurize our ontological integrity into polar extremes, constraining our potential into various actual – specific, concrete, particular – modes of being.[2] These conditions threaten us with utter dissolution, so existence brings with it a fundamental mood of *Angst*, or anxiety, about our being at "home" in the world – whether we explicitly recognize this mood or not in our everyday lives.[3] Wherever we are or, more importantly, *how*ever we are, there lingers an uncanny sense of not really being at home, no matter how much at home we might take ourselves to be. In other words, conditions of existence estrange us from ourselves, each other, and our rootedness in a world.[4] As Tillich writes: "The state of existence is the state of estrangement."[5]

We are, fundamentally, strangers here. As such, any sense of being at home is a *fragile achievement* whereby we traverse the "secret rift" that is our existence.[6] A genuine experience of being at home reveals, rather than conceals, what Ricoeur articulates as "the fragile synthesis of [human being] as the *becoming of an opposition*."[7] At stake presently is the specific opposition of individualization and participation. As Tillich writes:

---

[1] Paul Tillich, *Systematic Theology, Vol. I* (Chicago, 1951), pp. 176–7.

[2] Paul Tillich, *Systematic Theology, Vol. II* (Chicago, 1955), p. 21.

[3] Martin Heidegger, *Being and Time: A Translation of* Sein und Zeit, trans. Joan Stambaugh (Albany, 1996), pp. 177, 255–6. See also Søren Kierkegaard, *The Sickness Unto Death*, trans. Howard and Edna Hong (Princeton, 1983).

[4] Tillich, *Systematic Theology, Vol. II*, pp. 44–5.

[5] Ibid., p. 44.

[6] Paul Ricoeur, *Fallible Man*, 2nd edn (New York, 1993), p. 141.

[7] Ricoeur, *Fallible Man*, p. 141, emphasis in original.

> In the state of estrangement [human being] is shut within [itself] and cut off from
> participation. At the same time, [human being] falls under the power of objects
> which tend to make [it] into a mere object without a self. If subjectivity separates
> itself from objectivity, the objects swallow the empty shell of subjectivity.[8]

Estrangement poses an ontological challenge in the face of which we struggle to realize a self-fulfillment or proper integration of both individuality and participation. How can we realize this happy integration and achieve the fragile sense of being at home with ourselves?

I do not wish to move too quickly to reiterate Tillich's and Ricoeur's suggestions that this polarity between independence and interdependence forms a productive tension for our being in the world without first developing the radical difference between these two dimensions of our lives. Alone with ourselves, we experience an uncanny unease of need for more in order to realize we are home. In sociality with others, we experience an uncanny unease of need for less in order to realize we are home. At times we feel we need to be alone, and at other times we feel we need to be with others. But in either case, we sometimes find ourselves not feeling completely at home, not achieving a fulfilling sense of being at home.

In order to develop this difference more sufficiently, particularly with regard to the theme of being at home with ourselves and others, I turn to two historical resources who present radically opposed pictures of each pole of our divided selfhood: Kierkegaard and Aristotle. Aristotle argues that individuals are "at home" with one another in complete character friendship, urging that such friends live together by sharing in conversation and thought – unlike cattle grazing in the same pasture.[9] Kierkegaard, alternatively, insists on the radically subjective character of faith, that the so-called "knight of faith" cannot disclose himself in the universal except through irony.[10] This suggests that a person of faith cannot realize the kind of living together available in complete friendship that Aristotle asserts is constitutive for selfhood, because such a person cannot properly share in conversation and thought with another. And yet, for Kierkegaard, faithfulness is the full realization of authentic selfhood and a refuge whereby one is at home with oneself.

Do these inheritances force upon us a hard choice, an estrangement between either faith or friendship in our effort to be a self?[11] Or, alternatively, does this tension provide us with an opportunity to realize a more complex self-understanding? May these two structural conditions – authentic individuality

---

[8]   Tillich, *Systematic Theology, Vol. II*, p. 65.

[9]   Aristotle, *Nicomachean Ethics*, trans. Terence Irwin (Indianapolis, 1995), p. 150.

[10]   Søren Kierkegaard, *Fear and Trembling/Repetition*, trans. Howard and Edna Hong (Princeton, 1983), pp. 113 and 118.

[11]   See Paul Ricoeur, "Religion, Atheism, Faith," in *Conflict of Interpretations* (Chicago, 2007), pp. 440–67.

and human connection – be integrated into a greater whole of self-attestation? Can we build a home on this fault line in the human heart? I find these questions particularly pressing today in Western culture's saturation with irony and reflexivity, as well as its emphasis on independent individualism. As we will see, irony ideally forms the proper mode of expression for authenticity. So, with the surplus of irony in contemporary medias, we can assume that our culture tends toward the affirmation of individualistic faith to the detriment of friendship and genuine participation in greater social wholes. However, with the surplus of irony and reflexivity, have we reached the point of unmanageability in our efforts to realize authenticity? Is not irony today precisely a symptom of our homelessness? In light of the contemporary surplus of individuality (to the point of self-enclosure), it seems that a crucial responsibility of contemporary thinkers is to retrieve and practice life-affirming ways of being with others. Such a practice ought to prove to be part of the antidote to today's pervasive homelessness.

In what follows, I first sketch Aristotle's and Kierkegaard's divergent philosophical anthropologies to develop more fully the difference between friendship and authenticity. What this inquiry shows is that our being in the world in the life of faith fundamentally differs from our being in the world in the life of friendship. Juxtaposing these two philosophical anthropologies also exposes their limits, especially the limits as they are concretely realized in discursive practice. In light of this, I move to sketch extents to which faith and friendship are operative in our discursive practices of irony and dialogue. Through this delimitation in our discourse, we can be empowered to coordinate faith and friendship, neither granting privilege to one or the other, nor succumbing to the pressure of one over other. I conclude by suggesting that through each one's proper timing we can compose a polyrhythm, balancing the timing of dialogue with the timing of irony, and vice versa. The model of the polyrhythm is crucial here because such a piece integrates two distinct rhythms into a greater whole without canceling out each rhythm's uniqueness. A polyrhythm is precisely the fragile achievement of a home within the fundamental opposition that we are. I leave us with a question that I hope will empower each of us to compose our own polyrhythmic discourse: when is the fitting time for my irony and when is the fitting time for our dialogue? Let us turn to our intellectual predecessors.

Conflicting Philosophical Anthropologies

Aristotle

Aristotle's development of participation in complete friendship needs to be situated within its conceptual backdrop: his philosophical anthropology. The fundamental distinction here is between "body" and "soul," or in broader terms between "matter" and "form." We find neither of these empirically as such; rather, we always perceive particulars that are composites of both.[12] As Aristotle suggests, we can distinguish these upon reflective analysis for the sake of understanding.[13] With regard to the human self, the body is the concrete medium in which all acting, thinking, and feeling are actualized. Differing from modern Cartesian dualism, the body is not another part of the self distinct from the mind; it is the actuality of the thinking, acting, and feeling being that we are.[14] If we are ever at home, it is always concretely embodied.

Aristotle delineates three discrete dimensions of "soul."[15] Before examining these dimensions, it should first be noted that by the term "soul," we are speaking about the ways in which living things move. This can be brought out by rehabilitating our sense of "soul" in appealing to the Greek word for soul, *anima*. Our word "animal" is etymologically derived from this notion, but so too is our word "animation," and even contemporary Anime. An inanimate object is something lacking in organic life and movement. So when we are looking at Aristotle's distinctions, it is crucial to note that we are talking about discrete kinds of movements in speaking about the "soul." Participation in friendship entails being caught up in a peculiar sort of movement, a movement whereby we achieve a deep yet uncanny sense of belonging and being home with others.

All organic life shares the movement denoted by the phrase "nutritive soul."[16] The kind of movement proper to nutrition is absorption, digestion, and growth. Animals possess increased capacities for movement; unlike plants, we are mobile. And Aristotle denotes this kind of movement proper to animals as "appetitive soul."[17] I take this to capture the increase of movement where animals have the capacity to be even more mobile than plants, a mobility that makes us more effective in gratifying our desires. Telescoping in on human beings in particular, the movement unique to us is denoted by the phrase "rational soul," or what I prefer to translate as "discursive soul."[18] I deliberately translate "logos" as "discourse" in order to circumvent any modernist anachronism that reads Cartesianism back into the construal of reason for ancient Greeks. Reasoning, as discourse, is inherently public and social, concretely realized bodily, and so whatever privacy can be acquired, it is only to the degree that one reasons in constrained social environments – rather than broadcasting one's messages to undifferentiated audiences, one can instead develop thought with select others, an elite group of compatriots.

---

[12]   Aristotle, *Metaphysics*, III:4 and VII:4, in *The Complete Works of Aristotle*, trans. Jonathan Barnes (Princeton, 1983), pp. 1578–9 and 1625.

[13]   Aristotle, *On the Soul*, II:1, in *The Complete Works of Aristotle*, p. 657.

[14]   Ibid., p. 656.

[15]   See Aristotle, *Metaphysics*, VII:9, in *The Complete Works of Aristotle*, p. 1635. See also Aristotle, *On the Soul*, II:3; and Aristotle, *Nicomachean Ethics*, p. 9.

[16]   See Aristotle, *Nicomachean Ethics*, pp. 9 and 149.

[17]   Ibid.

[18]   Ibid., pp. 163–5.

This constricted publicity in our discursive practices should not, then, be conflated with what we will describe as the ontological elusiveness of the transcendental subject in Kierkegaard's philosophical anthropology. Furthermore, the rational-discursive way of moving – peculiar to humans – takes place as living language. Uniquely human movement is, at least when it comes to friendship, dialogue.[19] Dialogue houses the home achieved through our bodily movements and efforts to share in thought with a friend. Stressing this dimension of human being will become increasingly significant in our juxtaposition of Aristotle on self-realization in complete friendship and with Kierkegaard on self-realization in faith.

Maximal flourishing for the unique kind of beings that we are is realized, for Aristotle, in conversation. In fact, Aristotle identifies *eudaimonia*, or human happiness, as "study," something which, he says, we can presumably do more effectively with others than in isolation.[20] Of course, by "study," Aristotle is not referring to our contemporary practices of taking notes during a lecture and memorizing information to be regurgitated for exams; instead, study for Aristotle is when we affirm events as opportunities for dialogue and the realization of understanding. Whenever I teach this theme to students, I illustrate this point by asking them: how many of you have been to Disney World? How many of you go alone? Through these questions we come to see that talking about experiences is what helps us integrate them, enrich them, remember them, and appreciate them. (In other words, we *study* them.) When we travel to a place like "Disney World," or any place other than home, the presence of friends allows us to find the uncanny flavor of home elsewhere.

Aristotle specifies that the most appropriate context for dialogue is within "complete" or character friendship.[21] Character friends, for Aristotle, live together in the sense of sharing in conversation and thought. And he distinguishes this mode of living together from mere physical proximity, where cattle can be said to live together to the degree that they graze in the same pasture. Simply sharing the same physical shelter with other people does not make us friends. Living in separate dwellings does not mean that we are not friends either. Rather, it is when persons dwell within shared ideas and understandings, more or less independent of physical proximity, that they can be said to be friends. Character friendship is a fragile achievement, whereby we make an uncanny home with another. This can be illustrated by those instances in which marriages dissolve even after the achievement of being together for over 30 years. In such cases, the dissolution exposes the relationship to have been merely sustained by "grazing

---

[19]   Ibid., p. 150.

[20]   Ibid., pp. 162–3 and 165, where Aristotle says: "For what is proper to each thing's nature is supremely best and most pleasant for it; and hence for a human being the life in accord with understanding will be supremely best and most pleasant if understanding, more than anything else, is the human being. This life, then, will also be happiest."

[21]   Ibid., p. 150.

in the same pasture," rather than shared living through conversation and thinking together. However, why can't we sustain conversation all the time? Why do good conversations come to an end?[22] While these questions are also important, let us end here by saying, with Gadamer and Holderlin: since a conversation we are.[23]

Since we are here taking the fully realized human life as the life of study, as occurring within dialogue, we need to briefly turn to delineate the structure of dialogue as it relates to understanding. To understand is to come to terms with conversation partners and to have our questions responded to.[24] To understand meaning is to understand it as an answer to a question.[25] Through sharing questions we can transfer meanings from one person to the other. And, depending on what we understand, we can enact what we learn in applying the meanings to our own lives. In this way, dialogue as the sharing and exploring of questions – particularly the sustained dialogue of character friendship – allows for an increase of being and self-understanding. It is through participating in conversation, in effect, that we realize who we are. Thus, the conversation forms the proper household for the kind of being at home, the fragile and uncanny home, achieved by character friends.

Suspending momentarily this development of the life of friendship in dialogue, let us turn to Kierkegaard's thoughts on the life of faith and radical subjectivity.

Kierkegaard[26]

Working within the milieu of modern philosophy influenced by Descartes' turn to the subject, Kierkegaard presupposes an entirely distinct philosophical anthropology to Aristotle. We first need to clarify this anthropology before isolating his notion of radically individualized faith. A useful way of explicating Kierkegaard's assumed anthropology and its implications for his conceptualization of faith is to draw out implicit ways in which he extends and critiques Kant.

Rather than rehearse Kant, though, I will here only briefly isolate two distinct themes which are particularly relevant for our reading of Kierkegaard. First, human thinking is fundamentally structured by two faculties: the faculty of perception through which thinking is given particulars in field of sensibility; and the faculty of conception which issues concepts to thinking in the field of intelligibility.[27] Thinking is, in large part, synthesizing particulars with concepts, as can be illustrated through the grammatical analysis of a judgment. The grammatical subject

---

[22]   Ibid, p. 158. The problem is, of course, that we are not divine.

[23]   Hans-Georg Gadamer, *Truth and Method*, 2nd revised edn, trans. Joel Weinsheimer and Donald G. Marshall (New York, 2004), p. 370.

[24]   Ibid., p. 371.

[25]   Ibid., p. 368.

[26]   For the purposes of this chapter, I refer to the author of *Fear and Trembling* as "Kierkegaard" rather than the pseudonym, Johannes de Silentio.

[27]   Immanuel Kant, *Critique of Pure Reason*, trans. Norman Kemp (New York, 1965).

of a sentence identifies and refers to a particular percept; predication, though, is the conceptual location of that percept in a field of intelligibility.[28] Thinking is, then, an operation of synthesis, which Kant calls "transcendental apperception," the agency which Fichte and later idealists and phenomenologists identify as the "transcendental I." Rather than analytically dividing the self between body and soul, Kant's transcendental critique exposes the split in the self between the transcendental I and the empirical me. To the degree that modernists emphasize the Cartesian subject, especially through natural scientific methodologies that exclude particular human engagement (or "biases"), we can identify this emphasis on the transcendental subject as a ground for the contemporary homelessness accompanying individualism.

Second, in the field of practical action, human beings purportedly realize their freedom through legislating to themselves maxims that are in accord with the fundamental moral law, the supreme principle of morality, the Categorical Imperative.[29] An individual's autonomy is realized when, through this coordination, I tell myself what to do rather than when someone or something else tells me what to do. It is only through legislating such actions to ourselves that we realize a "good will," the only thing that, for Kant, can be said to be good without qualification.[30] Already we can see a radical difference in anthropologies between Aristotle and Kierkegaard (anchored in Kant), located primarily in the turn to the subject in all modern philosophy after Descartes. It appears that neither metaphysically nor morally can the modern subject ever achieve the kind of being at home available in Aristotle's ethics.

Rather than clarifying and explicating the constitutive and procedural laws that structure relations between the transcendental "legislating" I and the empirical "legislated" me, Kierkegaard tirelessly emphasizes and imaginatively explores the intricacies of the existential burden of becoming a self. It is not simply that I legislate rational laws to myself, but that every instance of such choice is shrouded in fear and trembling or anxiety. It is not simply that I synthesize percepts and concepts, or that I legislate maxims to myself in accordance with the moral law. In my very being in the world, I am constantly confronted with the existential fact of my actuality and individuality, of actually being the one judging and acting in the world. And under the conditions of existence, I am burdened with the weight of making something of myself. Kierkegaard brings the subject back into direct, even immediate, relation with the world, and in so doing makes possible an alternative way to achieve being at home. His existential insight here licenses his critique of modern moral philosophy – though we must note that it is unclear at this point

---

[28]   Paul Ricoeur, *Interpretation Theory* (Fort Worth: Texas University Press, 1972), pp. 10–12. See also David Klemm, *The Hermeneutical Theory of Paul Ricoeur* (East Brunswick, 1982), pp. 10–12.

[29]   Immanuel Kant, *Grounding for the Metaphysics of Morals*, trans. James W. Ellington (Indianapolis, 1993), pp. 26 and 49.

[30]   Ibid., p. 7.

just how applicable his critique of ethics extends to ancient ethics and Aristotle in particular.

The fundamental question articulating Kierkegaard's critique of Kantian and Hegelian morality is: if the universal is the highest, then is ultimate fulfillment anything other than reconciliation with the universal any time one either is tempted to or in fact does assert her individuality as above the universal?[31] If this is all there is, then what becomes of Abraham? The significance of this question cannot be stressed enough. Since Abraham is considered to be the father of faith for three major monotheistic religions (Judaism, Christianity, and Islam), what is it about him that makes him great? If Kant is correct about the good will, Kierkegaard thinks, then Abraham is lost, incapable of achieving a state of being at home. Alternatively, if Abraham really is the model of faithfulness, that is, a fully realized human being, then there must be something "higher" than the universal, there must be an existential possibility that teleologically suspends the universal.[32] However, as we laid out above, the universal – or in other words the conceptual – is the sieve through which particulars can be understood. Thus, according to Kierkegaard, Abraham is beyond understanding and thus beyond the kind of being at home realized in character friendship.

It is not simply that Abraham as a biblical character exceeds our understanding as such; Kierkegaard lucidly illustrates all *the various ways* in which he exceeds understanding. He tirelessly stresses how he cannot adequately speak about Abraham. The first section of *Fear and Trembling*, for example, consists of multiple failed attempts at adequately (re)narrating Abraham's story in an alternative way to that preserved in the biblical texts.[33] While he can tell the story of classical tragic heroes and unfulfilled lovers, he simply cannot tell the story of Abraham in any other way. What did Abraham say on the way back down Moriah? What could possibly be supplied in order to adequately fill in the ellipsis? For a further comparison, while we can write a love song or love poem, what would it look like to write a "faith" song?[34] Praise would not be sufficient. Furthermore, let the irony of *Fear and Trembling* as a whole not be lost on us. The pseudonym is named Johannes de Silentio (John the Silent) and with regard to the apparent subject matter (Abraham and faith) he remains silent – either by virtue of the subject matter itself resisting thematization or by virtue of the limitations of his own thinking and imagination. If Abraham is capable of being at home, it certainly is not with another.

Simply because an existential possibility cannot be understood does not mean that the existential possibility cannot be lived. As Kierkegaard is often quoted as saying, "Life can be understood backwards, but must be lived forwards."[35]

---

[31]   Kierkegaard, *Fear and Trembling*, p. 54.

[32]   Ibid., pp. 54–60.

[33]   Ibid., pp. 10–14.

[34]   See ibid., pp. 32 and 61.

[35]   This is not Kierkegaard's exact wording. In his journals and papers, he writes: "It is quite true what philosophy says: that life must be understood backwards. But then one

Rather than implying that faith does not exist, Kierkegaard emphasizes the radically subjective and individualistic character of faith (throughout most of his early pseudonymous writings). Indeed, this is consistent with the idealist tradition's characterization of the transcendental I and its systematic elusiveness – in other words, its homelessness. The radically subjective character of faith is not without historical precedent to Kierkegaard either. Indeed, Kierkegaard's debt to Hegel may be overestimated when we consider relevant themes in Hegel's contemporary, Schleiermacher. On the theme of the radically subject character of faith, consider Schleiermacher's characterization of "religion" as an "intuition of the universe" unique to each individual.[36] In overcoming moralism by teleologically suspending it, Kierkegaard asserts that Abraham realizes an "absolute relation to the absolute," where the individual is higher than the universal,[37] thus stressing, like Schleiermacher, the radically individualized realization of religious consciousness as the essential home of human being. We have a deep and fundamental belonging with the universe and we can realize this when we dissolve the occlusions of it by metaphysics and moralisms.

Just as the proper mode of discourse for friendship is dialogue, we can ask what the proper expression is for faith, this radically subjective existential possibility. What form of discourse houses the home of authenticity? What can Abraham say? Just as for Kant, for Kierkegaard informative discourse brings particulars into the light of intelligibility, the light of the universal. As an example, I can discuss a particular chair in the hall through reference and predication, lifting up the particular through the subject term and situating it within a field of intelligibility through predication. As Kierkegaard shows, we are unable to do that with Abraham. But it is not simply that one cannot adequately predicate something of Abraham, it is also that Abraham himself cannot speak in descriptive discourse. Kierkegaard examines Abraham's response to Isaac's question: where is the sacrifice? Imagining Abraham answering with "It is you" would disclose Abraham in the universal as weak and in need of moral reconciliation. Were he to answer "I do not know," he would be lying, and thus in need of reconciliation again. Neither of these statements could be consistent with the ideal of the father of faith.[38] In both cases, he would be forgoing his home in radical individuality for the sake of mere participation in a greater moral whole.

---

forgets the other principle: that it must be lived forwards. A principle which, the more one thinks it through, ends exactly with the thought that temporal life can never be properly understood precisely because I can at no instant find complete rest in which to adopt the position: backwards." Søren Kierkegaard, *Journals and Papers, Vol. IV* (Indianapolis, 1975), p. 164.

[36] See Fredrich Schleiermacher, *On Religion*, trans. Richard Crouter (Cambridge, 1996).

[37] Kierkegaard, *Fear and Trembling*, pp. 55–6.

[38] Ibid., pp. 118–19.

The only recourse Abraham has for expressing himself faithfully is irony.[39] Kierkegaard defines irony in *Fear and Trembling* as saying something and yet not saying anything. I am inclined to interpret this through Robert Scharlemann's differentiation between reflection and reflexivity.[40] Reflection demands direct descriptive discourse, demands asserting either the affirmation or denial of a claim in correspondence to a reality. Reflexivity, however, says two things at the same time, both yes and no. In this way, irony both says something and doesn't say anything simultaneously. And this "speaking in tongues"[41] is the proper mode of expression for the radically subjective character of authentic individuality. Irony houses the home of authenticity. It is the concrete embodied achievement. When Abraham responds to Isaac's question with "The Lord will provide," he is both saying something and not saying anything. And he is at home with himself there.

Thus, it seems that we are faced with a hard choice: dialogue or irony? Friendship or faith? On the one hand, from Aristotle we receive an ontology of human being as intrinsically public and participatory, and on the other hand, from Kierkegaard we receive an ontology of human being as intrinsically individual and private (at least when it comes to the constitution of authentic selfhood). I want to suspend this choice, however, and I hope to provide a different space for resolutely persevering in ambivalence between these poles. I turn now to carve out this space of opportunity by identifying limits of dialogue and limits of irony, and thereby coordinate friendship and faith as coeval existential possibilities for the constitution of selfhood, neither of which is ontologically subordinate to the other. It is my wager that such delimitation empowers us in our effort to be and to integrate disparate dimensions of our selves. In this way, may we come to achieve an uncanny home with both ourselves and others.

Integration through Delimitation of Limits

If conversation is the ideal context for friendship, and irony is the proper expression of faith, is it possible for two ironists to enter into conversation and reach an understanding? Allow me to briefly turn to trace the limits of subjectivity and friendship with regard to their specific expressions. Before turning to this, though, I want to make a crucial distinction between existential dispositions and expressions of those dispositions. Both dialogue and irony can be conceived of as existential dispositions rather than mere expressions. That is, we can describe a person as being disposed toward dialogue in always being ready to affirm events as opportunities for a good conversation. Alternatively, we can describe a person as possessing an ironic disposition in that she comports herself with regard to the world in an ironic or reflexive way. In order to avoid confusion, I label these

---

[39]   Ibid., pp. 117–18.

[40]   Robert Scharlemann, *The Being of God* (New York, 1981), pp. 26–9.

[41]   Kierkegaard, *Fear and Trembling*, p. 114.

dispositions as "friendship" and "faith." For present purposes, I hold dialogue and irony merely to be ways of expressing ourselves that are indicative of and (usually) correlative to their proper existential dimensions.

The Limits of Friendship (Dialogue)

I seek to identify the limits of friendship and participation through recourse to determinations of the limits of dialogue. What are the limits of dialogue? For one, are there not things that simply cannot be thematized as an object of discourse, such as transcendental subjectivity (which is systematically elusive to consciousness) and what Paul Ricoeur refers to as "limit experiences" (like the experience of evil or the ultimate beginning of being)?[42] Such "things" – if that is even the right word to use here – can only be pointed to obliquely through mythopoetics. Moreover, some people, or all people at different times or with regard to certain topics, seem too emotionally invested in one particular view to perform suspensions necessary for exploratory conversation, particularly when it comes to interpersonal or political conflict and heated misunderstandings (especially when things turn moralistic). Furthermore, some events are so urgent and practical that appropriate response seems to require immediate action rather than reflective dialogue, such as physical trauma. It is also worth considering that sometimes we either just aren't interested in or just aren't committed to realizing an understanding, which perhaps severs the communicative bonds that – at least in part – make us human. And, perhaps, some topics appear so fraught with risks that we lack the courage to muster up something to say, such as criticizing a boss. Perhaps most importantly, faith itself as "the absolute relation to the absolute" eludes direct expression.

What I am trying to point out with the above brief reflection on the limits of dialogue is simply that dialogue cannot be and ought not to be conceived of as the universal solvent, which is what many do today in popular multicultural discourse. As John Durham Peters indicates, such calls for dialogue are naïve and undermine our ability to recognize the value and virtue of other modes of communication.[43] Other actions besides dialogue are often called for. Without vigilantly attending to the limitations of dialogue, the humility it can embody disintegrates into humiliation.

The Limits of Subjectivity (Irony)

As with friendship and dialogue, I seek to identify the limits of subjectivity through recourse to determinations of the limits of irony. What are the limits of irony? Does it not seem inherently against understanding? Or can we instead say that irony, particularly Socratic irony, itself expresses the mode of understanding

---

[42]   See Paul Ricoeur, *Symbolism of Evil* (New York, 1986). See also Paul Ricoeur, "Biblical Hermeneutics," *Semeia* 4 (1975): pp. 123–45.

[43]   John Durham Peters, *Speaking into the Air* (Chicago, 2001).

that one does not understand? Either way, irony does seem to lack the necessary conditions of friendship: mutual goodwill, recognition, reciprocity, etc.[44] Why is it that in our inherited classical literatures we rarely, if ever, witness two ironists in face-to-face dialogue? Can we even image a dialogue between two Socrateses or between two Jesuses? Wouldn't this be like trying to hold together the positively charged ends of two magnets?

Kierkegaard himself had to face this problem of ironic saturation when the national press subjected him to "Danish humor" and the "Copenhagen laugh" through a series of cartoons accenting his various eccentricities, such as his uneven trousers, hunched back, and umbrella.[45] This tribal revenge taken on Kierkegaard robbed him of his public body and he could no longer take advantage of his existential presence in the same way (with his life's work reduced to a matter of the length of his trousers and the arch of his curved back).[46] Since the entire town had become ironic, he could no longer sustain his ironic mode of indirection. As Roger Poole summarizes this: "For one cannot efficiently manage irony in the face of irony."[47] Like Kierkegaard, we also live in an environment saturated with irony and reflexivity, to such an extent that we can, with impunity, wonder whether it is correlated to authenticity any longer or whether it is merely a technology. Thus, one crucial limit of irony is its unmanageability in its surplus. Identification of an age as saturated with irony discloses the hubris of escalated irony rather than preserving it in its proper place of pride.

Neither dialogue nor irony can be considered a "universal solvent" for existential self-realization and authentic self-expression. While both house significant dimensions of existential fulfillment and while both can help us achieve a sense of being at home, both have their limits. This recognition of limits, however, need not be experienced as disabling estrangement, because we can recognize this polar juxtaposition as an opportunity for the enactment of our freedom and thinking, to discern within each moment whether dialogue or irony are called for in building a fragile home over the fault line of existential estrangement.

The Effort to Integrate

Allow me to conclude with a brief reflection on the timing of participatory dialogue and the timing of irony in order to suggest one way in which we can get a nose for navigating between friendship and faith. I am thinking here of Qoheleth's gathering reflections on proper timing – that to everything there is

---

[44]   See Aristotle, *Nicomachean Ethics*, pp. 120–1.

[45]   Roger Poole, *Kierkegaard: The Indirect Communication* (Charlottesville, 1993), p. 15.

[46]   Ibid.

[47]   Ibid., p. 21.

a season. I believe, perhaps naïvely, that we are capable of building an uncanny home in this multiplicity – a home that is an explicit recognition and expression of the fragile balance between individualization and participation. Perhaps there are times that house what is of ultimate importance and the sacred intimacy of faith, and we must set these times apart via the shroud of irony. Perhaps there are those times that house what is of interpersonal importance, and at those times we must publicize this significance in a good conversation. The pride of the time of irony always needs to be kept in check by the humility of the time of dialogue and vice versa. Coordinating these times is our opportunity to realize a polyrhythmic life. Through each one's proper timing, we can compose a polyrhythm, balancing the timing of dialogue with the timing of irony. The model of the polyrhythm is crucial here because such a piece integrates two distinct rhythms into a greater whole without canceling out each rhythm's uniqueness. A polyrhythm is precisely the fragile achievement of an uncanny home within the fundamental opposition that we are. How are we to tell the difference? Let us suspend our response until another time.

References

Aristotle, "Metaphysics," in *The Complete Works of Aristotle*, trans. Jonathan Barnes (2 vols, Princeton: Princeton University Press, 1983), pp. 1552–728.

Aristotle, "On the Soul," in *The Complete Works of Aristotle*, trans. Jonathan Barnes (2 vols, Princeton: Princeton University Press, 1983), pp. 641–92.

Aristotle, *Nicomachean Ethics*, trans. Terence Irwin (Indianapolis: Hackett, 1995).

Gadamer, Hans-Georg, "Friendship and Self-Knowledge: Reflections on the Role of Friendship in Greek Ethics," in *Hermeneutics, Religion, and Ethics*, trans. Joel Weinsheimer (New Haven: Yale University Press, 1999), pp. 128–41.

Gadamer, Hans-Georg, *Truth and Method*, 2nd revised edn, trans. Joel Weinsheimer and Donald G. Marshall (New York: Continuum, 2004).

Heidegger, Martin, *Being and Time: A Translation of* Sein und Zeit, trans. Joan Stambaugh (Albany: SUNY Press, 1996).

Kant, Immanuel, *Critique of Pure Reason*, trans. Norman Kemp (New York: Macmillan & Co., 1965).

Kant, Immanuel, *Grounding for the Metaphysics of Morals*, trans. James W. Ellington (Indianapolis: Hackett, 1993).

Kierkegaard, Søren, *Journals and Papers, Vol. IV* (Indianapolis: Indiana University Press, 1975).

Kierkegaard, Søren, *Fear and Trembling/Repetition*, trans. Howard and Edna Hong (Princeton: Princeton University Press, 1983).

Kierkegaard, Søren, *The Sickness Unto Death*, trans. Howard and Edna Hong (Princeton: Princeton University Press, 1983).

Klemm, David, *The Hermeneutical Theory of Paul Ricoeur* (East Brunswick: Associated University Press, 1982).

Matustik, Martin, and Merold Westphal, *Kierkegaard in Post/Modernity* (Bloomington: Indiana University Press, 1995).

Peters, John Durham, *Speaking into the Air* (Chicago: Chicago University Press, 2001).

Poole, Roger, *Kierkegaard: The Indirect Communication* (Charlottesville: University Press of Virginia, 1993).

Ricoeur, Paul, *Interpretation Theory* (Fort Worth: Texas University Press, 1972).

Ricouer, Paul, "Biblical Hermeneutics," *Semeia* 4 (1975): 123–45.

Ricoeur, Paul, *Symbolism of Evil* (New York: Beacon Press, 1986).

Ricoeur, Paul, *Fallible Man*, 2nd edn (New York: Fordham University Press, 1993).

Ricoeur, Paul, "Religion, Atheism, Faith," in *Conflict of Interpretations* (Chicago: Northwestern University Press, 2007).

Scharlemann, Robert P., *The Being of God* (New York: Seabury Press, 1981).

Schleiermacher, Friedrich, *On Religion*, trans. Richard Crouter (Cambridge: Cambridge University Press, 1996).

Smith-Pangle, Lorraine, *Aristotle and the Philosophy of Friendship* (Cambridge: Cambridge University Press, 2003).

Strawser, Michael, *Both/And: Reading Kierkegaard from Irony to Edification* (New York: Fordham University Press, 1997).

Taylor, Mark C., *Journeys to Selfhood: Hegel and Kierkegaard* (New York: Fordham University Press, 2000).

Tefler, Elizabeth. "Friendship," *Proceedings of the Aristotelian Society*, New Series 71 (1970–1971): 223–41.

Tillich, Paul, *Systematic Theology, Vol. I* (Chicago: Chicago University Press, 1951).

Tillich, Paul, *Systematic Theology, Vol. II* (Chicago: Chicago University Press, 1955).

Vanier, Jean. *Made for Happiness: Discovering the Meaning of Life with Aristotle*, trans. Kathryn Spink (Toronto: Anansi Press, 2001).

Walsh, Sylvia, *Living Christianly: Kierkegaard's Dialectic of Christian Existence* (University Park: Pennsylvania State University Press, 2005).

Chapter 9

Homecoming as Damnation

Thomas J.J. Altizer

Homecoming has become empty if not the very opposite of itself, as so forcefully embodied in our literature and most decisively so in our drama, a drama that in a Beckett or O'Neill absolutely reverses everything that we have known as home. Homecoming itself can now only finally be a descent, and a decent not only into darkness but ultimately into Hell. Above all other nations, America has been most universally open to Hell, as reflected in its drama and literature, and at a time when theology is virtually closed to Hell, with the great exception of the disenactment of Hell in Barth's *Dogmatics* (II,2), Hell continues to be enacted in our deeper American dramas, including our dramas of homecoming. Perhaps it is homecoming which most awakens us to Hell, or most awakens us to an absolutely dark destiny, a destiny that we inevitably know when we are most awake, a destiny entailing the necessary and inevitable loss of home, a home which we have most actually known as a paradise lost.

For us to know paradise is inevitably to know a paradise lost, but the loss of paradise is damnation itself, as so forcefully enacted throughout 2,000 years of Christian history, and that history does not perish with the end of Christendom; rather, it moves even more deeply within, as a new interiority is born that is the darkest or emptiest in our history. This is the interiority which can only know homecoming as damnation: now all innocence has vanished, or all actual innocence, and our primal grounds reverse themselves, or are transformed into their very opposite. Inevitably we must know the way to home as a return, and an ultimate return, but it is just an ultimate return that is most closed to us, and if realized at all by us could never be realized as an eternal Heaven but only as an eternal Hell. Thus, our imaginative images of an ultimate destiny have far more been images of Hell than images of Heaven, and just as the *Inferno* is far more overwhelmingly real to us than is the *Paradiso*, all too significantly it is the *Inferno* that inaugurates a uniquely modern imaginative realism.

This realism goes far beyond any realism of the ancient world, even including the Hebrew Bible, and the Hell that we have tasted in our imagination is a truly realistic Hell, one not only inducing an ultimate terror, but an ultimate emptiness going beyond any other emptiness in its absolute vacuity, an absolute vacuity that is absolutely real. This all-too-realistic Hell has had an enormous effect upon the world, and perhaps most decisively so in America, an America where even today there are far more mentally ill people than anywhere else. *Moby Dick* is the great American epic, where an American destiny is enacted that is a killing of the White

Whale or the absolutely alien God, thus realizing a uniquely American destiny or homecoming, a homecoming to absolute sacrifice itself. But since this is the sacrifice of Moby Dick, or the absolutely alien God, it inevitably issues in an eternal death or Hell, a Hell consuming the enactors of this murder or sacrifice, accordingly a Hell that is the very destiny of America. While that destiny is hidden in our common life, it is dislodged in moments of crisis, moments re-enacted again and again in our literature and drama, but also re-enacted in the most powerful expressions of American religion, expressions creating an ultimate terror, yes, yet a terror consumed by grace in the most ecstatic moments of American religion.

These moments occur in our imaginative creations just as they do in actual religious moments, where they are decisively realized as moments of destiny, and of an eternal destiny, one theologically known and named as Predestination. Predestination is unknown in Eastern Christianity, but it is proclaimed by every major Western theologian, and in the West if not the East is primal in Pauline tradition, the richest of all Western theological traditions, one wherein grace *is* Predestination. And all too paradoxically, it is precisely here that freedom is richest and most substantial in the West, the depths of freedom being unknown apart from Predestination; such depths are absent from nature, and from every expression of nature and of nature alone, depths that are only possible through the actuality of grace. As such, only damnation is possible apart from grace, and an eternal damnation, one decisively called forth when we are open to grace, or when we engage in a homecoming to our original condition. Such homecoming is inevitably profoundly threatening, for our original condition is deeply our own, and as such stands outside of grace or outside of the actuality of grace.

Only Predestination actualizes grace, an eternal Predestination that is the origin of salvation and damnation at once, a salvation wholly unreal apart from damnation, and a damnation wholly real in actuality itself, or in that actuality that is actual to us. It is precisely by tasting damnation that we most purely taste our own actuality, tasting it apart from everything that is seemingly our own, thereby transcending if only for a moment all of those illusions that we have created or that have been given to us, and given to us wholly apart from grace. Thus, it is damnation that is most purely home to us, most purely our own and not another's, and most purely reality and not illusion. Indeed, this is the reality that we have been given by grace, a grace that is judgment but nonetheless grace, a grace that could not be grace apart from judgment and is not grace apart from eternal judgment. This is the judgment that is only manifest to us through freedom or is only actual to us through the actualization of our freedom, a freedom commonly dormant or passive, and only enacted by way of actual challenges. Interior freedom is not born until the advent of Christianity, after which it is the very center of the epistles and the gospels, thereby making possible the ultimate breakthrough of Augustine, the most revolutionary of all Christian thinkers.

Perhaps Augustine is also our most paradoxical thinker, and is so as that thinker who discovered both an interior freedom and an eternal Predestination, each inseparable from the other, and each only real in relation to the other. While

Augustine only realized Predestination in his profound conflicts with Christian heterodoxy, a heterodoxy that he could know as being virtually everywhere, he discovered a uniquely Augustinian freedom in his own solitary voyages, a freedom inseparable from a new self-consciousness, and one issuing in the discovery of the genre of autobiography in the writing of the *Confessions*. Few realize how absolutely new an Augustinian self-consciousness is, or realize how inseparable it is from an absolutely new Predestination, a Predestination that is both an eternal Predestination and a Predestination that here and now is all in all. What is most unique about the Augustinian self-consciousness is that it is absolutely inseparable from grace, and from that grace of God that is closer to us than we are to ourselves, only thereby is Predestination all in all, and is all in all in an absolutely new and total immanence.

This is a uniquely Augustinian absolute immanence which is identical with a uniquely Augustinian absolute transcendence, when for the first time immanence and transcendence wholly pass into or flow into each other. Even if the overlap of absolute immanence and transcendence is introduced by the Incarnation, it only enters into or transforms consciousness itself in the Augustinian revolution. Yet this is also a revolution that knows damnation more deeply and more purely than it has ever been known before, an inevitable consequence of a new Predestination, one wholly discovered by Augustine, just as it is wholly alien to Eastern Christianity. Indeed, it is precisely Predestination that calls forth the absolute ubiquity of grace, or the absolute ubiquity of the will of God, one equally responsible for salvation and damnation, a damnation and salvation only possible through the will of God, and only enacted or actualized by the eternal will of God. This eternal will is absolutely free and its enactments are absolutely free enactments, and thus wholly independent of everything outside themselves.

Is it possible to imagine a homecoming to our eternal judgment or to imagine such a homecoming as not being one to our eternal damnation, for can we actually know our eternal condition as not being one of damnation? Christian apologists have long known that actually to evoke the name of God is to evoke an eternal judgment, a judgment that can only be an absolutely negative judgment apart from grace, and a judgment that is evoked in us by every genuine pronunciation of the name of God. This is the great secret of homiletics: fully to pronounce the name of God is to induce an ultimate shock, but this is a shock occurring in the imaginative realm as well, as fully manifest not only in *Moby Dick*, but in each of our great imaginative enactments, whose very greatness can even be measured by the degree to which they embody or evoke such a challenge or shock.

Now there simply is no greater shock than an initiation into our own damnation, and if Jonathan Edwards is our greatest preacher, this is most purely manifest in his sermons on damnation, which are certainly the most famous and influential sermons in America, sermons inevitably inducing an ultimate terror, and one intended to issue in conversion. William James captured this beautifully in his lectures on conversion in *The Varieties of Religious Experience*, just as he embodied it in his understanding of the "sick soul," and even as only the sick soul is capable of conversion, only the damned are capable of redemption. Perhaps this is the most dramatic realization of a uniquely Christian *felix culpa*, a fortunate fall apart from which there could be no redemption and apart from which there could be no actual realization of absolute glory. This is the very point at which we can become most resolutely aware of a deep and ultimate ground of Christian art, literature, and music: a profound negativity is absolutely necessary for a uniquely Christian imagination, and one found nowhere else in the world.

This is the negativity that is so profoundly and so universally called forth by Hegel, but so too is it primal in Dante, Milton, and Blake, a negativity apart from which no ultimate life or energy is possible, and if damnation is a pure negativity, it is nevertheless finally inseparable from its very opposite. That is precisely why damnation is a *felix culpa*, a fortunate fall in its ultimate effect, a fall apart from which there could be no realization of absolute glory, and not even a realization of the absolute glory of the Godhead. Here, the primal word "real" is all important, for there is an overwhelming difference between the primordial and the actual, or between primordial Godhead and a fully realized or fully actual Godhead, an actuality only possible by way of an absolute transcendence of primordial Godhead, a transcendence realizing a wholly new actuality, and therefore an absolutely new Godhead. This is the Godhead that is the consequence of apocalypse itself, hence it is an apocalyptic Godhead, and if only thereby one wholly transcending primordial Godhead.

The most ultimate Christian temptation is the call of primordial Godhead, one purely realized in Gnosticism, or a uniquely Christian Gnosticism, a Gnostic Godhead that in being absolutely other is absolutely other than itself, and thus is itself its own "other," and hence is necessarily a dualistic or dichotomous Godhead. Christian orthodoxy was only born by way of an ultimate conflict with Gnosticism, a conflict that has never come to an end, and just as orthodoxy is inseparable from heterodoxy, the orthodox God is inseparable from the Gnostic God and can be realized only by opposition to Gnosticism. While the Gnostic God is certainly not to be identified with primordial Godhead, it does evoke a Godhead prior to the Creator, and a Godhead absolutely opposed to the creation, a creation here known to be absolute evil, as for the first time there is an epiphany of absolute evil itself. It is seldom recognized that the idea or symbol of absolute evil is only fully born with the advent of Gnosticism, for even if Satan is known as absolute evil, epiphanies of an absolutely evil Satan do not occur before Gnosticism.

A deep conflict with Satan occurs in the New Testament, and occurs here as it never does in the Hebrew Bible, and now and for the first time an eternal damnation is fully actual in consciousness, as what Nietzsche discovered as an absolute No-Saying is fully born. But this is a No-Saying wholly inseparable from the absolute Yes-Saying of apocalypse, or of what Jesus uniquely proclaimed as the advent of the Kingdom of God, an advent in which an apocalyptic redemption is wholly inseparable from an apocalyptic judgment, a judgment that quite simply is an eternal damnation. As Nietzsche knew so deeply, a *horror religiosus* dominates the New Testament and is wholly alien to the Hebrew Bible, for it was

Christianity that introduced the world to absolute terror, a terror inseparable from a uniquely Christian redemption. Perhaps Barth is the one modern theologian who can face this truth, but it is deeply known by Augustine, and is primal in genuinely Augustinian theological traditions, even including Aquinas. So it is that damnation dominates Christianity as it does no other tradition or way, and if this is alien to modern expressions of Christianity, including modern theology, it is not alien to the deeper expressions of the Christian imagination, as above all manifest in the Christian epic from Dante through Joyce.

The language of the Christian epic is far more deeply Biblical than is our theological language, as most marked by the absence of apocalypse in our theological language, an apocalypse that was at the center of an original Christianity, and likewise at the center of the Christian epic throughout its history. Even a deeply apocalyptic Paul had to be wholly transformed to be absorbed into theological language, but a far deeper theological transformation occurs of Jesus' language, as an apocalyptic Kingdom of God becomes an absolutely primordial Godhead. Only Christianity has undergone such an absolute historical transformation, and this is inseparable from the absolute dynamism of Christianity, a dynamism embodying continual transformations, and even a transformation of the purely sacred into the purely profane, one creating an absolutely new and an absolutely unique secularism.

Has damnation undergone a comparable transformation in Christianity? Is it possible to speak of a purely profane damnation, or a damnation liberated from every possible sacred ground, or a damnation that can only be known or manifest in a wholly secular world? Now it could be affirmed that it is only after the death of God, or after the historical realization of the death of God, that pure or absolute evil is fully manifest or fully real. Accordingly, no previous evil is so horrible as are the horrors of Nazism and Stalinism, never previously was pure evil so purely itself, and after this advent it becomes impossible to think purely or even clearly about evil. Yet the depths of evil can now be imaginatively enacted, and this occurs after the death of God far more profoundly than ever previously, so that even the *Inferno* can appear to be more open to the good than any major expression of the late modern imagination.

Late modern prophets such as Blake and Nietzsche can know damnation to be universal in their worlds, and how revealing that they can name and enact damnation far more decisively and profoundly than can our theologians, as from their perspective damnation is absolutely alien to the world of theology. But if damnation is now unspeakable theologically, does that make it any the less real or any the less actual in our deeper centers? Indeed, could this be a sign that it is all the more real, as fully manifest in a Blake or a Nietzsche, or a Kafka or a Beckett, absolutely primal figures in late modernity who wholly transcend all theology? Yet, as here enacted, damnation itself is a truly transcendent condition, one going far beyond our common condition and wholly transcending a common humanity, and even if this occurs by way of an absolute negativity, that negativity is an actual source of an actual transcendence. This is the negativity that is now the deepest mystery, and even if it becomes absolutely rational in Hegelian thinking, a purely Hegelian thinking or reason or *Vernunft* has now either wholly disappeared or become wholly opaque or disguised, as decisively manifest in the disappearance of all genuine universality. Unless damnation is the one universality that now is truly actual and real, a damnation wholly alien to Hegel, and at no other point is Hegelian thinking more alien to us.

Now if Augustine and Kierkegaard and Nietzsche are the great masters of damnation, thinkers whose deep understanding of damnation is fully paralleled in our great imaginative creators, does a genuine understanding of damnation necessarily demand a full acceptance of it, as deeply occurs in Nietzsche, Kierkegaard, and Augustine? Once it was common to refer to all three of these thinkers as "Existentialists," and theirs is a thinking that illuminates a uniquely human existence as does no other, except for Heidegger, who incorporates all three of them in his thinking. But how revealing that it is thinking about damnation that most illuminates our existence, for even if this is deeply Pauline and deeply Augustinian, it is apparently alien to that secular world that so dominates our lives. Or is it? Does it reveal that world, too? And thereby absolutely reverse our common banality? Indeed, does this not occur in the great dramas of late modernity and in its great novels, too? One has only to think of Joyce and Proust, and if they gave us a universe of damnation, it is also a universe of absolute joy, and a joy perhaps only possible by way of an absolute damnation.

Thus, all too paradoxically a universe of damnation is ultimately a universe of Joy, no such ultimate joy is known or realized apart from damnation, which is why the Christian can know the original fall as a fortunate fall, a fall apart from which neither redemption nor apocalypse would be possible. If Christianity inaugurates an ultimate or absolute damnation, as so purely recorded by Paul and enacted by the Book of Revelation, only that damnation makes an absolute apocalypse possible, one uniquely embodied in Christianity, and in that ultimately new world made possible by Christianity. Here is a truly absolute *coincidentia oppositorum*, one progressively enacted by the Christian epic, as so purely manifest in the deeper and purer enactments of Dante, Milton, Blake, and Joyce. Thus, if an absolute apocalypse is alien to our theologies, it is not alien to the Christian imagination or to our most deeply Christian philosopher, Hegel, whose absolute self-emptying and self-negation realizes a universal apocalypse. Now even if that apocalypse can be reversed by Kierkegaard and Marx, this is a reversal and not a dissolution, one initiating a new totalitarianism and a new nihilism, but that absolute negativity finally makes possible the realization of absolute apocalypse.

PART III:
Uncanny Mediations of Homecomings

Chapter 10

Revolt Against the City? Art and Home in Iowa

Joni L. Kinsey

The year 2011 marked the seventy-fifth anniversary of the Iowa Writers' Workshop, one of the University of Iowa's most important and enduring claims to fame. Begun as a gathering of writers and students brought together in 1936 by University of Iowa English professor Wilbur Schramm, it is the oldest graduate creative writing program in the country and an internationally renowned center that has fostered the work of hundreds of acclaimed authors.[1]

Even though the anniversary conference included readings such as "The Writer as Outsider" and "The Necessity of Estrangement," writing about Iowa, about home and belonging, has been extremely significant for many in the Writers' Workshop and for the identity of the program more generally.[2] Building on the 1922 decision by Dean Carl Seashore that creative work could be submitted for advanced degrees at the university, the Workshop has long asserted that significant writing could and indeed *must* come from a place like Iowa, and that drawing from one's origins and locale can be an important source of creative and intellectual power.[3]

Although not all the work that emanates from the Iowa Writers' Workshop is either about Iowa or is a direct response to the authors' residency in the state, connections between Midwesternism and the program's identity have been persistent. It is surely not coincidental that many of the most compelling and well-regarded recent books to emerge from the program are set in Iowa—Marilynne Robinson's *Gilead* and *Home* being prominent examples.[4] And, in addition, there is something about Iowa City that makes it an appealing place for the work of writing, whether that ultimately refers to Iowa or not.[5] Many Workshop members have remarked upon this congeniality, expressing appreciation for the city that

---

[1]   http://www.uiowa.edu/~iww/about.htm [accessed July 30, 2012].

[2]   http://iww75th.uiowa.edu/reunionschedule.html [accessed July 30, 2012].

[3]   http://www.uiowa.edu/~iww/about.htm [accessed July 30, 2012].

[4]   Marilynne Robinson, *Gilead* (New York, 2004); *Home* (New York, 2008). Robinson is a member of the faculty of the Iowa Writers' Workshop.

[5]   Iowa City was designated a UNESCO City of Literature in 2008. See http://www. writinguniversity.org/index.php/main/unesco [accessed July 30, 2012].

facilitates and appreciates their labor and their art.[6] That this program exists in Iowa seems to many both quaint and a little exotic, a peculiarly exciting combination that offers an added ironic luster to the program's excellence.

Given the support that the University of Iowa has offered the arts since 1922 and the spectacular success of the Iowa Writers' Workshop since the 1930s, it may be surprising that the relationship of other arts on campus—or at least the visual arts—with Iowa and the Midwest has been noticeably more troubled and troubling. In contrast to the Workshop's pride in its luminaries and the celebration of their work, even when they have a regional flavor, the University of Iowa's visual and performing artists are rarely acknowledged in the institutional publicity, especially those whose work focuses on this region and its subtle and ironic charm. Even the state's most famous artist, Grant Wood (1891–1942), while celebrated by the larger community of the state of Iowa and whose American Gothic (Art Institute of Chicago, 1930) has been credited with being second only to Leonardo da Vinci's *Mona Lisa* (Louvre, c. 1503–1519) as the most widely recognized painting ever produced, is virtually ignored on campus and in university publicity, despite the fact that he taught at the University of Iowa for the last decade of his life, led a movement that positioned the state and the Midwest in the forefront of the national art scene, and has been the subject of a spate of important books and exhibitions.[7] The disparity between the reputations of writing and the visual arts at the University of Iowa, both now and in the past, is intriguing and offers revealing insights into the issue of home and our conflicted relationship with it. For both programs, Iowa and the idea of it as home has often been a distinctive element of their reputations, but for one group this tie has been a sustaining factor that has nourished its growth and development, while for the other it has more often been a source of controversy and marginalization.

Grant Wood's brand of Regionalism was quintessentially about representing ideas of home and Americans' attachment to it, but even though his portrayals were hardly a simplistic celebration (they were often tinged with irony and a subtle critique of the foibles associated with his subject), he and Regionalist art were nevertheless ridiculed by some art critics (almost all urban-oriented individuals from the East) who could neither identify with the sense of belonging he and his fellows found so compelling nor appreciate the power and significance of that

---

[6]   See for example Eric Olsen and Glenn Schaeffer, *We Wanted to be Writers: Life, Love, and Literature at the Iowa Writers' Workshop* (New York, 2011).

[7]   The comparison of the relative fame of *American Gothic* and *Mona Lisa* has been made by many. For a recent example, see Stephen Biel, *American Gothic: A Life of America's Most Famous Painting* (New York, 2005). Key texts in the Grant Wood historiography include Wanda Corn, *Grant Wood: The Regionalist Vision* (New Haven, 1983); James Dennis, *Grant Wood: A Study in American Art and Culture* (Madison, 1985); Jane C. Milosch (ed.), *Grant Wood's Studio: Birthplace of American Gothic* (New York, 2005); Thomas Hoving, *American Gothic: The Biography of Grant Wood's American Masterpiece* (New York, 2005); and R. Tripp Evans, *Grant Wood: A Life* (New York, 2010).

fundamental relationship. Their rejection of Regionalism was part of a larger effort to make Iowa home to a different kind of art and ideology, one imported from elsewhere that was based in a profound alienation from place and that denounced the connections the Regionalist artists sought to reinforce. The dispute between these factions had a lasting impact on the reputation of Regionalism far beyond Iowa's borders, affecting attitudes toward art in the United States ever since. Although much of the story lies beyond the scope of this chapter, the idea of home and all of its convoluted associations links the varied elements, offering new insights into the conflicting perceptions of Regionalist art and relationships of ideology, place, and identity.

Of course, being at Iowa or even drawing upon Iowan experiences has not led to the downfall of all the visual artists who have passed through the art program at the state's flagship university. Several exemplary artists such as Elizabeth Catlett (b. 1915) and Ana Mendieta (1948–1985), both graduates of the art department, made their reputations precisely by building on personal identity issues fostered through close association with place, and they are still admired, even at their alma mater.[8] But during the formative period of both the Writers' Workshop and the visual arts program at the University of Iowa, issues of region as acceptable subjects for artistic expression took very different trajectories, ones that have had a lasting impact on perceptions of that art and its creators.

There are many reasons for these disparities, but surely one is that even before the founding of the Writers' Workshop, regionalist writing already had enjoyed a respected history, both nationally and locally, most notably, of course, in the work of Mark Twain, the celebrated nineteenth-century writer from Missouri who built his reputation on stories of the Midwest. The early decades of the twentieth century saw a strong body of regional literature emanating from such Midwesterners as Hamlin Garland, Sherwood Anderson, Willa Cather, and others, even if some of it was more satirical than complimentary.[9] By 1915, the State University of Iowa, as the University of Iowa was then called, was home to *The Midland* literary magazine, founded by undergraduate John T. Frederick, who would go on to teach in the University's English Department from 1921 to 1930.[10] Devoted to short stories, essays, and poetry, *The Midland* specialized in and celebrated Midwestern subject matter, and although not all of its contents dealt with the issue of home per se, much of it did in various ways, and it provided an important forum for the work of a number of young writers, including Iowans Frank Luther Mott, Jay Sigmund, and Ruth Suckow. By the 1930s, over 150 so-called "little magazines" were being

---

[8] See Melanie Herzog, *Elizabeth Catlett: An American Artist in Mexico* (Seattle, 2004); and Jane Blocker, *Where is Ana Mendieta? Identity, Performance, and Exile* (Durham, 1999).

[9] For more on this issue, see Tom Lutz, *Cosmopolitan Vistas: American Regionalism and Literary Values* (Ithaca, 2004).

[10] http://www.themidland.org/index.html [accessed July 30, 2012]. The University of Iowa Library has the complete series of *The Midland*.

published all over the United States, many of them focused consciously on writing about region, with titles like *Space, Prairie Schooner,* and *Frontier.* Both Mott and Suckow quickly established themselves through this genre, Mott with *The Literature of Pioneer Life in Iowa* (in 1923) before he went on to write his Pulitzer Prize-winning *History of American Magazines* in 1938, and Suckow with her first book entitled *Country People* (1924), which was quickly followed by others such as *Iowa Interiors* in 1926 and most notably *Folks* in 1934.[11] Midwestern literature was a respected genre with a distinguished history.

By the mid- to late 1920s, regionalism was increasingly recognized as a serious subject in a number of disciplines and arenas. In Oklahoma, for example, the Harvard-educated folklorist Benjamin Botkin was publishing his *Folk-Say* anthologies and would go on in the late 1930s to direct the New Deal's Federal Writers' Project, a program that hired hundreds of writers to canvas the country and document local history and folkways.[12] But while Eastern critics tended to scoff at the trends, few were more contentious than those in the visual arts. The United States did have a long and noteworthy tradition of landscape painting that celebrated various regions, but this genre had largely fallen out of favor in the 1880s with the advent of Impressionism and other modernist movements. Although many in the art world were still anxious to witness—or to create—what Georgia O'Keeffe called "the Great American Thing" that would launch a distinctive national art form once and for all, the trends of the 1920s that were deemed acceptable by most art critics were almost wholly modernist efforts and none dealt with the Midwest.[13] Most art that addressed issues of place, at least west of the Hudson or outside the exotic Southwest where many modernists painted, was decidedly out of fashion during the 1920s. Even in the later part of the decade, as collectors such as Abby Aldrich Rockefeller were being drawn to early American folk art (often for what appeared to be its modernist form as much as its historical significance), the art world was still reticent to embrace subject matter that did not emanate from urban centers or that did not have decidedly modern qualities.[14]

---

[11]   Frank Luther Mott, *The Literature of Pioneer Life in Iowa* (Iowa City, 1923); Frank Luther Mott, *A History of American Magazines* (5 vols, Cambridge, MA, 1938); Ruth Suckow, *Country People* (New York, 1924); *Iowa Interiors* (New York, 1926); *The Folks* (New York, 1934).

[12]   For an overview of Botkin's career, as well as a fascinating study of FBI surveillance of his activities, see Susan G. Davis, "Benjamin Botkin's FBI File," *Journal of American Folklore* 122 (Winter 2010): pp. 3–30. For more on the Federal Writers' Project, see Jerrold Hirsch, *Project America: A Cultural History of the Federal Writer's Project* (Chapel Hill, 2003) or David Taylor, *Soul of a People: The WPA Writer's Project Uncovers America* (Hoboken, 2009).

[13]   For more on O'Keeffe and "The Great American Thing," see Wanda Corn, *The Great American Thing: Modern Art and National Identity, 1915–1935* (Berkeley, 2001).

[14]   Although not focused on Rockefeller's collecting, see John Michael Vlach, "Holger Cahill as Folklorist," *Journal of American Folklore* 98 (April– June, 1985): pp. 148–62 for a useful article on the development of folk art collecting in 1920s America.

However, the combined forces of new trends that were shattering old ways of life, farm crises, the economic collapse of 1929, and growing political tensions in Europe between the World Wars prompted new interest in rural and regional subjects and styles in the United States, in part because those traditions seemed either threatened in some way or because they offered some sense of psychological refuge—a touchstone of familiarity—in a time of great change. Artists of many sorts turned to subjects that were close to home and portrayed them increasingly in ways that were, if not old fashioned in their formal qualities, decidedly figurative or representational rather than purely abstract.[15] Many of the artists who would come to be associated with Regionalism in the 1930s, for example, had begun their careers in European-inspired styles and abstractly modernistic modes, but by the late 1920s were turning toward forms and subjects that had greater connections to issues of local relevance and expressed that connection in both form and content.

In 1930, for example, after a number of years of experimentation with fragmented Impressionistic brushstrokes used to depict foreign subject matter gleaned from several trips abroad, Grant Wood was newly embarking on what would become his signature style of precise rendering and smooth contours, applied to subjects that he knew well from long experience in Iowa. His entry onto the national stage came with that material; his iconic *American Gothic* was shown at the Art Institute of Chicago, was quickly purchased by that museum, and then widely reproduced.[16] People, even on the East Coast, were fascinated and oddly reassured by the dour couple who suggested in their stoic solidity that even in hard times, staunch, hardworking Americans would persevere. Wood was made into a household name through the painting, and he subsequently became one of the most prominent proponents for regional art that emanated from one's locale and personal experience.[17]

Although other states and regions experienced cultural renaissances about the same time, in the early 1930s, Iowa's home grown art was capturing the nation's attention in a variety of ways. In 1932, the same year as long-term Iowa Writers'

---

[15]   Grant Wood himself commented on this, saying: "In 1922, the *Survey Graphic* published a rural number and at that time, the editor, despite the most diligent searching, was unable to find creditable pictures (not photographs or romanticized landscapes) representing American life. Today were he faced with the same problem, the editor could select from an abundance of pictures dealing with rural themes, pictures that rank with the best that is being produced today in America art. He would find them the works of numerous artists treating various sections of our great agricultural areas and upon investigation would discover that in many cases, the artists live and work in the regions they depict." Grant Wood, "Rural Influence in Contemporary Art," *Regional America* (February 1936): pp. 41–3.

[16]   For discussion of contemporary reviews of the painting, see Evans, *Grant Wood*, pp. 96–7.

[17]   See Joni L. Kinsey, "Cultivating Iowa: An Introduction to Grant Wood," in Milosch, *Grant Wood's Studio*, pp. 11–33.

Workshop director and Cedar Rapids native Paul Engle submitted his M.F.A. thesis (a book of poems entitled *Worn Earth* that won the Yale Series of Younger Poets award and was published by Yale University Press), Iowa painters Grant Wood and Marvin Cone (1891–1965) and several others directed the first session of the Stone City Art Colony near Anamosa, a summer program that brought artists together to paint the surrounding landscape.[18] In 1933, Wood's work and that of those who would become his fellow leaders of the Midwestern Regionalist movement, Missourian Thomas Hart Benton (1889–1975) and Kansan John Steuart Curry (1897–1946), were exhibited together at the Kansas City Art Institute, and their paintings were touted as a new phenomenon that would be that longed-for Great American Thing. "One of the most significant things in the art world today," the New York curator Maynard Walker told the *Art Digest*, "is the increasing importance of real American art. I mean an art which really springs from American soil and seeks to interpret American life."[19] This was entirely consistent with Wood's own statement, "Rural scenes, characters, and events have emerged to a dominant position in our arts and letters and a great part of the creative work that is being done today is flavored with a close, solid relationship to the soil."[20] Emphasizing the broader significance of this, Wood added: "These modern artists ... are not producing picturesque landscapes or sentimental genre but are painting solid significant scenes of the great agrarian America which makes the industrial nation of machines and smoke possible." Furthermore, the region was, in Wood's opinion, superior to industrial America, since it was "the only region of the country that is not provincial."[21] In his view the Midwest was a compelling subject for works of art because it represented the fullness of the country's identity as no other area could; it was *home*.

As if to confirm the country's approval of this idea, a major turning point for Midwestern Regionalist imagery came in December 1934 when *Time* magazine featured Thomas Hart Benton's self-portrait on the cover—the first artist ever to be so honored—and photographs of Wood and Curry on the opening page of the story.[22] The three were, it said, leaders of a new movement that stood in "opposition" to "outlandish" European modernism, and it predicted that their art was the beginning

---

[18]   One of the best sources on the Stone City Art Colony is the website http://projects. mtmercy.edu/stonecity [accessed July 30, 2012]. Discussions of the Colony are also found in the books on Grant Wood cited in n. 7.

[19]   "Mid-West is Producing an Indigenous Art," *Art Digest* 7 (September 1, 1933): 10. See also James M. Dennis, *Renegade Regionalists: The Modern Independence of Grant Wood, Thomas Hart Benton, and John Steuart Curry* (Madison, 1998): pp. 57–9.

[20]   Wood, "Rural Influence in Contemporary Art," p. 41.

[21]   Wood was here quoting Thomas Hart Benton, who had said upon his move back to Missouri from the East Coast that "I am returning to live again in the only region of the country that is not provincial." Ibid., p. 42.

[22]   [Allen Jackson], "U.S. Scene," *Time* 24 (December 24, 1934): pp. 24–7.

of a trend that would "turn the tide of artistic taste in the U.S."[23] This was heady stuff, as was Wood's appointment that same year to the directorship of the Iowa Division of the Public Works of Art Program (PWAP), an early New Deal project that paid artists to paint murals in public buildings. Almost immediately the mural project and its federal funding came to the attention of the University of Iowa, and Wood was invited to conduct the project on campus, with his artists receiving college credit in addition to their government paychecks and Wood becoming a member of the art department faculty.[24] The alliance with the federal program and one of the new celebrities of the art world was enormously appealing to the university, whose art department had been languishing since the 1925 retirement of Charles Cumming, a painter from Des Moines who had modeled the program's curriculum on a century-old academic European model. When Wood arrived, he was considered a "modernist" who, with both his newfound celebrity and his novel mode of painting, was shaking things up.[25]

Wood and his regionalist fellows in a variety of arenas were shaking things up in other ways as well. Revolutionary New Deal programs were changing the nature of farming and many other aspects of rural America, a transformation in which Iowa's Henry A. Wallace played a leading role, first as Secretary of Agriculture and later as Vice President. Allied with these efforts was the federal government support for the arts, especially what it called American

---

[23]   Ibid.

[24]   The best study of Wood's involvement with the PWAP is Lea Rosson DeLong, "The Project: Grant Wood and the Public Works of Art Project in Iowa, 1933–1934," in *Where Tillage Begins, Other Arts Follow: Grant Wood and Christian Petersen Murals* (Ames, 2006), pp. 1–43.

[25]   The most tantalizing evidence of this is an incomplete copy of a document, dated June 1934, in the Edwin Green Papers, Grant Wood File, in the University of Iowa Special Collections. As the document explains, the original document was placed (and at the time of writing remains) in the cornerstone of what was, in 1934, the then new Art Building on the University of Iowa campus. Unfortunately only three pages of the copy in Special Collections (which is untitled) remain, but the first paragraph explains the situation: "This brief explanation of the present problem in the department of Graphic and Plastic Arts at the University is placed in this cornerstone in June 1934 with the thought that the outcome of the conflict between the conservatives and the liberals of the faculty will be known when this comes to light and can be interpreted with perspective. The leader of the conservatives is Professor Catherine McCartney, Acting head of the Department and an influential member of the Iowa Arts Guild established by Professor C.A. Cumming, while the leader of the liberals is Professor Grant Wood, who has played an important role in the Iowa Artists Club." The document continues with a review of the history of the department to that date, but the pages that describe the dispute in question are missing. At this writing, in late 2012, the fate of the now old Art Building is uncertain in the wake of the 2008 Iowa City flood which inundated the basement of the building. If the building is demolished, the papers in the cornerstone will be revealed and the nature of the 1934 dispute finally clarified.

Scene painting, a category closely related to Regionalism.[26] Regionalist issues, whether economic or cultural, became hot-button topics, both hailed and vilified, depending on one's perspective.[27] In the visual arts this polarization pitted Regionalism against Modernism, both stylistically and conceptually, with the latter favored unquestioningly by urban-oriented art critics and Eastern intelligentsia. As a result, each of the Regionalist movement's leaders—Benton, Curry, and Wood—faced withering criticism in the art press, even as the American public generally embraced their work and its ideas.[28]

Due to popular more than critical acclaim, Wood's work sold well, even during the economically depressed 1930s, was exhibited in major museums, and appeared prominently in many publications, including on the cover of *Time* in 1938 and in a number of issues of *Life* magazine.[29] He and the University of Iowa art department were the subject of a two-page spread in *Life*, and his message that painting what one knew best was the route not only to good art, but to a new and better future for American culture made him a sought-after speaker.[30] However, his detractors became increasingly vehement as the decade wore on, in part

---

[26]   There are a number of books on the subject, but see for example Roger Kennedy, *When Art Worked: The New Deal, Art, and Democracy* (New York, 2009); and Jonathan Harris, *Federal Art and National Culture: The Politics of Identity in New Deal America* (New York, 1995).

[27]   For more on this, see Robert L. Dorman, *Revolt of the Provinces: The Regionalist Movement in America, 1920–1945* (Chapel Hill, 1993).

[28]   In addition to the books on Wood, cited in note 7 above, see Dennis, *Renegade Regionalists*; Patricia Junker (ed.), *John Steuart Curry: Inventing the Middle West* (New York, 1998); and Henry Adams, *Thomas Hart Benton: An American Original* (New York, 1989).

[29]   The *Time* cover for September 23, 1940 depicted a Grant Wood drawing of the Iowa native Henry A. Wallace, who was then Secretary of Agriculture and Franklin Roosevelt's running mate for Vice President. The pair won the election and Wallace became Vice President in 1941. Grant Wood and his work were mentioned in at least 22 issues of *Life* in the 1930s alone (the magazine only began publishing in 1936). Some of these were merely passing references, but others were significant attention, as in the two-page color spread featuring his painting *Spring Turning*. "Grant Wood's Latest Landscape: *Spring Turning*," *Life* (February 8, 1937): pp. 34–5. Wood continued to be a focus of attention in *Life* in the 1940s, even after his death.

[30]   "The Flowering of the Valley: Iowa Trains Creative Artists," *Life* (June 5, 1939): pp. 54–5. The focus on the art program started the article, which continued through page 57, with discussion of the writing and theater programs at the University of Iowa. Longman, although chair of the art department, was not mentioned at all, a fact which surely irritated him, especially when Wood received not one but two photographs, one of which was a three-quarter page view. Wood was a speaker in many different cities throughout the United States in the mid-1930s. No comprehensive list of all his venues has been compiled, but see for example, "Easterners Look Wistfully at Midwest as Nation's Art Crown Brought to It: Wood Lionized on N.Y. Visit," *Cedar Rapids Gazette* (October 24, 1934): p. 4.

because of his popularity.[31] Among the most ardent of his enemies was his own department chairman at the University of Iowa, Lester Longman (1905–1987), a new Ph.D. in art history from Princeton University who arrived on campus in 1936 with the editorship of one of the discipline's flagship journals in hand, a growing network of prominent cronies across the U.S., and a determination to make Iowa the leading center for modern art education in the country.[32] Longman cast Wood as a reactionary who was at odds with the growing academic preference for what he called "internationalist" avant garde modernism, and the chairman launched a raging feud with the artist that dominated the remainder of Wood's life. It was hardly an in-house dispute; Longman publicly discredited Wood's work at national conferences, wrote scathing editorials in both his journal *Parnassus* and elsewhere about what he called the "dangers" of Regionalism, and he even leaked damning and salacious information about Wood to *Time* magazine that, to the artist's relief, was never published.[33] Furthermore, Longman's ideas were shared by a number of prominently positioned art critics across the country who worked in various ways to discredit American Scene painting in favor of avant garde modernism.[34]

Longman liked to criticize Wood for anti-intellectualism among other things, but Wood was hardly an isolated painter working outside the world of

---

[31]   The Grant Wood scholarship is filled with discussions of this issue, but one of the most compelling commentaries may be that of his friend Thomas Hart Benton, whose letter to the editor of *Life* appeared in that magazine's February 8, 1943 issue. Benton said that Wood (who had died a year earlier) had been hated by "narrow witted art professors, by nuts with aesthetic missions, by obliquely turned museum boys, boy [by?] professional intellectuals, by most of the psychopathic critical fry, by artists whose works were service imitations of those concocted on the boulevards of Paris—in short, by all of the sickly mob that hangs on the skirts of American Art." *Life* (February 8, 1943): 7.

[32]   A brief biography of Longman can be found at: http://www.lib.uiowa.edu/spec-coll/archives/guides/RG99.0031.html [accessed July 30, 2012]. Longman was the editor of *Parnassus*, one of two journals published by the College Art Association (the other being *The Art Bulletin*).

[33]   Longman's campaign is documented in the Special Collections archives at the University of Iowa (Edwin Green Papers, Grant Wood File). It is also discussed in several of the scholarly studies of Grant Wood, including my "Cultivating Iowa," pp. 26–32; and Corn, *Grant Wood: The Regionalist Vision*, pp. 46–61. Longman's editorials include "Better American Art," *Parnassus* 12 (October 1940): pp. 4–5; "The Art Critic," *Parnassus* 13 (January 1941): 53–4; and "Contemporary Painting," *Journal of Aesthetics and Art Criticism* 3 (1944): pp. 8–18. The incident with *Time* occurred in the fall of 1940 and is discussed especially in my "Cultivating Iowa," pp. 29–30 and in Dennis, *Renegade Regionalists*, p. 72.

[34]   The collaborative effort is revealed in Longman's collection of letters from prominent art historians, museum officials, and art critics to discredit Wood in 1940, all in the file in the University of Iowa Special Collections. See for example Longman's letter to Earl Harper, dated December 10, 1940, that forwards to university administrators a critical letter about Wood from Museum of Modern Art Director Alfred Barr.

the intellectual theories Longman favored. Not only was he a frequent traveler, but even at home in Iowa City, his friends and associates included a wide array of intellectuals. Wood and several men already mentioned, such as *The Midland* editor John Frederick and journalism professor Frank Luther Mott, for example, belonged to the *Times Club,* a group of some 300 individuals organized to invite creative thinkers to Iowa City for conversation. Among their guests were prominent writers, critics, journalists, and politicians, including Carl Sandburg, Robert Frost, Sterling North, Christopher Morley, Lincoln Steffens, Gilbert Seldes, and Henry A. Wallace. The official events were mostly serious affairs focused on discussions of contemporary politics, economics, and aesthetic and literary issues, but after the formalities the group often reconvened for drinks as the "Society for the Prevention of Cruelty to Speakers" (SPCS). The SPCS gathered in the rooms that are now, once again, called the Times Club, located on the second floor of what is now Iowa City's Prairie Lights Bookstore on Dubuque Street. There Wood and his friends socialized amid a space that Wood had himself decorated in what he gleefully called "the worst of the Victorian tradition." Sometimes the group even donned costumes, hilariously satirizing their own Regionalist interests and Midwestern manners more generally.[35] Regionalist frivolity was obviously great fun, but it was also a parody, consciously rebuking the contempt that Longman and his ilk heaped on all things Iowan, a joke those aesthetes would neither have understood nor appreciated.

In 1935, with help from Mott, Wood launched his own critical assault on the cultural animosities toward Regionalism in a booklet entitled *Revolt Against the City,* a manifesto that denounced the domination of European artistic styles and called painters, writers, playwrights, and others to a cultural homecoming—an emphasis on "native materials, an honest reliance by the artist upon subject matter which he can best interpret because he knows it best"—that would bring about a new era of cultural growth in America.[36] The text celebrated rural culture generally and censured the urban critics who had too long denied its significance, but, just as important, it was a strident validation of those who would focus on that regional culture in their work, whether visual, written, theatrical, or musical. It may be no coincidence that the Iowa Writers' Workshop was begun the next year. Certainly, Wilbur Schramm, its first director, was well aware of Wood, his work, and his interest in regional subject matter, as an early photograph of him and his wife mugging as the *American Gothic* couple reveals.[37] For Schramm and the other writers, revolting against the city and claiming home as the wellspring of their art, only helped solidify their claim as significant writers.

---

[35]	For more on the Times Club and images of the members of the SPCS, see Corn, *Grant Wood: The Regionalist Vision,* pp. 44–5; and Evans, *Grant Wood,* pp. 184–8.

[36]	It is generally accepted that Mott either ghost wrote or co-wrote with Wood the small booklet that is *Revolt Against the City* (Iowa City, 1935). The text is reprinted in Dennis, *Grant Wood,* pp. 229–35.

[37]	http://www.university-heights.org/jubilee/people.html [accessed July 30, 2012].

Wood and the visual artists were not so fortunate. Their activities, its success and widespread appeal, and Wood's embodiment of down-home Iowa qualities in his art and his personal demeanor, grated at Longman and many of his fellow art critics across the country who greatly resented the celebrated artist and what they considered his hopelessly provincial art. In a personal sense, the folksiness of Wood's imagery, the popular prints and illustrations he created, and the ideological call for the elevation of regional art not only went against Longman's own tastes and ambitions for his modernist program and American art more generally, but the pervasive appeal of those images and ideas, and Wood's position as the most famous member of his University of Iowa art department surely also fed the art historian's frustrations and insecurity at having landed in the hinterlands after a promising early career in Eastern universities. The accolades Wood and his Regionalist fellows received in the popular press seemed especially rankling to the department chair, who wrote withering and thinly veiled critiques of "illustration mongers who serve us for money and fame."[38] Wood's election to the National Academy of Design in 1935 and his several honorary doctorates in 1936–1937 only made matters worse, since this gave him real academic credibility, further provoking Longman's ire as he continually tried to dismiss the artist in overalls as a purely local sensation, a publicity hound, or a rube lacking in academic legitimacy.[39]

Longman's animosity for Wood and what he represented went far beyond personal antipathy, jealousy, and a basic disagreement about artistic taste. It devolved into a crisis at the University, corroding Wood's personal and professional life in his last years. Elsewhere I have cast the Wood/Longman dispute and the national controversy it mirrored in terms of *cultivation*. Each side, whether it was Wood and Longman or Regionalism and Modernism more generally, was dedicated to an idea of cultivation, but the term meant very different things for each.[40] Wood and his fellow regionalists in the arts devoted themselves to reconciling the two notions of cultivation, one that reveals human character through hard work with the soil and the other that aspires to create it through intellectual and artistic refinement. They believed that both could coexist in American art and that together they might help remedy many of the cultural conflicts of the era. They were enormously popular with those who identified with and appreciated their efforts, people who were themselves often cultivators, but they were vehemently opposed, ironically by individuals who considered themselves *cultivated* in the more abstract cultural sense.

---

[38]   Longman, "Better American Art," p. 5.

[39]   Wood was elected a National Academician at the National Academy of Design in 1935. He received an honorary Doctor of Letters degree from the University of Wisconsin, Madison in 1936, one from Lawrence College in Appleton, Wisconsin in 1938, and others from Northwestern University in Evanston, Illinois and Wesleyan University in Middletown, Connecticut in 1940.

[40]   See my "Cultivating Iowa."

Upon reflection, other perspectives seem even more compelling. As John Crowe Ransom theorized in his 1934 *American Review* article entitled "The Aesthetic of Regionalism," once humans have created a home out of the wilderness, "nature not only yields up her routine concessions, but luxuriates and displays her charm, and men, secured in their economic tenure, delight in this charm and begin to represent it lovingly in their arts ... It is the birth of natural piety, a transformation which may be ascribed to man's intuitive philosophy."[41] This piety, an affection for home that becomes a kind of spiritual attachment, lies at the heart of the controversy that divided Wood and his fellow Regionalists from their opponents in the world of modern art. The fundamental basis of modernism is arguably a response to alienation in the wake of any number of historical forces, from horrific wars to the vacuity of imperialist aesthetic styles. The result, both philosophically and in the formal constructs of modernist art imagery, is fragmentation, dissolution, and disorder, bordering on chaos. All of this, of course, is the very opposite of home and the domestic hope, if not promise, of connection, synthesis, and even redemption. These ideas, so important to Wood, even at his most ironic (as in *American Gothic*, for instance), were either regarded as hopelessly naïve by the modernists or utterly incomprehensible. Part of their reaction was surely an affected academic trait, still prevalent today, that privileges disconnection and critique and regards anything else as unsophisticated, but perhaps even more it was that the idea of home, of connection, identity, and spiritual renewal threatened the essence of their modernist mentality, that sense of being rootless, adrift, and alienated, that relies on spiritual despair. No doubt Lester Longman's exile in Wood's home state reinforced such conviction.

Before and after Wood's death, Longman wrote articles that stridently castigated Regionalism aesthetically and politically, and characterized the dispute not only as a matter of place, but also of class and nationalistic politics. "When an uninstructed public begins to pay money for what it considers art," he wrote, "... the temptation is great to paint pictures that sell like hot cakes instead of pictures that will last." He insisted that "Artists must still paint for history's elite jury," since only that class of judges could distinguish art that was good from the bad and identify that which was subversive, either aesthetically or politically. Mincing no words, he said, "Let those who know an anecdotal 'buckeye' point to it," and he called for the "defenders" of "true art ... to attack" that genre, a category of imagery that he called "communazi" art, since he claimed it had formal and conceptual similarities to the social realist imagery of Nazi Germany and the Soviet Union.[42] Just as damning, he called this entire aspect of American

---

41   John Crowe Ransom, 'The Aesthetic of Regionalism," *American Review* 1 (January 1934): p. 296.

42   Longman, "Better American Art," pp. 4–5. Longman described his own role in "The Art Critic," pp. 53–4, in which he wrote revealingly of his zeal in the Wood controversy: "[The critic] has a special interest in and devotion to the present and therefore directs all his breadth of knowledge into a single channel, which as it nears a contemporary and momentous problem narrows into a torrent of profound conviction."

art—a category which he never identified as Regionalism but which clearly was—as "the fifth column of American art" that was undermining our national culture from within.[43] If such reactionary art was not recognized for what it was and then rejected, he prophesied, it could only result in "a fascist revolution" led by "illustration mongers, who serve us for money and fame ... blood brothers of the new order that is so convenient to their material prosperity."[44]

Longman's vituperations became even more radicalized as the United States entered the Second World War, and he continued to express his animosity for Wood even after the artist's early death in 1942.[45] Longman remained at the University of Iowa until 1958, and indeed did turn it into a widely respected center for modern art, holding exhibitions of contemporary painting and emphasizing modernist styles in the curriculum. Among his more significant achievements was the acquisition of one of the pre-eminent works of Jackson Pollock for the college from his friend and modern art collector Peggy Guggenheim as a sort of signature piece for the school.[46] But over the course of his tenure and beyond, he and the art and art history faculty essentially obliterated Grant Wood's legacy on campus, leaving most students and faculty today unaware that the artist even taught at the University. Instead of being touted as an icon of the University of Iowa like the eminent writers of the Iowa Writers' Workshop, Wood and his achievements have been virtually ignored. The situation may be slowly changing, with Wood finally being welcomed home once again—in the form of a fledgling "Grant Wood

---

[43]   The term "fifth column" was very *au courant* when Longman wrote this. It originated in a 1936 radio address by Emilio Mola, a Spanish general who was describing a group of subversive forces. The term was picked up by Ernest Hemingway, who used it as the title for a play and a book in 1938, *The Fifth Column and the First Forty-Nine Stories*. *Encyclopaedia Britannica*: http://www.britannica.com/EBchecked/topic/206477/fifth-column [accessed July 30, 2012].

[44]   Longman, "Better American Art," p. 5.

[45]   Longman never mentioned Wood by name in the press to my knowledge, but he continued his thinly veiled attacks on Regionalism after Wood's death. Moreover, he continued to write letters disparaging his dead foe to his superiors at the University of Iowa, a diatribe that seemed obsessive, even to the deans, one of whom finally said "let the dead bury their dead." Earl Harper to Harry K. Newburn, December 12, 1942, Edwin Green Papers, Grant Wood File, University of Iowa Special Collections. For more, see this file and my "Cultivating Iowa."

[46]   The work *Mural* (1943, University of Iowa Museum of Art) was a gift from Guggenheim to the University in 1951. For more on the picture, see http://uima.uiowa.edu/mural [accessed July 30, 2012]. The work has been the subject of controversy several times over the years as the University—or more correctly the Board of Regents that oversee the University—has considered selling the prestigious painting. For more on this, see the University's report at http://www.regents.iowa.gov/news/Pollockquestions1008.pdf [accessed July 30, 2012]. For a differing opinion, see art historian Donald Kuspit's view at http://www.artnet.com/magazineus/features/kuspit/jackson-pollock-university-of-iowa-2-24-10.asp [accessed July 30, 2012].

Colony" at the University and an accompanying biennial symposium at the School of Art and Art History that began in 2008. But it is an uncanny homecoming that is necessarily accompanied by revelations of unpleasant aspects of the University's past, especially its conflicted dealings with Wood's closeted homosexuality and the vendetta of his department chairman against him.[47]

Just as troubling as Wood's marginalization in his home institution was the larger trend of modernists in the art world more broadly to dismiss Regionalism and its ideals not merely as a misguided and irrelevant moment in the history of American art, but as subversive—ironically even as un-American—and to nearly expunge the movement from the history students have been taught for the past half-century. The most noteworthy perpetrator of this campaign was Horst W. Janson (1913–1982), who taught at the University of Iowa briefly in Wood's last years and who despised him almost as much as Longman did. Janson left Iowa for Washington University in St. Louis in 1942 and subsequently wrote several important articles that characterized Wood and Regionalism as fascist.[48] But, even more importantly, he institutionalized a negative view of Regionalism through his 1962 survey textbook *History of Art*, which has been part of the training of generations of students, selling millions of copies over the decades and remaining in print today. Until the voluminous text was substantially rewritten in 2006 (long after Janson's death), Grant Wood was not mentioned at all over the course of six editions, and Regionalism received only one scant, negative paragraph which went unrevised for 44 years.[49]

Today, in the face of cataclysmic changes just as dramatic as those of the 1930s, as we consider the rise of a host of new movements that sound remarkably familiar, such initiatives as Localism, and with the rise of a spate of new painters

---

[47]   The biennial Grant Wood symposium was inaugurated in 2008, a collaborative effort of the School of Art and Art History and James Hayes, the owner of the Grant Wood/Hayes House on Court Street. Hayes has also already begun working with the University of Iowa to develop the Grant Wood house and several surrounding dwellings into an arts study center which will be named for Grant Wood. For an early announcement of this plan, as well as discussion of the growing awareness of Wood's homosexuality, which was the focus of Tripp Evans's book, *Grant Wood: A Life*, see Tom Snee, "New Book Explores Grant Wood's Tumultuous Time at UI," http://fyi.uiowa.edu/10/04/grant-wood-biography [accessed July 30, 2012], an online article from October 2010.

[48]   H.W. Janson, "The International Aspects of Regionalism," *College Art Journal* [*Art Journal*] 2 (May 1943): pp. 110–15; and "Benton and Wood, Champions of Regionalism," *Magazine of Art* 39 (May 1956): pp. 184–6, 198.

[49]   H.W. Janson, *History of Art: A Survey of the Major Visual Arts from the Dawn of History to the Present Day* (Englewood Cliffs, 1962). Janson died in 1982 shortly after the second edition of the book was published. His son Anthony Janson inherited the franchise and supervised four additional editions. The seventh edition, significantly revised by a team of scholars (and no longer including Anthony Janson) was issued in 2006 as *Janson's History of Art*. In it, and in subsequent versions, Grant Wood finally gets his due, with a color reproduction of *American Gothic* and several paragraphs of balanced discussion.

of the Iowa soil who portray the land in both its pastoral and industrialized states, it seems apt that we reconsider our history's lessons in light of new questions. Where is home in an age of globalism, the Internet, urban sprawl, and the destruction of the vernacular? What role does regional art—or art generally—play in locating us politically, psychologically, philosophically, or spiritually in a place or time, and what does that mean when our surroundings are increasingly indistinguishable from every other place? What are the differences and relationships between nationalism and regionalism and at what point do the distinctions become significantly problematic? How can we portray identity through place in meaningful ways? While the answers remain elusive and ever changing, art's ability to convey the pervasive power of home and homecoming remains, despite the efforts of those who would deny it, a visual reminder of our uneasy relationship with where we live and how that defines us.

References

Adams, Henry, *Thomas Hart Benton: An American Original* (New York: Knopf, 1989).

Benton, Thomas Hart, Letter to the Editor, *Life* (February 8, 1943): p. 7.

Biel, Stephen, *American Gothic: A Life of America's Most Famous Painting* (New York: W.W. Norton & Co., 2005).

Blocker, Jane, *Where is Ana Mendieta? Identity, Performance, and Exile* (Durham: Duke University Press, 1999).

Corn, Wanda, *Grant Wood: The Regionalist Vision* (New Haven: Yale University Press, 1983).

Corn, Wanda, *The Great American Thing: Modern Art and National Identity, 1915–1935* (Berkeley: University of California Press, 2001).

Davis, Susan G., "Benjamin Botkin's FBI File," *Journal of American Folklore* 122 (Winter 2010): pp. 3–30.

DeLong, Lea Rosson, *Where Tillage Begins, Other Arts Follow: Grant Wood and Christian Petersen Murals* (Ames: Brunnier Art Museum, 2006).

Dennis, James, *Grant Wood: A Study in American Art and Culture* (Madison: University of Wisconsin Press, 1985).

Dennis, James, *Renegade Regionalists: The Modern Independence of Grant Wood, Thomas Hart Benton, and John Steuart Curry* (Madison: University of Wisconsin Press, 1998).

Dorman, Robert L., *Revolt of the Provinces: The Regionalist Movement in America, 1920–1945* (Chapel Hill: University of North Carolina Press, 1993).

"Easterners Look Wistfully at Midwest as Nation's Art Crown Brought to It: Wood Lionized on N.Y. Visit," *Cedar Rapids Gazette* (October 24, 1934): p. 4.

Evans, R. Tripp, *Grant Wood: A Life* (New York: Knopf, 2010).

"The Flowering of the Valley: Iowa Trains Creative Artists," *Life* (June 5, 1939): pp. 54–5.

"Grant Wood's Latest Landscape: *Spring Turning*," *Life* (February 8, 1937): pp. 34–5.

Harris, Jonathan, *Federal Art and National Culture: The Politics of Identity in New Deal America* (New York: Cambridge University Press, 1995).

Herzog, Melanie, *Elizabeth Catlett: An American Artist in Mexico* (Seattle: University of Washington Press, 2004).

Hirsch, Jerrold, *Project America: A Cultural History of the Federal Writer's Project* (Chapel Hill: University of North Carolina Press, 2003).

Hoving, Thomas, *American Gothic: The Biography of Grant Wood's American Masterpiece* (New York: Chamberlain Bros., 2005).

[Jackson, Allen], "U.S. Scene," *Time* 24 (December 24, 1934): pp. 24–7.

Janson, H.W., "The International Aspects of Regionalism," *College Art Journal* [*Art Journal*] 2 (May 1943): pp. 110–15.

Janson, H.W., "Benton and Wood, Champions of Regionalism," *Magazine of Art* 39 (May 1956): pp. 184–6, 198.

Janson, H.W., *History of Art: A Survey of the Major Visual Arts from the Dawn of History to the Present Day* (Englewood Cliffs: Prentice Hall, 1962).

Junker, Patricia (ed.), *John Steuart Curry: Inventing the Middle West* (New York: Hudson Hills Press, 1998).

Kennedy, Roger, *When Art Worked: The New Deal, Art, and Democracy* (New York: Rizzoli, 2009).

Kinsey, Joni L., "Cultivating Iowa: An Introduction to Grant Wood," in Jane C. Milosch (ed.), *Grant Wood's Studio: Birthplace of American Gothic* (New York: Prestel Publishing, 2005).

Longman, Lester, "Better American Art," *Parnassus* 12 (October 1940): pp. 4–5.

Longman, Lester, "The Art Critic," *Parnassus* 13 (January 1941): pp. 53–4.

Longman, Lester, "Contemporary Painting," *Journal of Aesthetics and Art Criticism* 3 (1944): pp. 8–18.

Lutz, Tom, *Cosmopolitan Vistas: American Regionalism and Literary Values* (Ithaca: Cornell University Press, 2004).

"Mid-West is Producing an Indigenous Art," *Art Digest* 7 (September 1, 1933): p. 10.

Milosch, Jane C. (ed.), *Grant Wood's Studio: Birthplace of American Gothic* (New York: Prestel Publishing, 2005).

Mott, Frank Luther, *The Literature of Pioneer Life in Iowa* (Iowa City: University of Iowa Press, 1923).

Mott, Frank Luther, *A History of American Magazines* (5 vols, Cambridge, MA: Harvard University Press, 1938).

Olsen, Eric and Glenn Schaeffer, *We Wanted to be Writers: Life, Love, and Literature at the Iowa Writers' Workshop* (New York: Skyhorse Publishing, 2011).

Ransom, John Crowe, "The Aesthetic of Regionalism," *American Review* 1 (January 1934): p. 296.

Robinson, Marilynne, *Gilead* (New York: Picador, 2004).

Robinson, Marilynne, *Home* (New York: Farrar, Straus & Giroux, 2008).

Snee, Tom, "New Book Explores Grant Wood's Tumultuous Time at UI," http://fyi.uiowa.edu/10/04/grant-wood-biography [accessed July 30, 2012].

Suckow, Ruth, *Country People* (New York: Ayer Co Pub, 1924).

Suckow, Ruth, *Iowa Interiors* (New York: Ayer Co Pub, 1926).

Suckow, Ruth, *The Folks* (New York: Ayer Co Pub, 1934).

Taylor, David, *Soul of a People: The WPA Writer's Project Uncovers America* (Hoboken: Wiley, 2009).

University of Iowa Libraries, Special Collections, Iowa City; Edwin Green Papers, Grant Wood file.

Vlach, John Michael, "Holger Cahill as Folklorist," *Journal of American Folklore* 98 (April– June, 1985): pp. 148–62.

Wood, Grant, *Revolt Against the City* (Iowa City: University of Iowa Press, 1935).

Wood, Grant "Rural Influence in Contemporary Art," *Regional America* (February 1936): pp. 41–3.

Chapter 11

Domestic Doubles, Generic Cities and the Urban Uncanny: Constructing Home in *Synecdoche, New York* and *Marwencol*

Michael Baltutis

… the better orientated he was in the world around him, the less likely he would be to find the objects and occurences in it uncanny. (Sigmund Freud, "The Uncanny")

Most of the architecture that surrounds us we barely see; in architecture, familiarity breeds not contempt but complacency. (Paul Goldberger, *Why Architecture Matters*)

In "How to Build a City," the essay that opens the Harvard Project on the City's volume *Mutations*, Rem Koolhaas et al. provide a tongue-in-cheek template that provides readers with the do-it-yourself opportunity to apply the Western model of urban planning to any square of open space. The resulting generic city (or "genericity") will contain a number of features familiar to residents of cities located in those areas whose urban planning has been affected by a Latinate model of the city of Rome, which is to say the majority of the world's population. These components represent the hardware required for the city's survival and include: the architecturally flexible Basilica that can be used for commercial transactions and liturgical needs; the prominently displayed and monumental Arcus that commemorates military and legislative victories; and the infrastructural Limites that, taking the form of both walls and ditches, function to exclude barbarians, regulate trade, and establish "an interiorized urban condition."[1] Once all of these urban and imperial elements are in place, Koolhaas declares, "you have successfully installed your genericity … [and] you can begin proliferating your city."[2] This production and proliferation of urban spaces, based on a single central model, leaves readers with a sense of both amusement and discomfort: these Roman elements are easily recognized in the cities in which readers live, while the repetition of the constituent elements of every generic city compromises the formerly unique status that any individual city was once seen to possess.

This chapter will consider this production and proliferation of cities in the context of two films—Charlie Kaufman's 2008 *Synecdoche, New York* (hereinafter *SNY*) and Jeff Malmberg's 2010 documentary *Marwencol*—that depict similar examples of do-it-yourself urban construction. The main character of each film

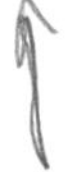

---

[1]   Rem Koolhaas et al., *Mutations* (Barcelona, 2001), pp. 12–15.

[2]   Ibid., p. 18.

engages in the meticulous (re)construction of a complex urban ecology via the production of the scale model of a city; in *SNY*, Caden Cotard theatrically reproduces New York City, and in *Marwencol*, Mark Hogencamp re-creates the fictional town of Marwencol, Belgium. Borrowing the language of *SNY*, we can see how each film treats its city as a synecdoche, the literary device that collapses the difference between part and whole.[3] Rather than simply creating ambiguity, however, these films employ the dual functionality of the synecdoche—in which the language of a constituent "part" is used to refer to a whole and the language of "whole" is used to refer to a part—in order to collapse the many potential referents of their symbolic cities. Thus, these model cities not only refer to the cities of which they are models (New York City and Marwencol, Belgium), but they also serve *both* functions of the synecdoche, as they simultaneously encompass the larger social and geographic worlds in which their architects live as well as the individual architects who built them.

Playing on Freud's notion of the uncanny, the theme of this volume, I will use the term "urban uncanny" as a means for understanding the significance of these built urban environments that replicate real and imagined cities. Though he did not consider film specifically, Freud asserted that works of fiction have the capacity to convey notions of the uncanny more clearly than does the real world. Works of fiction depict worlds whose terrifying settings and details lead viewers and characters to "that species of the frightening that goes back to what was once well known and had long been familiar."[4] The sense of the terrifying is encouraged in these films through their dual use of the synecdoche that recalls the opposing meanings that Freud asserted are inherent within the language of the *unheimlich*, the uncanny: "among the different shades of meaning that are recorded for the word *heimlich* there is one in which it merges with its formal antonym, *unheimlich*, so that what is called *unheimlich* becomes *heimlich*."[5] That which is *heimlich*, resonating with valences of domestic space, represents what is most familiar to us, but this familiarity easily shades into that which is most *unheimlich*, or concealed from us. The duality of the (*un*)*heimlich* reflects the central tension within each film, as its protagonists construct urban worlds that are both familiar and concealed, both domestic and public: reflective of the worlds in which their architects actually live, these model cities operate as alternative universes, concentric worlds, and shadows of their own urban selves.

Though these films utilize the double as their primary mechanism for depicting the urban uncanny, their architects do not randomly or coincidentally

---

[3]   In its part-to-whole function, the word "crown" can be used to refer to the king who wears it or even to the empire over which he rules, and in its whole-to-part function, the word "law" can be used to refer to an individual police officer whose job it is to uphold the law.

[4]   Sigmund Freud, "The Uncanny," in David McLintock (trans. and ed.), *The Uncanny* (New York, 2003), p. 124.

[5]   Ibid., p. 132.

encounter these doubles as they live and move in the universe. Rather, they actively construct these urban doubles and thus actively bring together the familiar and the concealed that lie at the heart of the uncanny. Far from avoiding the process of doubling that "often transforms a positive function into a negative effect"[6] and far from negating the double's primary valence of the "terrifying," the architects fully embrace the terrifying inherent in the double.[7] Both architects are repeatedly made aware of their own physical mortality, thus recalling Freud's assertion regarding the double: "having once been an assurance of immortality, it becomes the uncanny harbinger of death."[8] Neither architect is interested in simply dwelling on his past, however: each model city serves as a totalizing response to personal and relational crisis, and each architect places himself inside the new world he has created. (Caden refers to his double, and that of each character in his theater piece, as an "actor"; Mark refers to his, in more Freudian terms, as an "alter-ego.")

The dialectic of crisis and its geographic rectification that we see in these films plays off of other work in religious studies and anthropology. In using the term "crisis," I have in mind Robert Orsi's work on immigrant communities in Chicago and Harlem in the 1940s and 1950s, where the dual dis-locational crises of immigration and modernity affected "what people do with religious idioms ... and how [people] are fundamentally shaped by the worlds they are making as they make these worlds."[9] Karen McCarthy Brown, in detailing the alienation felt by Haitian Vodou practitioners in Brooklyn, uses the term "ecological dissonance" to describe the discordant relationships that sometimes obtain between urban architecture and traditional religious practice.[10] The urban idioms that the architects in these films employ reflect this dialectic of urban crisis and idiosyncratic but always strategic response that citizens deploy; these measured responses thus trouble "the mechanical creation of anxiety"[11] that Dawson attributes to the many "coincidental" literary examples that Freud provides of the uncanny and calls into question the standard response that the latter attributes to those experiencing the uncanny. Whereas for Freud, "The 'double' has become an object of terror,"[12] for Caden Cotard and Mark Hogencamp, the double has become a strategy for

---

    6   Robin Lydenberg, "Freud's Uncanny Narratives," *PMLA* 112/5 (1997): pp. 1072–86.

    7   Ibid., p. 1079.

    8   Freud, *The Uncanny*, p. 142.

    9   Robert A. Orsi, "Is the Study of Lived Religion Irrelevant to the World We Live In? Special Presidential Plenary Address, Society for the Scientific Study of Religion, Salt Lake City, November 2, 2002," *Journal for the Scientific Study of Religion* 42/2 (2003): p. 172.

    10   Karen McCarthy Brown, "Staying Grounded in a High-Rise Building: Ecological Dissonance and Ritual Accommodation in Haitian Vodou," in Robert A. Orsi (ed.), *Gods of the City* (Indiana University Press, 1999), pp. 86 and 99.

    11   Lorne Dawson, "Otto and Freud on the Uncanny and Beyond," *Journal of the American Academy of Religion*, 57/2 (1989): p. 293.

    12   Freud, *The Uncanny*, p. 143.

embracing the uncanny as they attempt to bring closure to their terrifying pasts and to negotiate a return home.

Synecdoche, New York

Charlie Kaufman's film *Synecdoche, New York* depicts the life, and apparently also the death, of Caden Cotard (played by Philip Seymour Hoffman), a theater director who lives in the upstate New York town of Schenectady. Feeling trapped by the limitations of its small theater scene—and constantly ruminating on his own death and that of others—Caden desires to move to New York City where he can direct more complex pieces for more appreciative audiences. His eventual relocation is spurred by two events whose simultaneity highlights the film's use of the double as a consistent strategy for communicating the total discomfort that Caden feels. His wife, Adele, an artist who paints in miniature, takes their daughter to her art show in Berlin, Germany, deciding at the last moment to leave Caden behind for their month-long trip. Crestfallen at their departure, Caden awkwardly and somewhat regretfully falls into the arms of Hazel, the red-haired woman who runs the box office at his Schenectady theater and whom Caden, longingly, will pursue for the rest of his life. This social crisis is met, however, with an artistic opportunity: Caden is awarded the MacArthur "Genius" grant, which urges him to "create something unflinchingly true, profoundly beautiful, and of unremitting value to your community and to the world at large." His response is to direct "something big and true and tough," a work of theater that depicts "the brutal truth" that he can finally put his "real self" into.

Despite the standard five-year length of the MacArthur grant, Caden's unnamed theater piece will take him the rest of his life.[13] More than simply one of the many clues as to the fantastical nature of his work, his theatrical production will utilize the double as "an uncanny harbinger of death" and the urban uncanny as a means for him to conquer death and to live forever. Kaufman's use of the double throughout the film underlies Caden's personal and terrifying confrontation with death, as Caden makes the function of his proposed piece clear to his cast at their first meeting: "We're all hurtling towards death, yet here we are for the moment alive, each of us knowing we're going to die, and each of us secretly believing we won't." Caden's summary is met with one response, uttered by Claire, an actress who worked with him in Schenectady and who will play (and become) his second wife. Her spontaneous response, "It's brilliant, it's everything," speaks to the universality of death that is the theme of Caden's piece as well as to the

---

[13]   Caden offers various titles for his as-yet unfinished theater piece throughout the film, each of which is apathetically rejected by the person to whom he proposes it: "Simulacrum," "Flawed Light of Love and Grief," "Unknown, Unkissed and Lost," "The Obscure Moon Lighting an Obscure World," and "Infectious Diseases in Cattle."

synecdochal structure—the doubles of both characters and setting—that will be established throughout the film.

Caden doubles his characters in a variety of ways. He directs individual actors to appear in different stages of their lives; he has several key actors play multiple characters (and vice versa); and, in playing these multiple roles, Caden's character (and those of other actors) undergoes a complete gender transformation as he begins to "lose even more of himself."[14] This duplication of characters is encouraged, even necessitated, by the concentric structure of Caden's urban model.[15] The setting for his piece, an abandoned warehouse in the heart of the city's theater district, provides one of the most concrete instances of the terrifying double; like the red-light district in the small Italian town to which Freud uncannily returns,[16] Caden's model city contains multiple cities in concentrically arranged warehouses inside the original to which he cannot help but return.[17] The urban uncanny is a result of Caden's architectural work that requires a precise doubling of, and thus a constant return to, his real life; Caden simply re-stages scenes in which actors in the inner warehouses, actors who receive notes that "correspond to the notes that I truly receive every day from my God," are required to play the actors who work in the outer warehouses, *ad infinitum* and *ad absurdum*. Though Caden's meticulous doubling allows him to gaze intently into the "murky cowardly depths of my lonely, fucked-up being," the precision with which he multiplies these incidents prevents him from fully rectifying the crises that comprise his life's story.[18]

Throughout the film, funerals serve as crucibles in which personal identities and intimate relationships are replayed and, inevitably, replicated. At her mother's funeral, Claire recalls that she "used to be a baby"; at his father's funeral, Caden learns of how badly he suffered and of how little was left of him at death; and at his mother's funeral, Caden has a one-night stand with Tammy, Hazel's double, though she later admits to having been hungover. The film's final funeral is that of Sammy, Caden's double, at which Caden says regarding his play: "I know how to do it now. There are nearly thirteen million people in the world … And none of those people is an extra. They're all leads in their own stories. They have to be given their due." Though every event in Caden's play occurs multiple times as he

---

[14]　This is paraphrased from an earlier statement made by Sammy, Caden's double, as he told Caden of his desired goal for Caden's re-performance of his life.

[15]　Lydenberg refers to Freud's own similar doubling of characters in 'The Uncanny," where "Freud defensively doubles himself in his personal anecdotes, splitting into controlling narrator and helpless protagonist." See Lydenberg, "Freud's Uncanny Narratives," p. 1080.

[16]　Freud, *The Uncanny*, p. 144.

[17]　*Synecdoche, New York*, like "'The Uncanny', reminds us not only that there is no place like home, but that, in another sense, there is no other place." See Hugh Haughton, 'Introduction,' in Freud, *The Uncanny*, p. xlix.

[18]　Caden's outburst here is a response to a question that an actor asks Caden at a "practice": "Caden … It's been seventeen years. When are we finally going to get an audience?"

stages it within each warehouse, Sammy's funeral is the only event that Kaufman actually *shows* multiple times. Providing a summarizing synecdoche between New York City and the entire universe, each staging of Sammy's funeral provides an opportunity for Caden to completely transcend his life-in-crisis and to arrive at a better understanding of his "true self."

During the first performance of Sammy's funeral, Hazel invites Caden home with her. Hazel's house, one of the most uncanny images in the entire film due to the fire that constantly burns there, serves as the double of Caden's broken home in Schenectady and as a harbinger of the death that haunts him. Hazel purchased this burning house, despite being alone at the time and despite her fear of dying in the fire. Following her final night in the house, and finally together with Caden, Hazel dies from smoke inhalation, just as she had feared. After hearing the news of her death, Caden begins to acknowledge the limitations of his geographically and chronologically sprawling piece and, echoing the knowledge he gained at Sammy's funeral, leaves this message on Hazel's answering machine: "I know how to do the play now. It will all take place over the course of one day, and that day will be the day before you died. And it's the happiest day of my life, and I'll be able to really live forever. See you soon."

The second performance of Sammy's funeral immediately follows both Hazel's death and a switch in director, as Ellen the cleaning lady temporarily changes roles with and becomes Caden, completing Caden's gender transformation. Frustrated by Caden's passively repetitive style of direction, and contrasting Claire's seemingly simplistic statement at Caden's initial proposal ("It's brilliant. It's everything"), Ellen protests, "This is tedious. This is nothing." As she comes out from behind the director's table where Caden typically remains, she immediately shoos the doubles of Caden and Hazel off the stage, whispering to them, "Your scene's over, would you leave the stage," and interacts with the remaining performers, providing them with advice, encouragement, and props. The result of her direction is a scene unlike anything Caden could direct: in the absence of Hazel, who is now dead, and of Caden as director, character, or actor, the performers eschew the simple replication of Sammy's funeral, emoting and improvising, and allowing their creativity not simply to double but to finally resolve the terrifying life of Caden Cotard.

Marwencol

Jeff Malmberg's *Marwencol* details Mark Hogancamp's construction of the fictional Second World War city of Marwencol, Belgium. Built on a 1/6 scale model following his severe beating by five men outside a Kingston, NY bar that left him in a coma and with a shattered right eye socket, the city of Marwencol provided a means for Mark to replay and re-create—through architecture, dramatic play, and photography—both the trauma of his attack and the ensuing possibilities as he transforms some of the most brutal moments in his life into a narrative of historical fiction. "This is my therapy," Mark states in reference both to his urban model and to the imagination that was to be the first part of his personal renewal. Just as Caden Cotard did in *SNY*, Mark carries out his renewal project through the mechanism of the urban uncanny: doubles of the people, places, and events in Mark's life are set within a Belgian town overrun by a Nazi SS squad, and his own personal double, the American officer Hogancamp, provides Mark with the opportunity both to recall the "vision of terror" that continues to plague him as well as to therapeutically move beyond it.

Hogancamp's arrival in Marwencol town reflects the suddenness of Mark's violent beating. After crash-landing his P-40 Warhawk into a field, he walks for several miles, where he discovers a town inhabited by 27 beautiful women and no men. Despite Mark's former life as an alcoholic having been physically beaten out of him, Marwencol's single bar—named Hogancamp's—represents the geographic and narrative center of town. Loosely modeled on the Anchorage Bar in Kingston where Mark works, Hogancamp's served as a shelter for the women and as the point of attraction for the Nazis who had earlier killed all the town's men. More than any other place in Marwencol, Hogancamp's allows Mark to narratively rebuild his life and to heroically protect the town's women from the attacking Nazis.

Like Caden's model city in *SNY*, Marwencol town is inhabited by family members and friends who have played significant roles in Mark's life before and after his attack. This includes Mark's mother, his roommate, the Anchorage Bar owner, the local district attorney who worked on Mark's case, and even the director of the film. Mark refers to their representative objects as "dolls"—the men are represented by eight-inch high G.I. Joe action figures that were popular in the 1970s and the women by plastic Barbies—and to each character as an "alter-ego," "a double that could do things that they could never do."[19] The projection of identities—usually heroic—onto these doubles allows Mark to further work out the issues of gender identity that he had been dealing with even before his Kingston attack, an attack immediately precipitated by his admission of cross-dressing. Reminiscent of how Caden undergoes a full gender transformation in the climax of *SNY*, Mark wrestles with the degree to which he can publicly display his private desire to wear women's clothing in public. All of these conflicts simultaneously come to a head near the middle of *Marwencol* in a series of scenes that make explicit the film's underlying gender issues.

Hogancamp and some friendly "town Germans" hatch a plan to infiltrate the SS and get their town back. Hogancamp is taken to the church as their "prisoner," but the SS quickly thwart their plans; he is detained, interrogated, and tortured, and the soldiers administer a long cut to the right side of his face, the side of his face that was injured in Mark's Kingston attack. Unwilling to wait for the townspeople's plan to free him, three women of Marwencol enter the church, still

---

[19]   These figures recall the doll Olympia in Hoffmann's "The Sand-Man," the short story that provides one of the significant narrative foundations of Freud's "The Uncanny."

filled with Nazi soldiers, with bottles of liquor in front of them and guns behind their backs. Several scenes graphically depict the women, having traded their military uniforms for Barbie clothes, dispatching their Nazi enemies: Jacqueline approaches one soldier from behind and cuts his throat, blood spilling down the front of his uniform; recovering Mark's revolver, Anna shoots at point-blank range the soldier guarding the church, leaving him disfigured and slumped over in a pool of his own blood; and Kris, dressed head to toe in pink, is shown pointing a gun at the "worst SS guy," whom the women had wounded and for whom they had bigger plans.

To inflict their revenge upon the Nazi regime for their attack on Hogancamp, Anna sends out a call to all the town's women to punish this one SS soldier. In the ensuing minute-long scene, we see half-a-dozen women, well-dressed in long skirts or short dresses, high-heeled shoes or thigh-high boots, ponytails or long flowing blond hair. With a nationalistic song playing in the background whose doubling refrain declares "We did it before, and we can do it again," the women of Marwencol subject him to a brutal beating: as he lies defenseless on the ground, they cut him with knives, kick him in the groin, and stomp on every part of his body, especially on the right side of his face. Finally, as a "good old fashioned eye for an eye, tooth for a tooth sort of thing," Svetlana finishes him off with a bullet to the head, his hand raised towards her as his last mode of defense. This narrative cycle of violence and revenge replays Mark's original attack at the hands of those whom he refers to as "the stronger ones," but allows him to rewrite the ending; the women's act of vengeance reasserts the primary function of Marwencol town, to provide Mark with a modicum of safety and security: "This is no town that you can push over, and take over," Mark explains, "this is what happens to people who mess with us." Appropriately, Hogancamp and Anna are married immediately afterwards, against a backdrop of executed Nazis strung up in the town's square.[20]

However, this brutal scene represents just one moment in the longer arc of Mark's narrative, as a second SS attack unravels the victory just won by the town's women. This second attack re-establishes the dialectic of crisis that lies behind the architecture of Marwencol, and this doubled (redoubled?) attack reminds us that Mark relives his own attack on a daily basis and that his model city, while providing a locus for his therapy, articulates only one point in his gradual healing process. The film ends as two different threads of this process continue, and continue to double. In the first, the therapeutic function of Marwencol town is stretched to its limits as Mark reluctantly sets out for New York City, where he will put his model and photographs of Marwencol on display at a Greenwich Village art museum. Confronting both his desire to wear women's clothes to the opening and his fear of the outside world, Mark turns to his town's female doubles who "know me better than I know me." In one of the film's most touching scenes, Mark photographs

---

[20] Mark had been married sometime before his attack, but the character of Anna represents more of a wish-fulfilment than a direct correlate of his former wife.

his wife Anna and three other women as they dress Hogancamp in silk stockings, preparing him for his artistic coming out.

In the film's conclusion, we see Mark's double, Hogancamp, now with "a lot of wear and tear on his mind" following his attack. Requiring his own means of therapy, he utilizes a familiar technique. As Mark and Caden Cotard had already done, Hogancamp constructs his own double—also on a 1/6 scale—who builds and photographs his own miniature urban world. Mark explains: "My character in the story had to create something for himself, to deal with the trauma that he still had from being attacked by five SS, and beaten and kicked, almost to death. He found comfort in building his own little world, his own little town…"

Conclusion

The construction of specifically urban locales to rectify social crises might seem ironic, as these filmic examples of the construction of the urban uncanny appear to stand in stark contrast to contemporary genericities as they exist in the so-called "real world." Louis Wirth, in his classic essay "Urbanism as a Way of Life," bolsters his largely negative portrayal of citizens' collective urban encounter with Emile Durkheim's concept of anomie and its concomitant loss of "the spontaneous self-expression, the morale, and the sense of participation that comes with living in an integrated society."[21] Urban theorist Saskia Sassen highlights the "Global City" as a place marked by such social and economic factors as transnationalism, a cross-border economy, the impact of electronic space on urban centrality, and the potential for new modes of citizenship. Furthermore, both Sassen and Koolhaas include as a necessary component of their cities (both generic and global) their communication with other cities, as these sites open up "possibilities for a geography of politics that links subnational spaces across borders."[22]

The urban worlds in these two films were constructed and inhabited not to extend the political or economic objectives of a Global City, but as therapeutic devices that provide an alternative world in which its architect can more safely live. This active, agentive, and constructive process comprises one of the key points in what I have called the "urban uncanny" and resonates with other types of construction. Drawing on the sociology of Peter Berger, for example, S. Brent Plate asserts a constructive function for the form and content of the very medium of film:

> World making, like filmmaking, is an active intervention into the space and time
> of the universe. It is the performative drama in which we humans partake when

---

[21]　Louis Wirth, "Urbanism as a Way of Life," in George Gmelch and Walter P. Zenner (eds), *Urban Life*, 4th edn (Long Grove, 2002 [1938]), p. 73.

[22]　Saskia Sassen, "The Global City: Introducing a Concept and its History," in Koolhaas et al., *Mutations*, p. 113.

we attempt to make meaning of the spaces, times, and people that make up our lives.[23]

The constructive processes entailed in Mark's and Caden's work similarly recall the medical/psychological healings common among shaman the world over. Lévi-Strauss describes one situation among the Cuna Indians, where the shaman cures a sick patient using symbol, ritual, and narrative to bring together (and thus to purposefully collapse and confuse) the realms of myth and physiology and hence to abolish all distinctions between them.[24] This categorical collapse is facilitated by the construction of a "mythical anatomy" or an "emotional geography" in which "conflicts materialize in an order and on a level permitting their free development and leading to their resolution".[25] In the case of the Cuna shaman, the resolution is a healthy, because readjusted, patient.

Like these tribal shaman (and like these filmmakers), the architects depicted in this chapter construct emotional geographies whose therapeutic value is undeniable. They, too, purposefully collapse symbol, ritual, and narrative in an effort to bring about the apotheosis of the urban uncanny. The dissonant relationships between these architects and the spaces in which they live constitute a crisis whose resolution is best sought on the level of the urban, despite (and also because of) the alienating anomie it necessarily entails. A resolution is reached, in part, as the temporal nature of each model is reinforced: Mark packs up Marwencol for an art museum in New York City, and Caden's urban model is destroyed by an explosion whose source requires no explanation; his theater piece ends when—and possibly because—everybody is dead. Each architect thus prevents his model from turning into a fetish, an object that "instantiates its meaning, and ultimately its power, by virtue of its very being"—as he uses his model as a means to *transcend* the model, using the urban as a means to re-establish a familiar, though ultimately terrifying, home.[26]

Premised on more than just a "'two worlds' view, in which the simulated world appears to be the 'real world,'"[27] these urban worlds and the doubling effect that recurs throughout them allow viewers to consider the genericities in which they live as similar loci for meditating on their own identities and mortality.[28] Despite the

---

[23]   S. Brent Plate, "Filmmaking and World Making: Re-Creating Time and Space in Myth and Film," in Gregory J. Watkins (ed.), *Teaching Religion and Film* (New York, 2008), p. 221.

[24]   Claude Lévi-Strauss, "The Effectiveness of Symbols," in Ronald L. Grimes (ed.), *Readings in Ritual Studies* (Upper Saddle River, 1995 [1963]), pp. 368–78.

[25]   Ibid., p. 375.

[26]   J. Sage Elwell, *Crisis of Transcendence: A Theology of Digital Art and Culture* (Lanham, 2011), p. 21.

[27]   Plate, "Filmmaking," 29.

[28]   S. Brent Plate, *Religion and Film: Cinema and the Re-creation of the World* (New York, 2008).

"fictive" nature of these urban worlds, then, they still embody the communicative nature of cities as Sassen and Koolhaas define them, as their architects move across the semi-permeable boundaries that they otherwise cautiously patrol. Despite the status of these models *as* models, then, these cities are not completely isolated: their architects effect an adjustment to the outside world not simply through the *model*, but through the relationships that are continually remade in their bars, apartments, streets, homes, and battlefields.

References

Andraos, Amale et al., 'How to Build a City: Roman Operating System," in R. Koolhaas et al. (eds), *Mutations* (Barcelona: Actar, 2001).

Brown, Karen McCarthy, "Staying Grounded in a High-Rise Building: Ecological Dissonance and Ritual Accommodation in Haitian Vodou," in Robert A. Orsi (ed.), *Gods of the City* (Bloomington: Indiana University Press, 1999).

Dawson, Lorne, "Otto and Freud on the Uncanny and Beyond," *Journal of the American Academy of Religion* 57/2 (1989): pp. 283–311.

Elwell, J. Sage, *Crisis of Transcendence: A Theology of Digital Art and Culture* (Lanham: Lexington Books, 2011).

Freud, Sigmund, "The Uncanny," in David McLintock (trans. and ed.), *The Uncanny* (New York: Penguin, 2003).

Goldberger, Paul, *Why Architecture Matters* (New Haven: Yale University Press, 2009).

Haughton, Hugh, "Introduction," in David McLintock (trans. and ed.), *The Uncanny* (New York: Penguin, 2003).

Kaufman, Charlie, *Synecdoche, New York* (Sony Pictures Home Entertainment, 2008).

Koolhaas, R. et al. (eds), *Mutations* (Barcelona: Actar, 2001).

Lévi-Strauss, Claude, "The Effectiveness of Symbols," in Ronald L. Grimes (ed.), *Readings in Ritual Studies* (Upper Saddle River: Prentice Hall, 1995 [1963]).

Lydenberg, Robin, "Freud's Uncanny Narratives," *PMLA* 112/5 (1997): pp. 1072–86.

Malmberg, Jeff, *Marwencol* (Cinema Guild, 2010).

Orsi, Robert A., *Gods of the City* (Bloomington: Indiana University Press, 1999).

Orsi, Robert A., "'Is the Study of Lived Religion Irrelevant to the World We Live In?' Special Presidential Plenary Address, Society for the Scientific Study of Religion, Salt Lake City, November 2, 2002." *Journal for the Scientific Study of Religion* 42/2 (2003): pp. 169–74.

Plate, S. Brent, *Representing Religion in World Cinema: Filmmaking, Mythmaking, Culture Making* (New York: Palgrave Macmillan, 2003).

Plate, S. Brent, "Filmmaking and World Making: Re-Creating Time and Space in Myth and Film," in Gregory J. Watkins (ed.), *Teaching Religion and Film* (New York: Oxford University Press, 2008).

Plate, S. Brent. *Religion and Film: Cinema and the Re-creation of the World* (New York: Wallflower Press, 2008).

Sassen, Saskia. "The Global City: Introducing a Concept and its History," in R. Koolhaas et al. (eds), *Mutations* (Barcelona: Actar, 2001).

Wirth, Louis. "Urbanism as a Way of Life," in George Gmelch and Walter P. Zenner (eds), *Urban Life* (Long Grove: Waveland Press, 2002 [1938]).

Chapter 12

Phenomenology and Uncanny Homecomings: Homeworld, Alienworld, and Being-at-Home in Alan Ball's HBO Television Series, *Six Feet Under*

David Seamon

In *Not at Home*, editor and art historian Christopher Reed assembled a set of essays arguing that domesticity, home, and at-homeness were largely suppressed in modernist art and architecture, which instead focused on "a heroic odyssey on the high seas of consciousness, with no time to spare for the mundane details of home life and housekeeping."[1] In the final essay in the volume, Reed and his co-author Sharon Haar contended that, in our postmodern era, domesticity, home, and at-homeness are again gaining prominence but in two contrasting ways: on the one hand, as a site of inertia and repression; and, on the other hand, as a springboard for change and autonomy.[2] To distinguish these two modes of postmodernist challenge to the modernist disfavor of home, Haar and Reed spoke of a postmodernism of *reaction* versus a postmodernism of *resistance*. The former refers to a *turning back* to nostalgia and tradition, whereas the second refers to a *turning forward* to empowerment, reform, and resistance of the status quo. Haar and Reed claimed that the postmodernism of reaction replaces "politics with aesthetics" and leads to "nostalgic celebrations of the home and nihilistic ruminations on its corruption" that counter any future commitment to personal and societal reform.[3]

Ultimately, Haar and Reed saw little positive value in a postmodernism of reaction and, instead, committed themselves to a postmodernism of resistance in which home is "not a symbol of an idealized past, but ... a space in which we enact a better future."[4] In this chapter, I draw on Haar and Reed's postmodernist designations to consider writer and director Alan Ball's popular Home Box Office cable-television series *Six Feet Under*, which completed its fifth and final

---

[1]   Christopher Reed (ed.), *Not at Home: The Suppression of Domesticity in Modern Art and Architecture* (London, 1996), p. 15.

[2]   Sharon Haar and Christopher Reed, "Coming Home: A Postscript on Postmodernism," in Reed (ed.), *Not at Home*, p. 253.

[3]   Ibid., p. 259.

[4]   Ibid., p. 253.

season in 2005.[5] In this comedy-drama, widowed mother Ruth Fisher (played by Frances Conroy), her teenage daughter Claire (Lauren Ambrose), and her two adult sons, 30-year-old David (Michael C. Hall) and 37-year-old Nate (Peter Krause), occupy the upper stories of a Pasadena dwelling that, on its ground and basement levels, houses the family mortuary business run by younger son David and his associate, embalmer and restorative artist Rico Diaz (Freddy Rodriquez). The series has been called "one of the great family dramas of our time," presenting "gloriously rich characters, situations, and ruminations on life and death."[6]

In this chapter, I contend that, on the one hand, there is much about the home life of the Fisher family that represents a postmodernism of reaction. On the other hand, I contend that in other ways—including the fact that the presence of death is always calling the world of the living into question—this series' portrayal of contemporary inhabitation reflects a postmodernism of resistance. Drawing on the phenomenological works of philosophers Anthony Steinbock and Kirsten Jacobson, I argue that *Six Feet Under* intimates the need for a lived mergence between reaction and resistance if home and at-homeness are to become Haar and Reed's "space to enact a better future."[7] To highlight the central theme of this edited collection, I end by considering how *Six Feet Under* uses the uncanny as a means to propel characters' personal transformations and thereby point toward a more progressive mode of home and at-homeness, not only for the Fisher family but for the series' viewers as well.[8]

---

[5]   Alan Ball and Alan Poul (eds), *Six Feet Under: Better Living through Death* (New York, 2003).

[6]   Davd Blum, "*Six Feet Under* Finds Its Footing," *Wall Street Journal*, February 28, 2003, p. 15; David Bianculli [Review of *Six Feet Under*], *Daily News* [New York], March, 1, 2002, p. 123.

[7]   Anthony Steinbock, *Home and Beyond: Generative Phenomenology after Husserl* (Evanston, 1995); Kirsten Jacobson, "A Developed Nature: A Phenomenological Account of the Experience of Home," *Continental Philosophical Review* 42 (2009): pp. 355–73.

[8]   Commentaries on home and at-homeness include: Gaston Bachelard, *The Poetics of Space* (Boston, 1964); Alison Blunt and Robyn Dowling, *Home* (New York, 2005); Shelly Mallett, "Understanding Home: A Critical Review of the Literature," *Sociological Review* 60 (2004): pp. 62–89; Lynn Manzo, "Beyond House and Haven," *Journal of Environmental Psychology* 23 (2003): pp. 47–61; Jeanne Moore, "Placing *Home* in Context," *Journal of Environmental Psychology* 20 (2000): pp. 207–17; David Morley, *Home Territories: Media, Mobility and Identity* (London, 2000); David Seamon, "Gaston Bachelard's Topoanalysis in the 21st Century: The Lived Reciprocity between Houses and Inhabitants as Portrayed by American Writer Louis Bromfield," in Lester Embree (ed.), *Phenomenology 2010* (Bucharest, 2010), pp. 225–43; Henry M. Seiden, "On the Longing for Home," in Brent Willock, Lori C. Bohm, and Rebecca Coleman Curtis (eds), *Loneliness and Longing: Conscious and Unconscious Aspects* (London, 2012), pp. 267–79; Gerry Smyth and Jo Croft (eds), *Our House: The Representation of Domestic Space in Modern Culture* (New York, 2006).

Six Feet Under as a Postmodernism of Reaction

Haar and Reed claimed that, in a postmodernism of reaction, "the attractions of adventure and change … pale before the pleasures of stasis."[9] They pointed to evidence of this reactional mode in the traditionalist architectural dwelling styles of architect Andres Duany's new urbanism, and in the dwelling phenomenologies of Gaston Bachelard and Emmanuel Levinas, grounded in what Haar and Reed identified as the "pabulum of Heideggerian nostalgia."[10] They accused Bachelard, for example, of conflating dwelling with convention through his argument that the home is constituted through supportive childhood memories. In other words, "inhabited space" is "the non-I that protects the I."[11]

There are many aspects of *Six Feet Under* that can be associated with a postmodernism of reaction. Architecturally, the Los Angeles house standing in for the Fisher home and business can easily be associated with the revival-style dwellings of new-urbanist communities like Seaside, Florida or Kentlands, Maryland. Built at the turn of the last century in an architectural style that would correctly be labeled "Craftsman mansion," the Fisher house is readily reinterpreted as a kind of American Victorian because of its peaked roofs, gabled dormers, prominent window bays, and generous wrap-around porch. As designed by the series' art director Marcia Hinds-Johnson, the first-floor interior where funerals are held continues the Victorian style, with wooden paneling, flowered wallpaper, plush, enveloping curtains, solid mahogany furniture, and potted ferns.[12]

The Fisher house readily reflects Bachelard's claim in *Poetics of Space* that the dwelling is both a vertical and centering being.[13] Bachelard placed the cellar as "the *dark entity* of the house, the one that partakes of subterranean forces."[14] In the Fisher house, the basement is the preparation room, where David Fisher and Rico Diaz earn their living by embalming corpses and making them presentable for open-casket viewing in the ground-floor viewing spaces, euphemistically called "slumber rooms."

The second and third stories of the house are the Fishers' living spaces; most prominently featured are the kitchen, sun porch, and dining room. The kitchen and the 1950s Formica table in the middle evoke Bachelard's centering quality of house in that many of the most significant events and exchanges propelling the series' storylines transpire there—for example, Ruth's learning that her husband Nathaniel is dead, or her asking older son Nate to stay on to help with family and business matters after Nathaniel's death. As Alan Ball explained in an interview,

---

9 Haar and Reed, "Coming Home," p. 257.

10 Ibid.

11 Ibid., p. 258.

12 Mandy Merck, "American Gothic: Undermining the Uncanny," in Kim Akass and Janet McCabe (eds), *Reading Six Feet Under: TV to Die for* (New York, 2005), pp. 61–2.

13 Bachelard, *Poetics of Space*, p. 17.

14 Ibid., p. 18.

the kitchen set was designed to create a cocoon-like atmosphere: "I wanted the kitchen to feel safe, almost like it has its own protective bubble."[15] The result is a space that seems firmly in place and unchanging. One is reminded of a nostalgic image of the solid 1950s American family, convivially gathered around a table of plenty, absolutely secure in their place.

Six Feet Under as a Postmodernism of Resistance

If, however, the Fisher house suggests a kind of enveloping domesticity associated with a postmodernism of reaction, it also evokes aspects of a postmodernism of resistance in that much environmentally is not what it seems. The house may at first glance echo the nostalgia of a well-ordered Victorian household, but the architecture also suggests elements of the Victorian Gothic associated with nineteenth-century Gothic novels and twentieth-century horror films: steep gables, pointed arches, mullioned windows, stained glass, and the cellar "prep" room where brothers David and Nate not only conduct business but sometimes play out repressed thoughts and feelings through corpses that seem to come back to life. The Fisher kitchen may appear cocoon-like, but the sense of containment is exaggerated by faded greens and browns, out-of-fashion appliances, and interior sun-porch windows looking into the kitchen, which in some scenes takes on the quality of a human "fish bowl" on display. The design aim, according to Ball, was "layers ... windows looking in on windows because the family is so insulated from each other and ... repressed."[16]

If the settings of *Six Feet Under* evoke aspects of both postmodernist reaction and resistance, so do the characters. When we first meet the Fishers at the start of the first episode, family life seems more or less ordinary and readily exemplifying a postmodernism of reaction. Other than the unusual fact that the house contains the family-run funeral business, the situation seems typical. It's the afternoon of Christmas Eve, 2000, and Ruth prepares a special family dinner that will include Nate, who is returning home from Seattle for the holidays. David has been reading an issue of *Mortuary Management*. His mother adjusts his tie as he gets ready for an early-evening funeral viewing in one of the slumber rooms downstairs. Ruth calls her husband Nathaniel, who drives his brand-new Cadillac hearse through downtown Los Angeles to meet Nate at the airport. As he lights a cigarette and sings along with Bing Crosby's "I'll Be Home for Christmas," Ruth tells him what groceries she needs and chides him for smoking: "You'll give yourself cancer and die a slow and horrible death."

---

[15]   Alan Ball, post-production commentary, episode 1, season 1, *Six Feet Under* DVD collection; see also Ron Magid, "Family Plot: HBO's Acclaimed Series *Six Feet Under*, Shot by Alan Caso, ASC, Bucks Television Conventions," *American Cinematographer* 83/11 (2002): pp. 70–2, 74–9.

[16]   Merck, "American Gothic," p. 62; Magid, "Family Plot," p. 74.

Nathaniel throws the unfinished cigarette out the hearse window, ends the call, and sings some more. Still craving a smoke, he reaches for another cigarette, his attention momentarily distracted. The hearse shoots through a red light and is t-boned and crushed by a Los Angeles city bus. Nathaniel dies instantly.

For the four major characters of *Six Feet Under*, their family patriarch's accidental death sets in motion a series of existential challenges that call into question taken-for-granted ways of living and impel individual and family efforts and breakthroughs that, in the final episodes, point toward a tentative actualization of Haar and Reed's "space in which we enact a better future." Over the five years of the series, the Fishers demonstrate that "living fully requires one to break away from social norms that are stifling and repressive."[17] Family members challenge viewers "to awaken and live with desire."[18] By confronting such "unspokens" as homosexuality, unfaithfulness, adolescence, promiscuity, mental illness, drug addiction, race, and class, the characters discover new "truths" concerning more traditional "certainties" relating to family, marriage, religion, and self-worth.[19]

For each of the major characters, this movement toward a more honest wholeness is different. As wife and mother at 17, Ruth never had the chance to discover who she is, and much of her story is determining whether she can find self-fulfillment as an older, independent woman. Ruth's adolescent daughter Claire is a troubled teenager and struggling artist who abuses methamphetamines, falls for unstable boyfriends, has an abortion, and feels she has missed out because no one noticed her growing up. Claire's older brother Nate left home when he was 17, partly because he and his father did not get along; much of Nate's story follows his finding something to live for, particularly after he learns near the end of the first season that he has a congenital malformation of blood vessels in his brain (AVM) and could die at any moment. Though at first he seems the most responsible and mature member of the Fisher family, younger brother David reveals himself in the first episode as a deeply closeted gay man whose story trajectory is gradually coming out, accepting himself, and allowing others, especially his family, to accept him.

Bridging Reaction and Resistance: Homeworld/Alienworld

Drawing on narrative evidence from *Six Feet Under*, I next ask whether a phenomenological perspective might bridge and even circumvent Haar and Reed's interpretive dichotomizing of reaction versus resistance. Is there a way to proceed phenomenologically so that one might portray a lived dynamic that encompasses

---

[17]　Thomas Fahy, "Introduction," in Thomas Fahy (ed.), *Considering Alan Ball: Essays on Sexuality, Death and America in the Television and Film Writings* (London, 2006), p. 15.

[18]　Ibid.

[19]　Ibid.

opposites and offers them space to meet in dialogue and perhaps constructively transform themselves? The need, in other words, is to move beyond Bachelard's domestic conservatism criticized by Haar and Reed, and to locate ways whereby home and at-homeness both stabilize *and extend* understandings and actions.[20] The recognition must be that "the house is very much of the world, that domesticity is as much an activity oriented toward the future as it is a state of mind rooted in the past."[21]

One conceptual way to envision a comprehensive, sustaining dialectic between stasis and positive adaptation and change is presented in the work of philosopher Anthony Steinbock, who drew on phenomenologist Edmund Husserl's lived reciprocality of *homeworld/alienworld*.[22] As Husserl interpreted it, the *homeworld* is the taken-for-granted, tacit sphere of experiences and situations marking out the world into which each of us is born and matures as children and then adults. The homeworld is always in some mode of lived mutuality with the *alienworld*, which is the world of difference and otherness but is only provided awareness because of the always already givenness of the homeworld.[23]

Drawing on Steinbock, philosopher Janet Donohoe described the homeworld as "a unity of sense that is manifest in a pre-givenness of the things of the world that constitute the norm by which we judge other worlds and by which the pre-givenness of other worlds becomes given."[24] Norms and normativity, in this sense, refer not to some arbitrary ethical or aesthetic system of right and wrong or better and worse but, rather, to "a foundational standard to which other places are compared in terms of our embodied constitution of the world."[25] The normative significance of the homeworld extends thoroughly into one's lived embodiment so that his or her lived spaces evoke a particular manner of comportment that "is not simply one's comportment toward this particular place, but simply one's comportment."[26]

Steinbock explained that the homeworld is a "normatively significant lifeworld" involving "an intersubjectively typically familiar territory in which we are 'at home'."[27] In relation to the homeworld, the alienworld presents norms different from what a person in his or her homeworld takes for granted. Steinbock argued

---

[20]   Haar and Reed, "Coming Home," pp. 257–8.

[21]   Ibid., p. 258.

[22]   Steinbock, *Home and Beyond*. According to Steinbock (p. 222, n. 5), Husserl's discussions of homeworld/alienworld are mostly found in manuscripts dating from 1930 to 1935, some of which are published in Edmund Husserl, *Zur Phänomenologie der Intersubjektivität* (The Hague, 1973).

[23]   Ibid., pp. 178–85.

[24]   Janet Donohoe, "The Place of Home," *Environmental Philosophy* 8/1 (2011): p. 30.

[25]   Ibid., p. 25.

[26]   Ibid., p. 31.

[27]   Steinbock, *Home and Beyond*, p. 171.

that the homeworld plays a central role in affording the identity we understand as ourselves:

> A homeworld is privileged because it is that through which our experiences coalesce as our own and in such a way that our world structures our experience itself. This constitutional privilege ... is indifferent to whether we like it or not, or to whether it makes us happy or miserable. The point is that the norms that guide the homeworld are our norms, our way of life, as that to which we have accrued.[28]

According to Steinbock, one crucial aspect of homeworld and alienworld is that they are co-constituted and co-relative in the sense that we always "carry with us the structure of our [homeworld] in the structure of our lived-bodies, in our typical comportment and in our practices"; we recognize the presence of the homeworld when we find ourselves in worlds different from that tacit typicality and normativity.[29] Steinbock explained the homeworld/alienworld co-constitution and co-relativity in terms of a *liminal* experience:

> By liminal I mean not merely that home and alien are formed by positing limits, but that they are *mutually delimited* as home and as alien, as normal and as abnormal. For this reason they are *co-relative* and *co-constitutive* ... [N]either homeworld nor alienworld can be regarded as the "original sphere" since they are in a continual historical becoming as delimited from one another. This is the sense in which home and alien are co-generative.[30]

Homeworld/Alienworld in *Six Feet Under*

If the homeworld is "an intersubjective sphere of ownness" and "our world," then, clearly, the Fisher homeworld in *Six Feet Under* is the unquestioned starting point and taken-for-granted world for each family member, though each character experiences and understands aspects of that homeworld differently.[31] Claire, for example, sees the Fisher homeworld as largely ignoring her; much of her narrative arc is "finding herself" in such a way that she recognizes the value of her family background but also realizes ways to move ahead that are true to who she is. Tellingly, the series' last episode ends on the morning that Claire says goodbye to her family on the porch and drives east to New York City to try her hand at becoming a photographer. In a different way, Nate, having left home because of conflicts with his father, must come to better understand who

---

28   Ibid., p. 232.
29   Ibid., p. 164.
30   Ibid., p. 179, emphasis in original.
31   Ibid., p. 232.

his father was and realize that he (Nate), though threatened with AVM, has a gift for helping others, of which he makes use by becoming a partner in the family mortuary business.

One way to understand the four major characters' transformative journeys in relation to homeworld and alienworld is to relate those journeys to modes of *liminal* experience that Steinbock, drawing on Husserl, identified as two—what he termed *appropriation* and *transgression*. On the one hand, appropriation involves situations of "the co-constitution of the alien through appropriative experience of the home."[32] On the other hand, transgression involves situations of "the co-constitution of the home through the transgressive experience of the alien."[33] In appropriation, we realize qualities of the homeworld through recognizing particular alienworld qualities as different from those of the homeworld. In a reciprocal way, in transgressive experiences, we encounter the alienworld and, through that encounter, recognize and perhaps accept in our homeworld potentially usable or helpful qualities of that alienworld.

For the four main characters of *Six Feet Under*, the Fisher homeworld continually shifts and transforms itself. Throughout the series' five-year narrative arc, this homeworld remains a resilient whole in spite of the fact that it is exposed to a wide range of appropriative and transgressive situations and experiences. On the one hand, there is a required shift in appropriation on the part of Ruth, who, remaining within the Fisher homeworld, comes to recognize and understand the alienworld of her son David's homosexuality so that it is no longer seen as "other" and becomes an accepted part of her homeworld. On the other hand, David, who is mostly closeted at the start of the series, must allow himself to move out into what is at first the alienworld of gay life and transgressively shift his homeworld accordingly so that his gayness can become an accepted part of his homeworld and that of his family. Similarly, Claire moves transgressively out into the alienworlds of drug use and mentally unbalanced boyfriends, but eventually discovers through the appropriative powers of her homeworld that much of the strength for her becoming a mature young adult lies in the positive familial homeworld support and love of her mother and brothers.

Steinbock described such shifts in homeworld as a "critical comportment" that "may entail the renewal of a homeworld's norms, revitalizing and renewing its internal sense; [this process] may even demand going against the prevalent normality, replacing old norms with a new ethical normality in an attempt to realize the homeworld more fully."[34] One of *Six Feet Under*'s most effective narrative devices to facilitate such critical comportment is starting almost every episode with a death—a young army veteran succumbs to Gulf War syndrome; a biker, on his Harley-Davidson, collides with a truck when riding to work as a department

---

32   Ibid., p. 179.

33   Ibid.

34   Anthony Steinbock, "Homelessness and the Homeless Movement: A Clue to the Problem of Intersubjectivity," *Human Studies* 17 (1994): p. 214.

store Santa; a porn star is electrocuted when her cat knocks heated hair rollers into her bath; a Thai convenience-store clerk is murdered in a robbery; a Latino gang member is shot by members of another Latino gang.[35]

In many episodes, these funerals provide a ready mechanism for bringing unusual alienworlds into contact with the Fishers' homeworld in ways whereby the Fishers themselves are often transformed, sometimes through appropriation and other times through transgression. Through a preparation-room encounter with the spirit of the dead pornographic-film star, for example, David comes to realize that his sexual attraction to men is normal, acceptable, and morally good, just as a similar encounter with the spirit of the dead Latino gang member gives him the courage to "be a man" in the sense of finding the courage to come out fully as gay. As the biblical aspect of "Fisher" intimates, the four main characters "are searching for an authentic way to live among others, according to their own internal rhythms, in defiance of any social [imaginaries]."[36]

With regard to Haar and Reed's postmodernist reaction and resistance, the broader point is that Husserl's language of homeworld/alienworld provides one descriptive and conceptual means for rejoining the division between home as static and conservative versus home as dynamic and in progressive relationship with worlds beyond. The split between reaction and resistance is reintegrated dynamically through the co-constitutive dialectic of homeworld/alienworld.

Bridging Reaction and Resistance: Being-at-Home

Besides Husserl's homeworld/alienworld, another helpful phenomenological conception is provided by philosopher Kirsten Jacobson, who explored the phenomenon of "being-at-home," which she envisioned as a tension between *passivity* and *activity*, or what I identify here as *inertia* and *impulsion*.[37] On the one hand, Jacobson pointed out that being-at-home "rests in the background of our experience and provides a support and structure for our life that goes largely unnoticed and is significantly beyond our 'conscious' control."[38] In this sense, being-at-home parallels Husserl's homeworld and involves a strong, inertial

---

[35]   There are two exceptions to all episodes beginning with a death: the first episode of the third season, "Perfect Circles," in which Nate has a brain seizure but survives death; and the series' last episode, "Everyone's Waiting," which begins with a birth and ends with a heartrending coda presenting how and when the major characters eventually die.

[36]   Dana Heller, "Buried Lives: Gothic Democracy in *Six Feet Under*," in Kim Akass and Janet McCabe (eds), *Reading Six Feet Under: TV to Die for* (New York, 2005), p. 78.

[37]   Jacobson, "A Developed Nature"; see also Kirsten Jacobson, "The Experience of Home and the Space of Citizenship," *Southern Journal of Philosophy* 48/3 (2010): pp. 219–45; Kirsten Jacobson, "Embodied Domestics, Embodied Politics: Women, Home, and Agoraphobia," *Human Studies* 34 (2011): pp. 1–21.

[38]   Jacobson, "A Developed Nature," p. 356.

force present most of the time but normally outside everyday awareness. On the other hand, Jacobson argued that being-at-home is "a way of being *to which we attain.*"[39] In other words, we may be motivated from within—i.e. impelled—to widen and deepen our world. In this sense, being-at-home incorporates a lived tension between unself-conscious stasis and self-conscious effort, and between inertia and impulsion. Jacobson wrote:

> We are beings whose experience of home is that of an *essential* and *inherent* background and foundation, but this foundation has been *developed* through our very efforts of *learning* how to dwell. So, although "to dwell" is inherent to our nature, "how" to realize this nature is something to be learned.[40]

Though Jacobson used the terms "passivity" and "activity" to identify the lived tension between the home's pre-givenness and transformative potential, I prefer "inertia" and "impulsion" because the words seem more appropriate for the lifeworld dynamics involved. From one perspective, the most essential quality of any lifeworld-as-it-is is its inertial dimension—in other words, most things and situations are taken-for-granted and not typically imagined otherwise.[41] In this sense, inertia is related to Husserl's homeworld of unself-conscious pre-givenness. This lived fact, however, does not mean that one is necessarily passive in regard to a lifeworld-as-it-is. Obviously, all sorts of efforts and actions arise in this lifeworld but, because they are mostly routinized and could not usually be supposed as otherwise, they remain in the taken-for-grantedness of the lifeworld-as-it-is. In this sense, these efforts and actions are *inertial.* In contrast, when one makes the effort to change one's lifeworld so that it becomes other than what it is (never an easy task), one *initiates* from within—there is an inner drive, or *impulsion,* as I have labeled it here.

I would argue that the narrative arcs of the major characters in *Six Feet Under* readily illustrate this lived tension between inertia and impulsion. For example, David's story is shedding traditional family structure, finding love, getting married, and making a family. On the one hand, this story arc is conventional but, on the other hand, it is arduous and even hazardous because David is a gay man who falls in love with and eventually marries African-American security specialist Keith Charles (Mathew St. Patrick), with whom he adopts two African-American siblings (Kendre Berry and C.J. Sanders).

What makes David's story particularly progressive and admirable is that his resolution of inertia and impulsion coalesce properties of both: a conventional

---

[39] Ibid., emphasis in original.

[40] Ibid.

[41] David Seamon, "Place, Place Identity, and Phenomenology," in Heman Casakin and Fátima Bernardo (eds), *The Role of Place Identity in the Perception, Understanding, and Design of the Built Environment.* (London, 2012), pp. 17–19; David Seamon, "Place, Placelessness, Insideness, and Outsideness in John Sayles' *Sunshine State,*" *Aether: Journal of Media Geography* 3 (2008): pp. 4–6.

humanist value system emphasizing family and kinship (postmodernist reaction) blends with gay and interracial marriage and interracial adoption (postmodernist resistance). In the last episode of the series, David becomes the sole proprietor of the Fisher funeral home and he, Keith, and their two sons resettle in the Fisher house. We learn that one son will eventually take over the funeral business from David, thus a cycle of being-at-home is repeated but in a progressive way not readily predicted. As Lorena Russell made the point, "Gay, yes. Interracial, yes. But still solidly middle class, centered on the futurity of children, and conservative in many ways."[42]

In evaluating the phenomenological interpretation of *Six Feet Under* offered here, one can ask how Jacobson's concept of being-at-home compares with Husserl's concept of homeworld/alienworld. Husserl's understanding is useful in that it assumes that otherness necessarily contributes to home and that one way in which the lived relationship between home and other can be understood is through appropriation and transgression. The homeworld/alienworld conceptualization is less useful in that it still intimates a stasis of place: the terms "homeworld" and "alienworld" suggest perhaps too much a kind of calcified lived geography rather than a dynamic process of human-becoming-in-and-through home place. Jacobson's conceptualization of being-at-home is helpful exactly for this reason. Her presentation offers a simpler, more processual portrait of how inertial and impelling life experiences and situations can shift the lived ground of homes and absorb otherness into at-homeness.[43]

For a phenomenology of home and becoming-at-home, one can say that an open sense of at-homeness, grounded in family and place, allows for personal and communal transformation for which both conceptions—homeworld/alienworld and becoming-at-home—provide useful interpretive possibilities. In this sense, one of the most affecting aspects of *Six Feet Under* is the main characters' transformative stories that might work as a vehicle through which television viewers recognize ways in which their own spheres of at-homeness might be impelled and transformed.

Six Feet Under and Uncanny Homecoming

In regard to this volume's theme of "uncanny homecomings," one can argue that, in *Six Feet Under*, the uncanny plays a central role in contributing to the potential transformation of home and at-homeness. If "uncanny" refers to unsettling moments in the homeworld when one suddenly encounters troubling experiences and understandings, then one recognizes that such situations fuel

---

[42] Lorena Russell, "Strangers in Blood: The Queer Intimacies of *Six Feet Under*," in Thomas Fahy (ed.), *Considering Alan Ball: Essays on Sexuality, Death and America in the Television and Film Writings* (London, 2006), p. 121.

[43] Jacobson was familiar with Steinbock's discussion of homeworld/alienworld and drew on his ideas in discussing how the home shapes perceptual experience; see Jacobson, "A Developed Nature," p. 265.

many of the actions, situations, and events in *Six Feet Under*.[44] Most obviously, the uncanny arises as people who die at the start of each episode often "return to life" and motivate the main characters to deal with some unsuspected or unclear aspect of themselves. In his essay on the uncanny, Freud explained how an intense emotional response can be introduced by the creative writer through "supernatural entities such as demons or spirits of the dead."[45] The result can be more powerful than the uncanny in everyday life: "the writer can intensify and multiply this effect far beyond what is feasible in normal experience ... he [or she] can make things happen that one would never, or only rarely experience in real life."[46] In regularly using "dead" characters to impel the Fishers toward a more ethical, humane homeworld, the *Six Feet Under* writers arouse in the viewer an unexpected emotional empathy that sometimes involves humor—for example, David's reactions to the "ghost" of the female porno star, who helps him understand that being gay is who he is. More often, however, these embodied spirits invoke deeper, spiritual emotions like regret, sorrow, resignation, or responsibility—for example, the rich sense of extended family and community that David feels when he, his brother, and his mother are invited to participate in the Latino gang member's funeral.[47]

---

[44] Freud, "The Uncanny," in Sigmund Freud, *The Uncanny,* David McLintock (trans.) (New York, 1919/2003), pp. 132 and 148. Useful discussions of the relationship between the uncanny, architecture, and place include: Susan Bernstein, *Housing Problems: Writing and Architecture in Goethe, Walpole, Freud, and Heidegger* (Stanford, 2008); Peter Homans and Diane Jonte-Pace, "Tracking the Emotion in the Stone: An Essay on Psychoanalysis and Architecture," in Jerome A. Winer, James W. Anderson, and Elizabeth A. Danze (eds), *Psychoanalysis and Architecture* (Chicago, 2006), pp. 261–83; and Anthony Vidler, *The Architectural Uncanny: Essays in the Modern Unhomely* (Cambridge, MA, 1992). David Lavery contends that the narrative genres present in *Six Feet Under* are complex; he suggests that, besides the uncanny, these genres also include the grotesque, the fantastic, and magical realism. See David Lavery, "'It's Not Television: It's Magic Realism': The Mundane, the Grotesque, and the Fantastic in *Six Feet Under*," in Kim Akass and Janet McCabe (eds), *Reading Six Feet Under: TV to Die for* (New York, 2005), pp. 19–33.

[45] Freud, *The Uncanny*, p. 156.

[46] Ibid., p. 157.

[47] Heller argued that these dead "only appear to the living, as manifestations of their inner questions and darker truths"; see Heller, "Buried Lives," p. 82. She referred to comments by Alan Ball, who explained that: "They're not really ghosts. They're a literary device to articulate what's going on in the living characters' minds, so I didn't want them to seem supernatural ... When death has touched your life in such a frighteningly intimate way, your entire world becomes surreal." In spite of what Ball claims here, one regularly feels in these encounters a certain eerie, other-world ambience that, in the moment, seems real and palpable. Moreover, these scenes are remarkably engaging emotionally, fostering a "suspension of disbelief" that is memorable and rare, especially in American television programming.

Another significant aspect of the uncanny in *Six Feet Under* relates to the frequent reappearance of dead Nathaniel, Sr. The uncanny, Freud wrote, "is that species of the frightening that goes back to what was once well known and had long been familiar."[48] Nathaniel's death exposes the four main characters to unsettling aspects of their personal and family identities that must be better understood and dealt with. Nathaniel's "ghostly" reappearance in almost every episode is an important narrative device for keeping unsettling aspects of the Fisher homeworld in sight. Through humorous or serious "after-life" encounters and conversations with his wife and children, the dead husband and father helps family members to see how their homeworlds in the past have mired them in place and how, for a more promising future, self-directed impulsion might move them ahead in transformative directions.

In this regard, one of the series' most moving scenes is at the end of the twelfth episode in season four, when David has been carjacked and almost murdered. Having just returned home from confronting the carjacker, now in prison, David is woken by a thunderstorm and walks out onto the balcony of his and his partner Keith's apartment to watch the rain. There on the balcony is Nathaniel, who says he's proud of his son for having the courage to face the incarcerated carjacker. "I thought it would set me free," says David, "but it didn't change anything." Nathaniel explains that he's missing the point: "You hang on to your pain like it means something—like it's worth something. Well, let me tell you: It's not worth shit. Let it go. Infinite possibilities and all he can do is whine." David retorts, "But what am I supposed to do?" His father replies: "What do you think? You can do anything, you lucky bastard. You're alive! What's a little pain compared to that?" David says that it cannot be that simple, but his father responds, "What if it is?" and places his arm around his son, whose head slowly moves to rest upon Nathaniel's shoulder. Through accepting his father's understanding and love, David suddenly realizes he should be grateful for what life has given him, including psychological suffering.

In its ingenious use of the uncanny to shed light on the unspoken, more hidden aspects of the Fisher homeworld, *Six Feet Under* offers provocative insight into Bachelard's claim that "All really inhabited space bears the essence of the notion of home."[49] If the homeworld is "our first universe, a real cosmos in every sense of the world," then a need is to understand and transform its more repressed, awkward, and unseemly situations and meanings into productive possibilities and results.[50] In this sense, *Six Feet Under* makes superb creative use of the uncanny to reconcile Haar and Reed's resistance and reaction and to move both characters and viewers toward a place "to enact a better future."[51]

---

[48]   Freud, *The Uncanny*, p. 124.

[49]   Bachelard, *Poetics of Space*, p. 4.

[50]   Ibid.

[51]   Haar and Reed, "Coming Home," p. 253.

References

Akass, Kim and McCabe, Janet (eds), *Reading Six Feet Under: TV to Die for* (New York: I.B. Tauris, 2005).

Bachelard, Gaston, *The Poetics of Space* (Boston: Beacon Press, 1964).

Ball, Alan and Poul, Alan (eds), *Six Feet Under: Better Living through Death* (New York: Home Box Office, 2003).

Bernstein, Susan, *Housing Problems: Writing and Architecture in Goethe, Walpole, Freud, and Heidegger* (Stanford: Stanford University Press, 2008).

Bianculli, David, [Review of *Six Feet Under*], *Daily News* [New York], March 1, 2002, p. 123.

Blum, David, "*Six Feet Under* Finds Its Footing," *Wall Street Journal*, February 28, 2003, p. 15.

Blunt, Alison and Dowling, Robyn, *Home* (New York: Taylor & Francis, 2005).

Donohoe, Janet, 'The Place of Home," *Environmental Philosophy* 8/1 (2011): 25–40.

Fahy, Thomas (ed.), *Considering Alan Ball: Essays on Sexuality, Death and America in the Television and Film Writings* (London: McFarland, 2006).

Freud, Sigmund, "The Uncanny," in Sigmund Freud, *The Uncanny*, David McLintock (trans.) (New York: Penguin, 1919/2003), pp. 121–62.

Haar, Sharon and Reed, Christopher, "Coming Home: A Postscript on Postmodernism," in Christopher Reed (ed.), *Not at Home: The Suppression of Domesticity in Modern Art and Architecture* (London: Thames & Hudson, 1996), pp. 253–73.

Heller, Dana, "Buried Lives: Gothic Democracy in *Six Feet Under*," in Kim Akass and Janet McCabe (eds), *Reading Six Feet Under: TV to Die for* (New York: I.B. Tauris, 2005), pp. 71–84.

Homans, Peter and Jonte-Pace, Diane, "Tracking the Emotion in the Stone: An Essay on Psychoanalysis and Architecture," in Jerome A. Winer, James W. Anderson and Elizabeth A. Danze (eds), *Psychoanalysis and Architecture* (Chicago: Institute for Psychoanalysis, 2006), pp. 261–83.

Husserl, Edmund, *Zur Phänomenologie der Intersubjektivität* (The Hague: Martinus Nijhoff, 1973).

Jacobson, Kirsten, "A Developed Nature: A Phenomenological Account of the Experience of Home," *Continental Philosophy Review* 42 (2009): 355–73.

Jacobson, Kirsten, "The Experience of Home and the Space of Citizenship," *Southern Journal of Philosophy* 48/3 (2010): 219–45.

Jacobson, Kirsten, "Embodied Domestics, Embodied Politics: Women, Home, and Agoraphobia," *Human Studies* 34 (2011): 1–21.

Lavery, David, "'It's Not Television: It's Magic Realism': The Mundane, the Grotesque, and the Fantastic in *Six Feet Under*," in Kim Akass and Janet McCabe (eds), *Reading Six Feet Under: TV to Die for* (New York: I.B. Tauris, 2005), pp. 19–33.

Magid, Ron, "Family Plot: HBO's Acclaimed Series *Six Feet Under,* Shot by Alan Caso, ASC, Bucks Television Conventions," *American Cinematographer* 83/11 (2002): 70–2, 74–9.

Mallett, Shelly, "Understanding Home: A Critical Review of the Literature," *Sociological Review* 60 (2004): 62–89.

Manzo, Lynn, "Beyond House and Haven," *Journal of Environmental Psychology* 23 (2003): 47–61.

Merck, Mandy, "American Gothic: Undermining the Uncanny," in Kim Akass and Janet McCabe (eds), *Reading Six Feet Under: TV to Die for* (New York: I.B. Tauris, 2005), pp. 59–70.

Moore, Jeanne, "Placing *Home* in Context," *Journal of Environmental Psychology* 20 (2000): 207–17.

Morley, David, *Home Territories: Media, Mobility and Identity* (London: Routledge, 2000).

Owens, Craig N., "When We Living Awake," in Thomas Fahy (ed.), *Considering Alan Ball: Essays on Sexuality, Death and America in the Television and Film Writings* (London: McFarland, 2006), pp. 124–38.

Reed, Christopher, "Introduction," in Christopher Reed (ed.), *Not at Home: The Suppression of Domesticity in Modern Art and Architecture* (London: Thames & Hudson, 1996), pp. 7–17.

Russell, Lorena, "Strangers in Blood: The Queer Intimacies of *Six Feet Under,*" in Thomas Fahy (ed.), *Considering Alan Ball: Essays on Sexuality, Death and America in the Television and Film Writings* (London: McFarland, 2006), pp. 107–23.

Seamon, David, "Place, Placelessness, Insideness, and Outsideness in John Sayles' *Sunshine State,*" *Aether: Journal of Media Geography* 3 (2008): 1–19.

Seamon, David, "Gaston Bachelard's Topoanalysis in the 21st Century: The Lived Reciprocity between Houses and Inhabitants as Portrayed by American Writer Louis Bromfield," in Lester Embree (ed.), *Phenomenology 2010* (Bucharest: Zeta Books, 2010), pp. 225–43.

Seamon, David, "Place, Place Identity, and Phenomenology," in Hernan Casakin and Fátima Bernardo (eds), *The Role of Place Identity in the Perception, Understanding, and Design of the Built Environment* (London: Bentham Science Publishers, 2012), pp. 1–26.

Seiden, Henry M., "On the Longing for Home," in Brent Willock, Lori C. Bohm, and Rebecca Coleman Curtis (eds), *Loneliness and Longing: Conscious and Unconscious Aspects* (London: Routledge, 2012), pp. 267–79.

Smyth, Gerry, and Croft, Jo (eds), *Our House: The Representation of Domestic Space in Modern Culture* (New York: Rodopi, 2006).

Steinbock, Anthony, "Homelessness and the Homeless Movement: A Clue to the Problem of Intersubjectivity," *Human Studies* 17 (1994): 203–23.

Steinbock, Anthony, *Home and Beyond: Generative Phenomenology after Husserl* (Evanston: Northwestern University Press, 1995).

Turnock, Rob, "Death, Limnality and Transformation in *Six Feet Under*," in Kim Akass and Janet McCabe (eds), *Reading Six Feet Under: TV to Die for* (New York: I.B. Tauris, 2005), pp. 39–49.
Vidler, Anthony, *The Architectural Uncanny: Essays in the Modern Unhomely* (Cambridge, MA: MIT Press, 1992).

Chapter 13

Coming Home and Places of Mourning

Janet Donohoe

In his memoir *Running in the Family*, Michael Ondaatje describes his return to his native home of Sri Lanka motivated by the death of his father who gasped the word "Asia" at his death. Ondaatje comments that his journey home to the places and people of his past was due to his desire to "touch them into words."[1] This return to a place rife with memories is coupled with the narratives that are shared about his family and his ancestors. Even in the absence of the people, the place calls them to mind and the memories come unbidden. It is this connection between place and narrative, between memory and mourning that is revealed in the homecomings that many of us, like Ondaatje, experience. These homecomings, however, are not simple retrievals of the past, but bring us to a confrontation with our own mortality and the loss of the past that is uncanny.

Ondaatje is not alone in his desire to return to a place of memory to retrieve narrative as an act of mourning. Journeys home are often made to bear witness to the dying and as pilgrimages in the aftermath of death, sometimes for burials or the commitment of ashes. Cemeteries are places we return to in memory as an act of mourning those who have gone before us to whom we are indebted for our traditions. These homecomings are often fraught with pain, uneasiness, and loss. They are *always* uncanny. This chapter investigates the role of homecoming in the preservation and construction of narratives through cemetery visits, and pilgrimages in the name of remembering and mourning the dead. By questioning how the memories of home are embedded in the landscape, the built environment, and the cemetery, this phenomenological analysis draws out the relationship between memory and place, focusing on the way homecomings bring us into relation with our own mortality as well as with our life traditions, with the narratives of self and family, and the uncanniness of our relationship to places of the past. Drawing upon the work of Martin Heidegger, I will explore the notion of the uncanny (*unheimlich* for Heidegger) in its connection with anxiety and the homelessness (*un-heimlichkeit*) that is bound up with our attempts to return home. For Heidegger, the uncanniness of human existence is characterized by the anxiety of our own being-towards-death and our utter homelessness on this earth, which is always in tension with our desire to recover a home where we can find comfort. I will argue, then, that our sense of place, our sense of mortality, and our narrative sense of self are all interrelated and all are characterized by an uncanniness.

---

[1]   Michael Ondaatje, *Running in the Family* (New York, 1993), p. 22.

Returning to the Cemetery or Site of Death

Why, we ask, do we feel the need to spend time in cemeteries or at places of death? Why do we want to visit the Nazi death camps or Ground Zero? What purpose do cemeteries serve such that we visit the graves of the departed? How do such places help us to mourn? Karsten Harries suggests that:

> The grave gestures toward the solidarity of mortals, even as it shatters such solidarity by facing each individual with his or her own mortality ... Bringing us home to ourselves, [the] grave at the same time lets us feel homeless in the everyday with all its familiar cares and concerns, bids us attend to the essential: our one death-bound life.[2]

We might say with Harries, then, that sites of death and cemeteries serve to remind us of our own mortality and our temporary stay on this earth. This is to confront us with our anxiety at being-towards death, as Heidegger would say, and therefore to confront us with the uncanniness of our own existence both in the sense of our mortality and our homelessness. Certainly, this is the case whether we thank goodness that we ourselves never had to face the gas chambers or leap from a burning high-rise, or whether we simply reflect upon the nature of our own death which comes inevitably but without warning.

But doesn't this seem, after all, a bit too simple? If this were truly and only the case, then it seems that any grave or death site would do. And to a point, perhaps any will do. Simply entering a graveyard can be an opportunity for reflection on the meaning of death or the meaning of life. Graveyards are often beautiful, manicured places that are peaceful and removed from the busyness of the everyday. But we normally do not go to graveyards for the simple effect of them. We do not seek out just any place of death. We may, of course, go for the aesthetic effect, but we most frequently go to visit the grave of someone in particular, someone we knew, maybe someone famous, or someone related to us or our family. We seek out the sites of death that have somehow affected us or our culture.

So, beyond the call to reflect upon our own mortality, what is it that graves and sites of death do for us? What is their role in the act of mourning? In cases of people we knew, the grave serves as a kind of mnemonic device of our loved one and our time together. Being in the place of the grave is time for recollection of that person and our shared memories. It may even be the cause of story telling to others about that person and our relationship to him or her. But for ancestral graves, to visit the grave is to call to mind the family connection, to place one in contact with a community of others—both those others who also visit the grave, the other living friends and relatives, and also those others whom we are only connected to in death. This foray to the grave of ancestors connects us with those

---

[2] Karsten Harries, *The Ethical Function of Architecture* (Cambridge, MA, 1998), p. 292.

of our family in our living, but also provides for a community of all in death – a community beyond clan and nation, beyond creed and race to the community of mortal beings.

This summer, for example, my family returned to my husband's country of birth, the UK. We spent two full days visiting sites of family heritage, the birth home of his father, the graves of grandparents and great-grandparents. In many cases these were not people my husband had ever met, but it was important to both him and his parents that our two young sons should see these places. This brings us to the recognition that while these graves were placed for those who died, they are more for those of us who live so that we may have a place to go in order to contemplate the loss as well as the heritage; that which has been received from these people whom we have never met.

Still, the role of the place of a cemetery or site of death as a mnemonic device does not quite get at the depth or the uncanniness of the relationship between narrative, memory, mourning, and place. We must do more to unearth that relationship.

Returning to the Death of our Past

It is not just cemeteries to which we return. We often make pilgrimages to places of our past as an act of mourning in memory of the deceased or to get in touch with our heritage by "returning" to places we have never actually been before. Visiting such places allows us to form a connection to the places of our ancestors, thereby helping us to incorporate the family or cultural heritage into our own narrative. But how indeed does that happen?

Normally when we think of narrative in terms of self-identity or communal identity, we think of it in terms of providing unity for a fractured temporality. The narrative organizes and clarifies our temporal experiences. What is not so frequently remarked upon is that the narrative also organizes our spatial experiences even while the place organizes our narrative. With every narrative plot, there is a narrative setting, which is not static and secondary, but is fundamental to the action of the narrative. Plot does not just happen, it happens *somewhere*. And the somewhere, insofar as it structures our knowledge, also structures our plot, meaning that the setting is not merely something objective from which we are separated. The plot doesn't just happen in a place, it happens in this particular place, which is just as important and influential for the experience and the memory as anything else. The places of experiences are living elements of those experiences and structure those experiences, which is why they can serve to make experiences present in their absence when we replace ourselves in them. Our habitual places structure our knowledge insofar as they provide us with an embodied style of being in the world that manifests itself in the constitutional act in such a way that certain things are salient while others are dormant. This is a way of constitution that includes the valuation of the salient, which is why it is salient. Such constitutional factors are passed along from generation to generation in the place and because of the place.[3] The stories we tell, then, have to do with how the world is constituted, as what we know of the world cannot be separated from how it is constituted. Narrative helps us to organize the spaces and places in which we find ourselves according to what aspects of those places make themselves felt by us.

The role of the place in constitution does not get passed along unchanged, nor does it remain unchanged even with any individual's repetitive constitution of the place. Just as every narrative involves an element of mimesis, so too does the narrative involve a platial resetting. According to Paul Ricoeur, any narrative transpires with a gap between the living of an event and the narrating of the event. The telling is not the living and the living is not the telling. But in the telling a particular perspective is taken up vis-à-vis the living such that the telling can only be performed from an already pre-formed position, style, and genre. This can be said, too, of the place of living and can thus explain part of the reason for the importance of returning to ancestral or childhood places. The narrative can reveal place and the place can reveal narrative.

Place and narrative must be fundamentally interrelated because we cannot consider the past independently of the particular people and objects of which it is composed. And those people and objects only interact within a particular place from which they cannot be separated. The atomic bomb was dropped by a particular person on a particular place. The French Revolution happened in a particular place and by means of particular actors. The places of history are not generic. They are important constitutive elements of the narrative of the past and not as simple settings for events, but as constitutive of the persons and things involved. This holds true for personal narratives as well. The places where one went to elementary school, had one's first kiss, or lost a beloved animal are integral to those experiences. And, as Jeff Malpas underscores: "The past cannot be prised away from the places ... This is so with respect both to the past that can be recounted as part of a personal biography and to the past that is articulated through communal narrative and history (and neither, of course, is wholly independent of the other)."[4] Narratives of one's personal past cannot be isolated from place or from the communal narrative.

Although the recollection of the past that often takes place through places is frequently romanticized—we wish to recapture nostalgically our past through a visit to grandma's old house or the old school we used to go to—it is important to recognize that pilgrimages can also take place to sites of trauma or tragedy. Such pilgrimages are hardly nostalgic, but play a slightly different role in perhaps incorporating the trauma into one's narrative of self or more concretely into the communal narrative. One look at the many websites advertising Jewish heritage

---

[3]   For more on the role of place in informing constitution, see my "The Place of Home," *Environmental Philosophy* 8/1 (2011). See also Jeff Malpas, *Place and Experience* (Cambridge, 1999).

[4]   Malpas, *Place and Experience*, p. 180.

tours to Eastern Europe is convincing enough that such tours are seen in part as an attempt to incorporate a horrific past into the communal sense of the future. One site suggests that the heritage tour allows one to "gain an in-depth understanding of how the European Jews handled their inconceivable predicament ... while exploring the wonders and mysteries of the time and place."[5] The act of returning to the place as an act of mourning serves as a way of reincorporating that bit of the past into a more unified narrative of self.[6] However, the unified narrative can never be completely singular, the heritage can never be full retrieved, and the past can never be totally incorporated. The gaps, the moments of lack of understanding, the inability to relive, retrieve, reinhabit confront us again and again with the uncanniness of our homelessness in the ancestral home.

In mourning, we frequently return to places of the past or make pilgrimages to places of heritage, or even to places once important to a lost loved one as an attempt to reconcile ourselves with the loss. This attempt can never provide complete reconciliation, but can contribute to a kind of knowledge of someone or a relearning of one's past that takes place through the narratives that are inherently connected with the places. This also means that the experience of loss and the mourning are inseparable from the experience of place. In returning to a place, we do not recapture that person with whom we shared the place, nor do we recapture the time. Remember, it is mimetic—there is a gap between the living of it and the re-encounter with the place. What we do is contribute to the narrative experience of ourselves. We come face to face with the march of time, with the loss of a younger self or a loved one, which is always juxtaposed with the movement away from the place, into old age, into change. Again, as Malpas notes:

> Not only, then, do the places and spaces of human dwelling change and disintegrate, but those places and spaces are themselves disclosed only through processes that bring change and alteration in their wake—indeed, such places and spaces are disclosed only in relation to movement, agency and, one might say, to change.[7]

To return to a place of the past is to experience the change of that place which is, on the one hand, an attempt to integrate the past into a unified narrative while at the same time recognizing the change of self and change of narrative that cannot but be connected to the place. One can fulfill a phenomenologically empty narrative by experiencing the place of the events narrated, but the experience will always

---

[5]   See http://www.arzaworld.com/jewish-heritage-tours/eastern-europe-tours.aspx [accessed August 2, 2012].

[6]   For some, that past has been so traumatic that the place is avoided in order to avoid incorporation of the past into the self. In other cases, the place is avoided as an act of respect for those who suffered the horror and trauma that the place embodies. But in neither case is the place itself inconsequential.

[7]   Malpas, *Place and Experience*, p. 191.

be in some way at odds since the place itself is different.[8] This presents one with an uncanny sense that cannot be readily or seamlessly incorporated into one's own narrative. It is uncanny precisely because it does not fit seamlessly together into a unified narrative. In being confronted with the change of place, one must confront the change of self, the unceasing march of self towards one's own death and the ever-present sense of our own homelessness in places of home. Within our narratives we treat such places as unchangeable, we regard them as places for us and as remaining the places of our past. The sense of the uncanny is brought on by the experience of the change of place, our homelessness, that is at the same time the change of self and the change of self that is the change of place. In returning to a place in mourning we are grappling with the change and the loss in an attempt to reconstitute the narrative of the place and of ourselves in light of the change.

Cemeteries have pretensions to a life eternal, which is, in part, an attempt to deny the change we have just been thinking through. Some even think of cemeteries as the preparatory ground for bodily resurrection. If such is the case, however, we fail to recognize the ways in which to be who and what we are is to be creatures who are in place, for whom places characterize our identities and our very experiences. To escape being in place is to cease to be human. To seek to return to one's homeland to be buried, or to retrieve one's heritage, or to mourn a loss is a matter of acknowledging the place-boundness that composes the narrative of one's self. It cannot, however, be separated from the loss of place that also composes the narrative of one's self. Thus, we turn to the uncanny, the way in which being bound to place creates for us a paradoxical sense of homelessness.

Place and the Uncanny

We need to make this connection between the uncanny homelessness and place more clear and explicit. It is nearly impossible to use the word "uncanny" in philosophy anymore without calling to mind Heidegger. He describes the uncanny in *Being and Time* as intimately connected with anxiety. I will not rehash the details of Heidegger's account of anxiety except to say that he claims primarily that anxiety for Dasein has to do with Dasein's own fundamental being-towards-death. In "What is Metaphysics?" he writes that "in anxiety, we say, 'one feels ill at ease'"; "one feels something uncanny."[9] For Heidegger, the desire to cast ourselves away from the anxiety, into a home, is always in tension with our feeling

---

[8]   I am drawing here upon a Husserlian concept of empty and filled intentions. An empty intention in one wherein the object of the intention is not itself present and thus the experience is not as detailed or refined as it could be. Such an intention can be fulfilled by a further experience of the thing in question or by the experience of more aspects of the thing in question, thus giving it more detail, making it richer and fuller, so to speak.

[9]   Martin Heidegger, "What is Metaphysics?" in David Farell Krell (trans.), *Basic Writings* (New York, 1977), p. 103.

of anxiety itself, with our homelessness. When we question our own traditions or heritage, we engage in a process that makes us uneasy. To live in this uneasiness, in the uncanny, is to refuse the comfort of traditional ways of thinking and to engage in questioning. What this also means, though, is that the process of questioning is always at the same time an attempt to recover a home, to bring us back to a home where we can find comfort. To be homeless is still to be bound up with home. For, to be genuinely at home in this world, one must affirm the homelessness that is essential to us. It means to recognize the essential uncanniness of our dwelling that can only be thought in relation to a home, but it is a home that withdraws whenever we seek to secure it for ourselves. For our project, then, to be confronted with the uncanniness of the graveyard or the altered cityscape or neighborhood of our youth is at the same time to be connected to the home. What is that connection? I would suggest that it is precisely the narrative of memory that allows us to mimetically represent the home through the uncanniness of our homelessness in the place of the home. The narrative both attempts to capture the home of the past while at the same time we know that any narrative is incomplete, insufficient, uncanny.

As we have just seen, when we endeavor to remember or to mourn those who have gone before us, we seek to return to the places of importance, we seek a home. Graveyards give us a place to mourn, impromptu memorials give us a place to mourn, we make pilgrimages to places of importance in order to call to mind the past and incorporate that past into a narrative. Again, as Malpas suggests, "Narrative is that which can be seen as structuring both memory and self-identity, as well as the places, the landscapes in which self identity is itself worked out and established."[10] I would suggest, however, that it is precisely the place-bound nature of this narrative act of mourning and remembering that makes the homecoming uncanny. For the places change and what we discover upon making the pilgrimage is that all is not how we expected it to be or how we remember it, or how the stories describe it. The tree where we loved to meet and play has been chopped down and paved over. The house where grandpa was born has been torn down and the school that grandma used to walk to has been renovated and doesn't look at all as grandma described it. With the change in place, we sense the temporal frailty of the narrative of the family and the community. We realize the transitoriness of our presence on this earth, but perhaps we also realize the great power of the narrative of self and community that is tied to these places. That narrative allows us to say "remember when this hairdresser's shop was great-grandpa's pork butcher shop? And after that it was an X-rated movie dealer?" The place in its particularity also shows to us the narrative of the community in its constantly evolving state—1940s middle-class British families gave way to immigrant Middle-Eastern families that gave way to a working-class Islamic community. They therefore rely upon place even while place cannot be secured from change, cannot be static. Narrative and place are intertwined in structuring the temporality of the subject such that a

---

[10]   Malpas, *Place and Experience*, p. 185.

homecoming or a return in mourning is always a narrative return to a place that is never without the uneasiness of the temporal frailty that is human.

However much a return to one's ancestral home or the graves of lost loved ones is intertwined with the narrative of one's self as well as one's community, the experience is at the same time the quiet reminder of one's loss of self and loss of world and others. This is because, no matter how important the places of one's shared past may have been to one, in returning to them, we note that they have not remained unchanged, they have not waited for us, they are altered and are indifferent to our memories. Even those places that have a fundamental influence upon our manner of constitution of the world such that our embodied experience is familiar in the feeling of the dry air upon our skin or the organization of the pans in the kitchen of our childhood home, for instance, even those places have been altered in other kinds of ways such that we cannot relive our childhood in them. Those with whom we shared the streets walk on different streets and do not even know enough to miss us. We recognize that the places that are so instrumental in the formation of our knowledge and our way of being-in-the-world are oblivious to us in our particularity. While the mark of place can sometimes be quite deep upon us, our mark upon the place is erased or buried so deeply as to be unnoticeable to the everyday. So, our narratives allow us to think that we have a home in the past and in a place, but experiences of return to those places confront us with our own temporality, our own mortality, and our homelessness. This too is uncanny.

Even the cemetery, then, as an attempt to secure a narrative, to stave off the mortality and the loss, is fraught with the relational nature of any experience of place that means it entails change and loss. One cannot make a pilgrimage to a cemetery in search of a grave as an act of mourning without at the same time engaging in a hermeneutic activity of the narrative of self and community that such a visit entails. Its narrative nature as well as the nature of place and self ushers into the experience change and loss, making the experience itself uncanny. The cemetery, then, can serve as a mnemonic device in triggering memories and stories of the lost loved one or the lost hero, but the experience in its complex relations of places to narrative, memories to narrative and narrative to self cannot remain immune to change and loss. It is thereby uncanny as a reminder of one's own mortality, one's own tentative identity, as well as the place-boundedness that just is what it is to be human.

Conclusion

So, why do we make pilgrimages? What is the draw of going home? Why do we visit cemeteries in mourning? The answer lies in the undeniable connection between place and narrative. We seek out the places of our prior others, our near and dear others, the others of our own past in mourning, for the sake of our own identity, our own narrative, as well as for the sake of communion with others. This is always an uneasy communion, an incomplete union fundamentally reminding us of the frailty of our own being and the frailty of our community with others, be they singular others or multiple, communal others. Immigrants who travel back to their homeland one last time before they die or who request to be returned to their homeland to be buried seem to recognize that their own narrative is tied to the land of their past, to that foundational home of their own existence. To return is to embrace the uncanniness of that home in the final stage of one's own narrative.

And what does the place have to do with the work of mourning? I have tried to argue here that mourning includes the process of recognizing the changing face of places that are so deeply intertwined with the person or identity that is lost. We mourn our own past and our own loss when we return to such places. The places in which our loved one is embedded are revisited as part of the mourning process. We begin to recognize that the places too change. The people with whom we spent our time are mourned, not because all of them are dead, but because many of them are in new places unknown to us. Perhaps they were a part of our everyday lives in the past, but their lives too have changed and moved on.

Like Ondaatje, we may make a journey home as an act of mourning. What do we seek to find? I have tried to suggest here that homecomings are an effort to fill in the narrative of self and family through experience of places of memory. At the same time, homecomings are uncanny precisely because of the change of place and the hermeneutic process which recognizes that any narrative as well as any place is always read or told anew. Narrative identity, whether we speak of an individual or a family or a community, in part because it is associated and imbued with place, is never constant, never static, never a completely restful home. As Ondaatje muses at the end of his memoir: "But the book again is incomplete. In the end all your children move among the scattered acts and memories with no more clues."[11] The narratives and the places are always incomplete, only giving a fraction of our communal identity, our communal memories, and our personal identity. And yet, with the places and the narratives, we have no option but to be uncannily content.

References

Donohoe, Janet, "The Place of Home," *Environmental Philosophy* 8 (2011): 1–15.
Harries, Karsten, *The Ethical Function of Architecture* (Cambridge, MA: MIT Press, 1998).
Heidegger, Martin, "What is Metaphysics?" in David Farell Krell (trans.), *Basic Writings* (New York: Harper & Row, 1977).
Malpas, Jeff, *Place and Experience* (Cambridge: Cambridge University Press, 1999).
Ondaatje, Michael, *Running in the Family* (New York: Vintage Books, 1993).

---

[11] Ondaatje, *Running in the Family*, p. 201.

Chapter 14
Poetic Habitats, Impossible Homecomings

Hanna Janiszewska

Poems are apt figures for the often-fraught experience of coming home. Reading a poem for the first time is like entering a home, but a home which is not ours. Only (but not always) by residing there long enough can we make it our own. But it is an experience rife with existential uncertainty; each reading at once makes it more habitable for us (by making it more familiar) but also more complicated. With each re-reading, we encounter the ghosts of readings past and strive to keep the experience self-consistent; with each reading, we face the possibility of disappointment, of being lost, of being bored. We want the memory of reading and its present to coalesce.

These remarks, of course, describe only a certain kind of reading—a reading which holds us captive to a specific emotional landscape, whose individual meaning we learn to inhabit by creating there an intimacy of our own. In re-reading such a poem, we feel as if we were coming home to ourselves, however elusive and illusory that self may be, because we feel we have made right something that had been amiss.[1] So far, I have only spoken of the experience of the reader, but what primarily concerns me here is the part this experience plays in poetic practice itself, that is, how poets themselves find homes through poems, and what this can tell us not only about our desire for home, but also about our desire for a reliable method to get there.

Romantic lyrical poetry is the paradigmatic poetry of memory and imagination: the primary tools of nostalgia. It is thus also the poetry of loss and recovery, of many attempted homecomings and much rootless wandering. The philosophical problem (whether in ontological or epistemological terms) of *how to be at home in the world* becomes a poetic one for the Romantics, that is, what sorts of poems and what kinds of poets can answer this question? Many Romantic lyrics become sites of recuperation, of holding still a vision of what is lost—whether home, friend or childhood—just long enough to experience it again or to imagine what that experience might be like, were it possible. In probing the limitations of a straightforward recovery, they find recompense of a different sort: the distant home, uncanny in its vividness and inaccessible, turns out paradoxically to be

---

[1]   I.A. Richards, whose discussion of poetry and beliefs informs my reading here, would call this feeling of "significance" "the conscious accompaniment of our successful adjustment to life." See I.A. Richards, *Principles of Literary Criticism* (London, 1967), p. 265.

more true. The feeling of strangeness becomes the postlapsarian's version of original comfort: the uncanny is the only home.[2]

One of the most famous of these poems is William Wordsworth's "Tintern Abbey" (1798), which relates the poet's return to a place uniquely meaningful to him. Older upon his return, he finds that he is no longer able to experience it in exactly the same way, and yet through the power of his imagination, which supplements the sight in front of him with the vision of the remembered one (and all that it evokes), he almost grasps it with a similar intensity of feeling. "Tintern Abbey" makes explicit what much of Romantic lyrical poetry suggests: that home is a state of mind. For Wordsworth, this state is a spiritual one as well:

> … that blessed mood,
> In which the affections gently lead us on,
> Until the breath of this corporeal frame,
> And even the motion of our human blood
> Almost suspended, we are laid asleep
> In body, and become a living soul
> While with an eye made quiet by the power
> Of harmony, and the deep power of joy
> We see into the life of things. (38–50)[3]

The "blessed mood" is attainable through memory and imagination, whose combined powers, when properly cultivated, are conceived by Wordsworth to be so great that we can depend on them to urge us into our true, timeless selves. By thus becoming more alive to the world in which we reside, we also come home—which for Wordsworth and the other Romantics amounts to feeling at home in this world.

And yet the idealist solution offered by "Tintern Abbey" (to the exile we all suffer as a result of growing up and growing old and disillusioned) leaves much to be desired. Wordsworth simply tells us *that* through the exercise of memory he arrives home, even if this home is compromised or partial. *How* and *that* are one to him: to know how to come home is to do so. Memory is a kind of ideology, a system that works because Wordsworth believes in the inviolability of the original experience. The Promised Land is not a place we travel to all our lives, but a vision we ascend to repeatedly. And so the present—however "weary" (40) or "unintelligible" (41), however full of "fear, or pain, or grief"

---

[2]   Some examples of Romantic lyrics include: Samuel Taylor Coleridge ("The Eolian Harp" (1796), "Sonnet to the River Otter" (1797), "Frost at Midnight" (1798)); William Wordsworth ("Lines Written a Few Miles above Tintern Abbey" (1798), "Ode: Intimations of Immortality from Recollections of Early Childhood" (1807)); and Percy Bysshe Shelley ("Mont Blanc" (1817), "Hymn to Intellectual Beauty" (1817)).

[3]   William Wordsworth and Samuel Taylor Coleridge, *Lyrical Ballads*, eds R.L. Brett and A.R. Jones (London, 1991), p. 114.

(144)—can always be redeemed by the past, by memories of the good. The home we have lost or can no longer return to is all the sweeter for having been lost, however unsavory that truism.

But what if the relationship between *how* and *that*, between having a method and following through on it, is more fraught? Wordsworth's contemporary and friend Samuel Taylor Coleridge entertained a somewhat different idea about how we overcome the sense of loss which inevitably accompanies us through life. "Sometimes," he writes in "This Lime-Tree Bower My Prison," "'Tis well to be bereft of promised good, / That we may lift the Soul, and contemplate / With lively joy the joys we can not share" (64–7).[4] And yet Coleridge has a more difficult time making himself at home in the world through poetry, despite his assertion that adversity can teach us to appreciate the world better. This is because Coleridge repeatedly attempts the act itself; he tries to make his poems[5] do the work of both telling the story of how he comes home and at the same time of bringing him there. In other words, while for Wordsworth poems are evidence of the efficacy of memory (we might even say that they are like relics of home: parts of the essential whole which, though it cannot be recaptured in its entirety, is nonetheless real in its partial manifestations), for Coleridge, they are the live means of making and inhabiting that home. A poem thus has both a metaphysical dimension and a phenomenal one.[6] It is an account (philosophical and spiritual) of the individual's place in the universe and the practice and experience of living in that space.

Central to Coleridge's thought was the desire to find unity in the heterogeneity of this world, and especially to find a language in which this unity could be expressed. Coleridge hoped that poetry was that language, that it could solve the irresolutions of philosophy and make manifest what philosophy could only describe: the essential relatedness of everything, the participation of the animate in the inanimate and vice versa. While philosophy could point us in the direction of such an intellectual home, it could never make us feel at home there. It was the province of poetry to bring that about, to make the mind feel as at home in the world as in its own representations, to help us, in other words, to overcome

---

    [4] Samuel Coleridge, *The Collected Works of Samuel Taylor Coleridge*, xvi: *Poetical Works*, ed. J.C. Mays, i: *Poems (Reading Text)*, 2 vols (London, 2001), i. 349.

    [5] I am referring specifically to the group of lyrics, written between 1795 and 1807, and known as the "conversation poems," which includes "The Eolian Harp" (1796), "Reflections on Having Left a Place of Retirement" (1796), "Frost at Midnight" (1798), "Fears in Solitude" (1798), "The Nightingale: A Conversation Poem" (1798), "This Lime-Tree Bower My Prison" (1800), "Dejection: An Ode" (1802), and "To William Wordsworth" (1817).

    [6] I say phenomenal in order to distinguish the following account from a phenomenological one, which would require a different kind of close reading from the one I offer here. For an account of the phenomenology of the imagination, see Gaston Bachelard and M. Jolas, *The Poetics of Space* (Boston, 1994).

the impatience with the inadequacy of knowledge (born out of dualism), and to end the homelessness which thought suffered as a result.[7]

Homeless thoughts, thoughts wandering towards home—these could be other names for the imagination. Such is certainly Wordsworth's story. There is a magnetic pull to all wandering; we wander and wonder, reaching after something, someplace, without knowing what it is or where until we have arrived at it. Therefore, just to wander is to admit the possibility of coming upon a home, but also knowing that home itself is just an aspiration, a notion that (paradoxically) ensures our continued movement away from the home itself. This is an optimistic version of wandering of course, which has its inverse: the punishing one of permanent exile, of the unavailability of hope. But any discussion of Romantic wandering and the imagination has to take the Romantics' strong belief in individual agency into account. And this belief is in fact the crux of the problem. Wordsworth's professed ability in hard times, "when the fretful stir / unprofitable, and the fever of the world / [hang] upon the beatings of [the] heart" (53–5), to turn to memories of childhood and "revive" the "picture[s] of the mind" (62)—those soothing landscapes of his early days—and thus to return to the comforts of home at will is uncanny indeed. We may train ourselves to escape malaise and we may even be successful in quieting what pains us, but unless we are fully cured, we would have to keep repeating the procedure.[8] To accept that living in this world, where each minute escapes our grasp, is to be sporadically ill with longing, to be homesick, to recognize the impossibility of a full cure, unless we change our frame of reference and understand coming home in the absolute terms of religion. And here I return to Coleridge.

Coleridge demonstrates just how difficult it is to sustain the Wordsworthian work of turning a habit of thought (that is, imagination) into a habitat (home). To the extent that home is a state of mind, its existence is always conditional. It is one thing to find solace in memories and another to believe that we can convincingly and consistently think ourselves into them at will and make the world in which we reside feel like the home we were meant for. Coleridge's conversation poems are a case in point. Even as Coleridge performs the emotional alchemy of turning into a home what he imagines should be one, he also unwittingly exposes the limitations of that act.

The typical narrative structure of a conversation poem runs as follows: we find the poet, fixed in place (sitting under a tree in his garden, by the fire in his house—always in or near his actual home), troubled by some thought or ill at ease or lonely; his thoughts gradually migrate from the confinement of his present environment to some remembered one, in which having surrendered himself to his circumstances, he was at ease; that memory grows in scope and urgency until the poet realizes

---

[7] For an extensive treatment of the paradox which is thinking, see Hannah Arendt, *The Life of the Mind* (New York, 1977), pp. 3–238.

[8] The idea of philosophy as a way of life—a learning to overcome anxiety—goes some way toward making this possible. For an examination of this idea, see Pierre Hadot, *Philosophy as a Way of Life: Spiritual Exercises from Socrates to Foucault* (Oxford, 1995), pp. 81–125.

that he no longer feels troubled; he returns from his imaginative flight, his vision enlarged, his surroundings, once limiting and imperfect, now a blessing, and a home, which he fully accepts as one. In all this Coleridge does not appear to differ much from Wordsworth. The imaginative flight restores, revitalizes, and brings about an internal adjustment. But the actual process is quite different, because it is driven not, as for Wordsworth, by a belief in the redemptive power of memory (and hence the emotionally sustaining weight of experience), but by a reliance on the strange powers of the will, encapsulated in Coleridge's concept of poetic faith.

Poetic faith, a term Coleridge invents, describes the curious cognitive state we find ourselves in while reading poetry. It is the same state necessary to submitting ourselves to the illusions of drama and which Coleridge famously called "the willing suspension of disbelief."[9] It is that which allows us to believe the improbable, to accept fiction as if it were reality, all the while remaining aware of the difference. And it is by means of poetic faith that Coleridge attempts to make his home through poetry. His use of the word "faith" in this context is curious and bears a brief biographical digression, because it not only demonstrates how no single term adequately conveys the experience of homecoming, but also shows the shortcomings of analogy.

As a result of reading too much philosophy as a young man, Coleridge suffered a crisis of faith and tried to reason himself out of it. But no amount of reasoning ever produced the certainty he was after: an unflinching belief in God's existence. He only arrived at it once he realized that faith is contingent on the possibility of exercising the will to reject it, that "its fundamental truth ... is ... such as might be denied."[10] It is then no accident that the "willing suspension of disbelief" is for Coleridge a condition of poetic faith, just as the willing suspension of doubt is necessary to faith in God. Both operate on the assumption that the tension between reason and belief is not only an inevitable part of belief itself but is indispensible to its authenticity. But this is where the helpful similarity ends, for while religious devotion may be said to provide a temporary home on earth in the anticipation of the heavenly one yet to be disclosed, to turn the habit (which is prayer) into a habitat (that anticipated home), a poem is no sure haven from the disquiet occasioned by our homelessness. It is not preparation for anything. And as the analogy with prayer suggests, homecoming is a formal business, a ritual which depends on the coherence and security of form. And as the example of Wordsworth demonstrates, therapy for homesickness works well when its tools are clear. There may be times when we are lucky and find ourselves at home by accident, but we certainly cannot count on this. We also cannot count on poetic justice. And yet this was Coleridge's hope: that in willingly suffering the lack of home, one would be given unto him. This is certainly an unsettling way to live and a lot to ask of poems. It is in essence to expect grace. I propose to look more closely at this procedure through a reading of Coleridge's "This Lime-Tree Bower My Prison" (1797).

---

[9]   Samuel Coleridge, *The Collected Works of Samuel Taylor Coleridge*, vii: *Biographia Literaria*, eds James Engell and W. Jackson Bate, 2 vols (London, 1983), ii. 6.

[10]   Ibid., i. 203.

Most often read as a redemptive tale of the power of the imagination and of God's infinite bounty, I take "This Lime-Tree Bower My Prison" to be Coleridge's paradigmatic exercise in self-abnegation. In brief summary of the plot: due to an injured foot, the poet is unable to join his friends on one of many long-anticipated walks; confined to his garden, he bemoans his lot by imagining what his friends are enjoying that he is missing. Soon these imaginings lift his spirits; he feels God's presence and concludes that what was once his prison has ceased to be so, and is in fact a lesson in God's grace. This trajectory, as one Coleridge critic helpfully put it, moves Coleridge from the solipsism of a "hyperbolic sulk" into "the poetics of participation."[11] In other words, he transcends the trance of his self-indulgent self-imprisonment and awakes to find himself more fully at home in the world and in his consciousness.

And yet it is not all as simple and especially not as natural as that. I will point out three moments in the poem that trouble this reading and will challenge the idea that home can be a matter of changing one's point of view, of acquiring double sight. The first such moment comes close to the beginning of the poem, in lines 10–20. In the preceding lines (1–10), Coleridge laments the fact that he is unable to join his friends on a favorite walk, and in lines 10–20 offers a detailed description of what he is missing—the beauties of the dell they are visiting:

> Well, they are gone, and here must I remain,
> This lime-tree bower my prison! I have lost
> Such beauties and such feelings, as had been
> Most sweet to my remembrance, even when age
> Had dimm'd mine eyes to blindness! They, meanwhile,
> Friends, whom I never more may meet again,
> On springy heath, along the hilltop edge,
> Wander in gladness, and wind down, perchance,
> To that still roaring dell, of which I told;
> The roaring dell, o'erwooded, narrow, deep,
> And only speckled by the mid-day sun;
> Where its slim trunk the ash from rock to rock
> Flings arching like a bridge;—that branchless ash,
> Unsunn'd and damp, whose few poor yellow leaves
> Ne'er tremble in the gale, yet tremble still,
> Fann'd by the water-fall! and there my friends
> Behold the dark green file of long lank weeds,
> That all at once (a most fantastic sight!)
> Still nod and drip beneath the dripping edge
> Of the blue clay-stone. (1–20)

---

[11]   Susan J. Wolfson, *Formal Charges: The Shaping of Poetry in British Romanticism* (Stanford, 1997), p. 80.

Something is amiss here. The repetition of the word "still"—"still roaring" (9), "tremble still" (15) and "still nod" (19)—which controls the deployment of motion in the dell and holds the frame of this experience in place betrays Coleridge's anxiety that the dell be "still" so that he can see it just as he first saw it in its original state. But there is something artificial about this scene. Coleridge calls the "lank weeds" in line 17 "a most fantastic sight" (18). "Fantastic" here is another name for the improbable—that which the imagination, in suspending disbelief, makes possible but whose unlikely meaning it represses. The sights of the dell are "fantastic" because they look like nature imitating herself; the "yellow leaves" (14) don't "tremble in the gale" (15) but look as if they did, because they are "fanned by the water-fall" (16). This effect of seeming animated from within and yet not being so, which the plant life in the dell exhibits, can be extended to Coleridge's voice in this poem. It sounds like inspired speech but is in fact merely an echo of one. It is a narrative, Coleridge admits, he has already "told" (9). He is repeating himself.

This artifice continues in the next part of the poem in lines 21–43:

> Now my friends emerge
> Beneath the wide wide Heaven—and view again
> The many-steepled tract magnificent
> Of hilly fields and meadows, and the sea,
> With some fair bark, perhaps, whose sails light up
> The slip of smooth clear blue betwixt two Isles
> Of purple shadow! Yes! they wander on
> In gladness all; but thou, methinks, most glad,
> My gentle-hearted Charles! For thou hast pined
> And hunger'd after Nature, many a year,
> In the great City pent, winning thy way
> With sad yet patient soul, through evil and pain
> And strange calamity! Ah! slowly sink
> Behind the western ridge, thou glorious Sun!
> Shine in the slant beams of the sinking orb,
> Ye purple heath-flowers! richlier burn, ye clouds!
> Live in the yellow light, ye distant groves!
> And kindle, thou blue Ocean! So my friend,
> Struck with deep joy, may stand, as I have stood,
> Silent with swimming sense; yea, gazing round
> On the wide landscape, gaze till all doth seem
> Less gross than bodily; and of such hues
> As veil the Almighty Spirit, when he makes
> Spirits perceive his presence. (21–43)

The poet moves with increasing momentum from the picturesque (lines 22–6) to the sublime (lines 33–7); his solipsism vanquished in the intensity of inspired experience. But this apotheosis comes about as an effect of purposeful choreography.

He bids this superlative, blazing vision into being (mark his imperatives in lines 33, 35, and 36, "slowly sink," "Shine in the slant beams," "richlier burn"). And the imperative mode quickly becomes a summons and ushers "the Almighty Spirit" in. Inspiration, it seems, invites grace (it brings God into the world) and grace, in turn, makes even the uninspiring and the mundane seem remarkable, and thus in the next movement of the poem, the poet willingly returns to his prosaic condition in the bower, as if it was the place, the home he was always looking for and not the one he sought refuge from.

This, in essence, is Coleridge's poetic faith—suspending the knowledge of the inhospitability of the bower by investing it with an alluring strangeness, both reminiscent of the "fantastic" dell and illuminated by the setting sun. And so in line 44, Coleridge exclaims:

> A delight
> Comes sudden on my heart, and I am glad
> As I myself were there! Nor in this bower,
> This little lime-tree bower, have I not mark'd
> Much that has sooth'd me. Pale beneath the blaze
> Hung the transparent foliage; and I watch'd
> Some broad and sunny leaf, and loved to see
> The shadow of the leaf and stem above
> Dappling its sunshine! And that walnut-tree
> Was richly ting'd, and a deep radiance lay
> Full on the ancient ivy, which usurps
> Those fronting elms, and now with blackest mass
> Makes their dark branches gleam a lighter hue
> Through the late twilight: and though now the bat
> Wheels silent by, and not a swallow twitters,
> Yet still the solitary humble-bee
> Sings in the bean-flower! (44–60)

What we have here is the form of conversion—signifying a new way of being and seeing—but not necessarily the substance of one. For Coleridge's conversion is a matter of the will (and more specifically of the willing suspension of disbelief) and not grace: it points to an imaginative routine whose repetition is necessary to that conversion's continuance and which as a result produces inevitable psychological and poetic strain. The home it has founded is still a prison, even as captivity itself has become captivating—"a delight." Coleridge's new delightful bower does not actually exist, except as a thing of the past. It is delightful because it is already ripe for recollection (mark the past tense in this passage). Its actual presence fades from sight in "the late twilight" (57), having been only briefly illuminated by the thought of the "Almighty Spirit." Against this fading, Coleridge sustains himself with the belief that an alternative to life as it merely is—the prison of our feelings—may be found in suspending its claims on us. Coleridge's point that it felt "As I myself were there" spells out the terms of this covenant: we can live in this world as if we were "there" not here; we can turn this world into a fable.[12]

And in the remaining part of the poem, Coleridge does just that. Henceforth, he says:

> ... I shall know
> That nature ne'er deserts the wise and pure;
> No plot so narrow, be but Nature there
> No waste so vacant, but may well employ
> Each faculty of sense, and keep the heart
> Awake to Love and Beauty! and sometimes
> 'Tis well to be bereft of promised good,
> That we may lift the soul, and contemplate
> With lively joy the joys we cannot share.
> My gentle-hearted Charles! when the last rook
> Beat its straight path along the dusky air
> Homewards, I blessed it! deeming its black wing
> (Now a dim speck, now vanishing in light)
> Had cross'd the mighty Orb's dilated glory
> While thou stood'st gazing; or, when all was still,
> Flew creaking o'er thy head, and had a charm
> For thee, my gentle-hearted Charles, to whom
> No sound is dissonant which tells of Life. (60–76)

Henceforth, in other words, home is everywhere as long as we are willing to believe so and willing to accept every "vacant" lot as an opportunity for, or perhaps even a call to, finding ourselves anew in this world. But this lesson, which Coleridge wants to believe, is undermined by the uncanny appearance of the solitary rook, crossing "the mighty Orb's dilated glory" (72).

After all this, it is not the blazing sun descending below the horizon that is the symbol of the unattainable, ever-mysterious, original home, but the "mighty" moon, which captures that sun's departed rays and gives them a proper home. The story of how we are in the world, imaginatively situating ourselves inside/outside, above/beneath an imagined home, always in relation to it as if it were a thing apart, a unity to be gained, is also the story of poetic language, which moves us in the direction of home. But where exactly is that?

---

[12]   For an extended account of just such fables, see Stanley Cavell, *In Quest of the Ordinary: Lines of Skepticism and Romanticism* (Chicago, 1988), p. 9. Cavell writes: "The everyday is ordinary because, after all, it is our habit, or habitat; but since that very inhabitation is from time to time perceptible to us – we who have constructed it – as extraordinary, we conceive that some place elsewhere, or this place otherwise constructed, must be what is ordinary to us, must be what romantics ... call 'home.'"

Where the rook is traveling is unclear, except that it is "homewards." When we think we have come home, it turns out, we are really only traveling towards it, never to arrive. Even if the moon brings us a little sun, it can never bring us to the sun itself. In fact, the closer we approach the moon, the further we move from the sun. This infinite regress is akin to walking backwards, and if we are indeed walking backwards, then we will not recognize our home until we have already passed it. Such too is memory. It compensates us for the loss of our home by helping us understand what a home is. In the final analysis, Coleridge "grasps" the nature of home, just as he releases his grip on it. The procedure of poetic faith makes this possible but leads to an unsettling conclusion. Either, we have to concede, the authenticity of this epiphany is predicated on the fact that it is the "last" epiphany (like the "last rook ... vanishing in light") and so cannot be repeated because it is the apocalypse of disillusionment, the unintended consequence of longing too hard; or that all that poetic faith can do for us is to keep alive the hope that our need alone confirms the reality of home, that the fact of direction itself suggests that we have somewhere to go. A meager faith indeed, and one that Coleridge ultimately abandoned a few years after writing "This Lime-Tree Bower My Prison." And yet homewards through words is not in itself impossible, but the emphasis we have to remember must always rest on the incompleteness of that motion. Home continues for us as long as we continue in our search of it. It is a place before language: and though poetry aspires to be its grammar, the best we can do, to borrow a phrase from Pierre Hadot, is to remain "spiritual[ly] vigila[nt]" to the "the fundamental rule of life: that is, the distinction between what depends on us and what does not."[13] Coleridge's error was to suppose that the distinction could be overcome through poetic faith. This need not discourage us from entrusting ourselves to poems. They can still fulfill a more modest end—to keep us vigilant against the temptation to conflate the need for comfort (for homely familiarity with our environment) with the need (and responsibility) to truly get to know our home, this world.

References

Arendt, Hannah, *The Life of the Mind* (New York: Harcourt Brace Jovanovich, 1977).

Bachelard, Gaston, and Jolas, M., *The Poetics of Space* (Boston: Beacon Press, 1994).

Cavell, Stanley, *In Quest of the Ordinary: Lines of Skepticism and Romanticism* (Chicago: University of Chicago Press, 1988).

Coleridge, Samuel Taylor, *The Collected Works*, vii: *Biographia Literaria*, eds James Engell and W. Jackson Bate (2 vols, London: Routledge & Kegan Paul, 1983).

---

13   Hadot, *Philosophy*, p. 84.

Coleridge, Samuel Taylor, *The Collected Works*, v: *Lectures 1808–1819 On Literature*, ed. R.A. Foakes (2 vols, London: Routledge & Kegan Paul, 1987).

Coleridge, Samuel Taylor, *The Collected Works*, xvi: *Poetical Works*, ed. J.C.C Mays, i.

Poems (Reading Text) (2 vols, London: Routledge and Kegan Paul, 2001).

Hadot, Pierre, and Davidson, Arnold Ira, *Philosophy as a Way of Life: Spiritual Exercises from Socrates to Foucault* (Oxford: Blackwell, 1995).

Richards, I.A., *Principles of Literary Criticism* (London: Routledge & Kegan Paul, 1967).

Wolfson, Susan J., *Formal Charges: The Shaping of Poetry in British Romanticism* (Stanford: Stanford University Press, 1997).

Wordsworth, William and Coleridge, Samuel Taylor, *Lyrical Ballads*, eds R.L. Brett and A.R. Jones (London: Routledge, 1991).

Chapter 15

When the Dead Share the Table: The Uncanny Colonial Home in James Joyce's "The Dead"

Ayesha Malik

The house is past. The bombing of European cities, as well as the labour and concentration camps, merely proceed as executors, with what the immanent development of technology has long decided was to be the fate of houses. These are now good only to be thrown away like old food cans. (Theodore Adorno)[1]

In human consciousness, the notion of home has been intertwined with a private and intimate space that invokes a sense of security, unconditioned warmth and rootedness. Home is the nexus of affiliation and camaraderie within a community that transcends the personal space into the public and generates communities and nations. However, home, in addition to facilitating communal bonding, endows the individual with psychological and emotional underpinnings. It becomes the "body and soul" of an individual that fuels the imagination, as Gaston Bachelard points out in *The Poetics of Space*, and without the *"felicitous space"* of home, a person would be a "dispersed being."[2] According to Bachelard, the "house" is thus a *"tool for analysis* of the human soul."[3] Furthermore, home is the repository of indelible memory—an unfading past—that refashions the present of its inhabitants. Home facilitates the daydreams of the person that shapes his or her present circumstances and becomes a shelter of the imagination: the highest benefit a house can offer, as Bachelard establishes. Although tinged with nostalgia, it is the first abode that remains in the memory and is constantly revisited.

However, home is a malleable concept as it is associated with human imagination and many factors, as Adorno's epigraph insinuates—social, economic, cultural, psychological, and political—continue to disrupt and refashion the utopian image of the word "house." As examples, natural disasters, ostracism, and immigration constantly transform the normative patterns of home. However, this chapter analyzes the effects of power in the colonial setting and the reconfiguration of the concept of home in a colonized community. How does the colonial power disintegrate the established normative structures of home within a community?

---

[1]   Theodor Adorno, *Minima Moralia: Reflections from Damaged Life* (London, 2005), p. 39.

[2]   Gaston Bachelard, *The Poetics of Space* (Boston, 1969), p. 43.

[3]   Ibid., p. 36.

How do these cast-off structures, sources of nostalgia and loss, affect the sense of community and belonging among the colonized? And is power capable of reinventing a new "home" that satiates the emotional and psychological needs of the colonized? In order to answer these questions, it is pertinent to analyze the workings of power and its effects on the immediate lives of individuals.

Foucault's essay "The Subject and Power" delineates the "dividing practices" of power that transform the relationship among the individuals and either divide the subject inside himself or divide him from others and initiate the process of objectivation. Foucault summarizes the process as:

> power that applies itself to immediate everyday life categorizes the subject, marks him with his own individuality, attaches him to his own identity, imposes a law of truth on him that he must recognize and others have to recognize in him. It is a form of power that makes individuals subject.[4]

The relationship of the individual to power is inherently violent and its force consumes him. The law of truth, imposed by the power, takes the form of a percept that "invents" a new community, which individuals are forced to recognize. Power thus transforms the imagination of a community through belligerence. Colonial power works in a similar fashion: aggressive binaries of power create subjects to formulate new submissive communities. Colonial power alienates the subjects not only from the community, but also from a shared common past, a home. As "others" inflict the law and its accompanying violence, the "invented" colonial communities become characterized by an uncanny aura as the nucleus of the community—that is, home—is tarnished by excessive power. Homely space turns into a hostile, combative space. Haunted by the annihilation of a shared past connected with home and an infelicitous present in a colonial setting, the subjects are reduced to ghostly appearances in the community.

Freud describes the "uncanny" as "that species of the frightening that goes back to what was once well known and had long been familiar" but is "intended to remain secret, hidden away and has come into the open."[5] The uncanny is a variety of the familiar that has been repressed and is consciously dead, but unintentionally returns. Freud, building on Schelling's definition of the uncanny, mentions a variety of "frightening things" that no longer are frightening and in fact are uncanny in nature:[6]

> This species of the frightening would then constitute the uncanny, and it would be immaterial whether it was itself originally frightening or arose from another

---

[4]   Michel Foucault, *Power* (New York, 2000), p. 331.

[5]   Sigmund Freud, *The Uncanny* (New York, 2003), pp. 124–32.

[6]   Ibid., p. 132. Freud quotes Schelling's definition as "the term 'uncanny' (*unheimlich*) applies to everything that was intended to remain secret, hidden away, and has come into the open."

affect. In the second place, if this really is the secret nature of the uncanny, we can understand why German usage allows the familiar (*das Heimliche*, the "homely") to switch to its opposite, the uncanny (*das Unheimliche*, the "unhomely"), for this uncanny element is actually nothing new or strange, but something that was long familiar to the psyche and was estranged from it only through being repressed. The link with repression now illuminates Schelling's definition of the uncanny as "something that should have remained hidden and has come into the open."[7]

Freud's definition of the uncanny can be stretched to illuminate the transformation of the home from a source of comfort and familiarity to a perverse uncanny space. The detrimental power and subject relationship culminates in the consumption of the individual. During this process, power severs the connection of solace and memory connected with home, transmuting it into an uncanny space. But colonial power is generally characterized by more aggression and enmity and instills a prodigious sense of alienation. As Fanon points out, "In the colonies the foreigner imposed himself using his cannons and machines" and "the ruling species is first and foremost the outsider from elsewhere, different from the indigenous population, 'the others.'"[8] The colonizer and the imposition of force and aggression displace the colonized into uncanny territory.

Furthermore, as Freud establishes, uncanny feelings are evoked by something that is hidden and secret; by the uncertainty of the animate and inanimate objects; by the factor of repetition and by the ghostly figures of the dead. And the colonial setting of "The Dead" manipulates all the tropes required to depict the uncanny home of the subjects.

James Joyce's concluding story in *Dubliners*, "The Dead," captures the mutations of the imagined concept of home within a family and correlates to the somber and moribund state of emotional displacement of its habitants under colonialism. The living individuals are transformed into shades under the crippling colonial power, and the dead cohabit the home with the living. The ghostly figures of the dead become uncanny as they dwell in the past, in the memory of the living, and are obliged to live there. The story complicates the traditional act of remembering the dead by providing a meaning to the essential formlessness of the dead, making them indispensable to the living. Under colonial power, the dead refashion the living, creating a home where the dead and living dwell together. But their unwelcomed presence overrides the present of the living and creates an uncanny atmosphere.

"The Dead" opens at the annual dinner party of Miss Morkans, held in the "dark, gaunt" home of two elderly ladies, Kate and Julia. Though a Christmas party epitomizing the Irish generosity, warmth and culture that, for years and

---

[7]   Ibid., pp. 147–8.

[8]   Frantz Fanon, *The Wretched of the Earth* (New York, 2004), p. 5.

years, has never "fallen flat," the opening passages set the mood of loneliness, miscommunication and entrapment, which belie the fissures in the family home.

The locale of a home in a colonial setting informs the "topo-analysis" that consequently explains the "topography of our intimate being" in Bachelard's words.[9] The locality and construction of a house as well as the material objects inside it describe and explain the emotional and psychological intricacies of its habitants. Colonial power deploys unnatural topographical mutations to accentuate unfamiliarity among indigenous people. Allan H. Simmons, in an essay entitled "Topography and Transformation," establishes Dublin's topography in *Dubliners* as a reminder of British colonial rule in Ireland but with a subversive counter narrative of resistance.[10] Colonial monuments and roads and street names reflecting British rule inescapably resonate in the daily life of Ireland and become the manifestation of indigenous subjugation. Physical space thus becomes a site of contention between the colonizer and the colonized for power and the right of ownership. But, as Simmons notes:

> Of course, realist fiction tends to be located in the real geographical settings, but, as Joyce demonstrates in *Dubliners,* this context contributes a narrative of its own. Indeed, as Joyce presents it, Dublin contains so many architectural and nomenclatural reminders of colonial domination that it is difficult not to read the locale as an expression of colonial (and postcolonial).[11]

In addition to establishing a counter narrative of resistance on the part of the colonized, locality also informs the uncanny and cataclysmic effects of power.

Miss Morkans' previous home was located in a lower-class neighborhood in Northwest Dublin. The "new" house, where the story opens, is far less an upgrade of the previous one, as Usher's Island was a rather dismal neighborhood at the time. From the beginning, we are reminded that the home is not located in the urbanized, metropolis of Ireland but in a deteriorating neighborhood. When the guests enter the house, Lily, the caretaker's daughter, is seen helping the gentlemen off with their coats in the "little pantry" and the bathroom is converted to the "ladies' dressingroom."[12] The first glimpse of the neighborhood and entryway of the house establishes the physical space as confined and congested, and a sense of claustrophobia prevails. The ease and comfort of movement associated with a home visited for 30 years is in jeopardy.

---

[9]   A term borrowed from Gaston Bachelard referring to the "doctrine" of home analysis that constitutes psychoanalysis and phenomenology.

[10]   Allan H. Simmons, "Topography and Transformation, A Postcolonial Reading of Dubliners," in James MacKillop (ed.), *Joyce, Imperialism, and Postcolonialism* (New York, 2008).

[11]   Ibid., p. 28.

[12]   James Joyce, *Dubliners* (New York, 2006), p. 156.

In addition to spatial limits, the house is poorly lit and the murkiness of the setting fuels the uncanny milieu of the story. Darkness is associated with concealment and obscurity and metaphorically to death. The recurring motif of darkness in Miss Morkans' house transforms the setting into a mysterious abode from the start. It further enhances the unfamiliarity of a home that is no longer a familiar place. The guests use the stairs from the pantry to reach the upper quarters, but throughout the story the stairs are "dark" in the Morkans' house. Stairs connect the different floors of the house and ensure the communication between the guests, but their darkness betokens an imminent rift in the house as well as among the guests. The gaslight in the house further complicates the sense of disconnectedness and unfamiliarity. The physical attributes of the characters are distorted and assume a ghostly appearance in the dim gaslight. Gabriel, the favorite nephew of the Morkans, arrives after long anticipation and is helped by Lily in the pantry. But the gaslight makes Lily appear paler than she is. With the progression of the story, familiar faces tend to become unrecognizable shades. For instance, later in the story, the effect of darkness becomes so pervasive in the minds of the characters that Gabriel, gazing from the "dark part of the hall," cannot recognize Gretta, his wife: "A woman was standing near the top of the first flight in the shadow also."[13] After his gaze follows the intricacies of her dress, the colors of which change into black and white in the dim light, the revelation comes as a stroke of finality, "It was his wife."[14] The familiar and mundane faces become unrecognizable in the darkness of the house, generating an uncanny feeling.

The topography shifts from the poor neighborhood to the grand, urbanized metropolis toward the end of the story when Gabriel and Gretta return after the party to a fancy hotel to spend the night in the center of Dublin. Again the promising climax of intimacy and a shared bond between Gretta and Gabriel is pulverized by the ubiquitous darkness of the story. Though the availability of the electric light (the Morkans' house was lit by gas lamp) is an indication of the elegance of the place, Gabriel refuses to have any light in the bedroom, preferring the "ghostly light from the street lamp."[15] The murky interior of the room intensifies the transformation of the familiarity of things and people into ghostly objects and spirits, respectively. Gabriel realizes how "One by one they were all becoming shades."[16] After the revelation of Gretta's past, Gabriel's final revelation ends the story with snow "falling on every part of the dark central plain."[17] The oppressive darkness and gloom that besets the story creates an uncanny atmosphere, resembling the Morkans' home, where familiarity becomes unknown. In the darkness of the hotel

---

13   Ibid., p. 182.

14   Ibid.

15   Ibid., p. 188.

16   Ibid., p. 194.

17   Ibid.

room, Gretta and Gabriel become strangers and Gabriel is forced to ponder as if "he and she had never lived together as man and wife."[18]

In *The Uncanny*, Freud narrates a story he read in the English *Strand Magazine* where a young married couple moves into a house with a crocodile-carved table and:

> Towards evening an intolerable and very specific smell begins to pervade the house; *they stumble over something in the dark*; they seem to see a vague form gliding over the stairs—in short, we are given to understand that the presence of the table causes a ghostly crocodile to haunt the place, or that the wooden monster *come to life in the dark*, or something of that sort.[19]

Freud commends the story for its "remarkable" ability to evoke uncanny feelings that are associated with the darkness of the evening when things are opaque, when reality seems to evade the sight. Darkness in "The Dead" accentuates the unfamiliarity of the physical space of the house and generates uncanny feelings. Social relationships break down in the dark nature of the unknown and the oppressive colonial power alienates the subject from his home and family. The familiarity of past relations and connections is lost in the present moment. Lily is no longer the girl Gabriel knew; the memory of Gabriel's mother is tarnished by her "slight phrases" of Gretta "being country cute."[20] And apparently the most substantial bond in the company shrivels away in the face of the past. Gretta is not the wife Gabriel married; she is not even the woman he married. The familiarity of past "home" and people is tarnished without a reassuring future.

Bachelard defines home as a place of integration and conformity, but colonial homes revert the process. It becomes a place of fragmentation and dissonance. During the party, an additional sense of alienation, a cause of unfamiliarity, is evoked in the characters through misunderstandings and moments of quiescence. A sense of dismay regarding each other oppresses the characters from the beginning. Lily is provoked by Gabriel's remarks about her matrimonial prospects.[21] Gretta is distraught by Gabriel's forceful continental mannerism. Gabriel is discomforted by the thought of intellectually primitive company and reconsiders his dinner-table speech in honor of his aunts. Even the high-spirited nationalist Miss Ivors whispers her resentment at Gabriel's aspiring collusion with the British Empire on the dance floor. In addition to the discomfort of the relations, the guests commit many faux pas. For instance, Freddy Malins, an old friend of the Morkans, comes to the party inebriated and ungainly refers to the "*negro chieftain* singing in the

---

[18] Ibid., p. 193.

[19] Freud, *The Uncanny*, p. 13, emphasis added.

[20] Ibid., p. 162.

[21] In response to Gabriel's question of her matrimonial prospect, Lily retorts: "The men that is now is all palaver and what they can get out of you." See Joyce, *Dubliners*, p. 154.

second part of the Gaiety pantomime" during the dinner.[22] The story is replete with such episodes that illustrate the quantization of the community as a result of imperial power: subjects are divided among themselves. The disquietude of the guests alienates them further from each other.

The room at the hotel promised a fastening of personal relations and a reinvigoration of hope and optimism at the end of the story. However, house (or later the hotel room: a provisional home) as a physical entity, synonymous with solace and compensation, ceases to function in the traditional manner in a colonial setting and acquires an uncanny quality. The Morkans' home correlates to the disintegration of the traditional idea of home in a colonized country. The house thus becomes a violent space in a colonized country due to oppressive and excessive power dynamics: a space that is no longer familiar and connotes ghastliness and hostility. Splintering home, both at the physical and emotional levels, and the darkness of the night correspond to the uncanny colonial state of mind and setting that we encounter in "The Dead."

Ghosts, the return of the dead or half-dead in literature, are a recurring uncanny theme that, according to Freud, reflects the primitive fear of death, of the unknown, and is repressed due to logical reasoning.[23] Freud points out that the mysterious quality of ghosts and spirits is the combination of two factors: our "emotional reaction" and inadequacy of the "scientific knowledge" about death.[24] In addition, the dead are part of the past and their return to life has an eerie quality. The uncanny feeling of the ghosts or the living-dead is the fear of their clandestine powers over the living. But these dead figures become indispensable for the colonial subjects. Home is the abode of a past that integrates a being through memory. But the past in a colonial home brings back the dead and turns the living into ghostly figures.

"The Dead" depicts a haunted house populated with the dead and half-dead. Contrary to the festive nature of the party, the title of the story belies the occasion; death and a bygone past enter the house with the guests. Bernard Benstock noted that the first sentence of the story indicates the deprecated nature of the house where Lily, the caretaker's daughter, is literally and figuratively "run off her feet." He further notes: "Three levels of these dead become apparent upon close examination: the deceased, the moribund, and the living-dead, the composition of the last group expanding with the progression of the story."[25] All the principal characters are introduced at some level of physical decay, approaching death or in a death-like trance. Aunt Julia is "quite grey" with a

---

²²   Ibid., pp. 172–3.

²³   Freud, *The Uncanny*, pp. 148–9.

²⁴   Ibid., p. 148.

²⁵   See Bernard Benstock, "The Dead," in Clive Hart (ed.), *James Joyce's Dubliners* (New York, 1969), p. 153. Benstock notes that "Lily's tag name, that of the funeral flower, serves as a symbol of death ... the smell of graveyard is in our nostrils." See also Janet Dunleavy's "The Ectoplasmic Truthtellers of 'The Dead'," *James Joyce Quarterly* 21/4 (1984): pp. 307–19 for the "invisible ghosts" of the story.

"flaccid face" and the "appearance of a woman who did not know where she was or where she was going," while Aunt Kate is "too feeble to go much about" with a face like a "shrivelled red apple."[26] Freddy Malins with "heavylidded eyes" and his disheveled hair is drunk and sleepy.[27] Gabriel enters with a "fringe of snow" on his overcoat and "restless eyes" that indicate the burden of the past and a piteous end. Even Lily, apparently the youngest of the company, is pale and feeble. Gretta, with the progress of the story, becomes a phantom of the past who turns into a "symbol of something" by living with the memory of a dead lover. And Gabriel prepares himself at the end for a "westward" journey and annihilation.

The uncanny ambience of death, loss, and decrepitude prevails in the narrative. Gabriel tries to pay homage to the eminence of Ireland's past that he fails to see in the "thoughttormented" and "hypereducated" generation of the present. He is nostalgic with others for the "absent faces" of the past who instill a sense of pride in the present and who will never die. However, the speech becomes an empty rhetoric of mawkish clichés. Gabriel and the guests are fully aware that the inadequate memory of a dazzling past cannot sustain the disintegrating present. A fractured past, the inaccessibility of the present, and no promise of a future leave the Morkans' household frozen in an uncanny time.

Gabriel's dead mother's portrait, dead tenor singers whose voices are still mentioned with reverence, monks living in coffins in a monastery, a dead lover outside the window in a wintry night, the *Lass of Aughrim*, the ghosts of betrayed Irish political leaders crawl the house imperceptibly and blur the dividing line between the living and the dead. The dead display an uncanny life, while the living have a death-ness about them. Gabriel's mother is dead but her life-size portrait is the insignia of her presence, which brings back bitter memories. Gretta's dead lover lingers as vividly as any living in the present moment. She is filled with the memory of his love rather than her husband. The spirits and ghosts, hovering in the memory of the living, who come to life in the story, are not freakish creatures with severed heads and arms. There is nothing terrifying about the ghosts in "The Dead"; in fact, some of them once enjoyed a close rapport with the characters, for example, Gabriel's mother, Michael Furey, and Gretta's dead lover. The dead cohabit the house due to its colonial setting. The memory of the ghostly figures becomes indispensible for the present of the living as they bring back the memories of the past, tarnished by the sense of present alienation. The inadequacy and discontent of the present compels the characters to seek refuge in the past, but the marks of the present soil the past as well.

The paralysis of the living in "The Dead" borders on the uncanny. Time seems to be frozen in a colonial setting and the linear progression of past, present, and future is halted, providing an additional layer of uncanniness. Under colonial

---

[26]   Benstock, "The Dead," pp. 152–5.

[27]   Ibid., p. 160.

power, the present and the future of the characters in the story are weighted down by the past, which extends uncannily into the present. Conversations revert to the flashbacks of familiar times. Gabriel recalls Lily while in the pantry, "as a child" who "used to sit on the lowest step nursing a rag doll."[28] But after Lily's bitter retort that left a gloom over his behavior, aunt Kate confirms Gabriel's doubt about the girl: "She's not the girl she was at all."[29] Gabriel wants to enquire about Lily, but aunt Kate breaks off suddenly to check her sister. Lily doesn't see any future in her matrimonial prospects. Gretta wants a vacation in Galway, her home, but is snubbed by Gabriel's ambitious continental plans. There is no mention of any future event among the guests. Only Gabriel, after the party, egoistically envisions an amorous night at the hotel. But he too discovers the mysterious "symbol" that Gretta had become in the home and which he could not imagine during the party. Gretta is transformed into the past that burdens "her frail shoulders" and collapses before Gabriel's erotic desires. The last mention of future time is found in Gabriel's epiphany about traveling "westward," a journey of snowy death. Linear temporality is halted at the Morkans' dinner party. The future is either bitterly resented, in the case of Lily, or hindered, in the case of Gretta, or is defective, in the case of Gabriel. The combination of the lack of imagination about the future and the amalgamation of the past and present insinuate inertia and paralysis in the characters that Joyce notoriously wanted to depict in "plain roast goose without any apple sauce," discarding Mary Jane's idea of a change in the menu.[30] The party could be indistinguishable at any time of the year. The defenselessness of the characters and the quagmire of repetitive time and death tinge the narrative with an uncanny feeling.

"The Dead" is replete with the elements of a colonial uncanny experience. Darkness, uncertainty, unfamiliarity, ghostly figures, the walking-dead, temporal paralysis, and an unintended vicious repetition manifest the uncanny effects of the coercive colonial power over individuals. As noted earlier, the transformation of topography in Ireland is associated with the alienation of the individual from his milieu. The pervasive presence of the British Empire dissociated individuals from their pasts and, consequently, from familiarity and home. The violence of the present besmirched a collective past, producing nostalgia and inertia. Familiarity, a shared past, and familial bonds constitute the idea of a home. But the Dublin of "The Dead" is deficient to nourish the memory of home in its habitants. Instead, death, a ghostly past, and alienated habitants occupy the shrinking space. Colonial power disrupts the traditional imagination of "home" and the past associated with it and, through dividing practices, alienates the subject residing in the home. Home is no longer a place of solace and "daydreaming," but a ghostly abode of dead and half-dead.

---

28 Ibid., p. 154.

29 Ibid., p. 157.

30 Ibid., p. 171.

References

Adorno, Theodore, *Minima Moralia: Reflections from Damaged Life* (London: Verso, 2005).

Bachelard, Gaston, *The Poetics of Space* (Boston: Beacon Press, 1969).

Benstock, Bernard, "The Dead," in Clive Hart (ed.), *James Joyce's Dubliners* (New York: Viking Press, 1969).

Dunleavy, Janet, "The Ectoplasmic Truthtellers of 'The Dead'," *James Joyce Quarterly* 21/4 (1984): 307–19.

Fanon, Frantz, *The Wretched of the Earth* (New York: Grove Press, 2004).

Foucault, Michel, *Power* (New York: The New Press, 2000).

Freud, Sigmund, *The Uncanny* (New York: Penguin, 2003).

Joyce, James, *Dubliners* (New York: Norton, 2006).

Simmons, H. Allen, "Topography and Transformation, A Postcolonial Reading of Dubliners," in James MacKillop (ed.), *Joyce, Imperialism, and Postcolonialism* (New York: Syracuse University Press, 2008).

Index

Bold page numbers indicate illustrations.